Praise for

A Thousand Days in Tuscany

"Another savory slice of de Blasi's life . . . an object lesson in living fully from a genuine sensualist unabashed by her emotions." —*Kirkus Reviews*

"A great mixture of travel, cooking, philosophy, and love."
—*Salisbury Post* (North Carolina)

"De Blasi takes the reader step by step into the enchanting and sometimes frustrating adventure of rebuilding a rural life for herself and her Italian husband. . . . Through sensual descriptions of food preparation, country festivals and the rich oral history of the old-time villagers, the reader is invited to spend a pleasant afternoon with the equivalent of comfort food in a book." —*Chapel Hill News*

"Lyrical and poetic, the author's writing is a joy to the senses."
—*RT Bookclub* (Brooklyn, New York)

"A charming story of food, romance, and friendship, *A Thousand Days in Tuscany* beautifully portrays the customs of this ancient village."
—*Pages* magazine

"Enchanting . . . a veritable sumptuous feast of storytelling in both Italian and English." —*The Sanford Herald*

Praise for

A Thousand Days in Venice

"An irresistible grown-up love story." —*USA Today*

"An appealing tale of a true romance and a second chance . . . *A Thousand Days in Venice* is a little cioppino of a book, a tasty stew with equal parts travel and food and romance, spiced up with goodly amounts of fantasy-come-true." —*The Seattle Post-Intelligencer*

"Move over *Bridges of Madison County.* Here comes real romance—with recipes, yet . . . a beautifully written memoir . . . The 'happily every after' is riveting and the recipes are mouthwatering just to read." —*The Philadelphia Inquirer*

"Marlena de Blasi makes us fall in love." —*St. Petersburg Times*

"The story sounds impossibly romantic [but] this moonstruck tale is absolutely true. . . . It is, surprisingly, a story with a happy ending—reached, as real-life happy endings must be, not by fiat but by accommodation." —*The Boston Globe*

"Charming . . . better than a romance novel, it's the real thing." —*New Orleans Times-Picayune*

A Thousand Days in Tuscany

BY MARLENA DE BLASI

Regional Foods of Northern Italy

A Taste of Southern Italy

That Summer in Sicily

A Thousand Days in Venice

A Thousand Days in Tuscany

The Lady in the Palazzo

Amandine

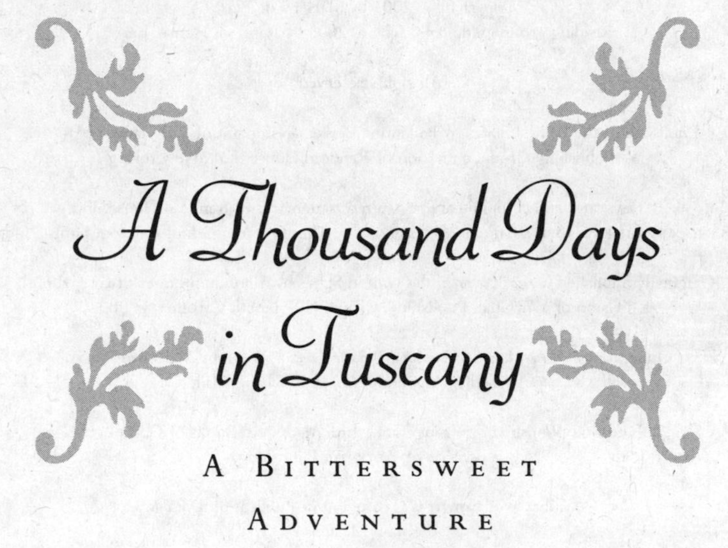

A Thousand Days in Tuscany

A BITTERSWEET ADVENTURE

• • •

Marlena de Blasi

Ballantine Books New York

2005 Ballantine Books Trade Paperback Edition

Published in the United States by Ballantine Books, an imprint of The Random House Publishing Group, a division of Random House, Inc., New York.

Originally published in hardcover in the United States by Algonquin Books of Chapel Hill, a division of Workman Publishing, Chapel Hill, North Carolina, in 2004.

This edition published by arrangement with Algonquin Books of Chapel Hill, a division of Workman Publishing.

Library of Congress Cataloging-in-Publication Data
de Blasi, Marlena.
A thousand days in Tuscany ; by Marlena de Blasi.
p. cm.
ISBN 978-0-345-48109-2
1. Cookery, Italian—Tuscan style. 2. Food—Italy—Tuscany.
3. Tuscany (Italy)—Social life and customs. I. Title.
TX723.2.T86D36 2004
641.5945'5—dc22 2004051589

Printed in the United States of America

www.randomhousereaderscircle.com

8 10 9 7

Text design by Anne Winslow

For Jill Foulston,

a beauty who, like Abraham's angels, stopped by

one evening and, being here, changed things,

enobled them forever.

"Because truly being here is so much; and because everything here
apparently needs us, this fleeting world, which in some strange way
keeps calling to us. Us, the most fleeting of all.
Once *for each thing. Just once, no more. And we too,*
just once. And never again. But to have been
this once, completely, even if only once:
to have been at one with the earth, seems beyond undoing."

RAINER MARIA RILKE

FROM *The Ninth Elegy*, TRANSLATED BY STEPHEN MITCHELL

Contents

Fall

Winter

Spring

Recipes

A Thousand Days in Tuscany

Prologue

"*Ce l'abbiamo fatta, Chou-Chou,* we did it," he says, using the name he gave to me, clutching the steering wheel of the old BMW with both hands, elbows out straight like wings, shoulders hunched in glee, wheezing up a conspiratorial laugh.

"Yes. We did it," I say, with only a crinkle of disdain riding on the "we." I look away from him and out the window to the lights of the Ponte della Libertà. The day still sleeps. Creamy shimmers of a waking sun curl about the fading moon, lowering now in the damp, dark blue of the lagoon sky. His child's joy and the whirring of the road beneath us make the only tracks on the silence. The weeping begins, tears pouring hot and fast no matter my will to hold them back. I don't want to go away from Venice. Still, I smile at the aptness of the bridge's name. Liberty. What better road for an escape? But this is *his* escape, *his* new beginning. Oh, I know it's mine as well. Ours. And much of me is rejoicing in this prospect of setting up house in the exquisite Tuscan countryside. Besides, we'll be a morning's drive away from Venice. We'll go back and forth. I know we will. But for now I must call on the enduring vagabond in me and hope she will oblige.

This Venetian husband of mine has unstitched every tie to his city. Having resigned from his work and sold our home, he is tearing up the remains of his past like a punishing letter, strewing the pieces out to a swallowing sea. This willful reformation he performed—plodding, sometimes, other times galloping—over these last thousand days since we met. His ending sealed, his says that *now* he can begin to be a beginner. Though inclined to melancholy, Fernando believes that beginnings, by nature, are joyful and flower-strewn passages, forbidden to pain. He thinks old ghosts won't find their way to Tuscany.

As we hit terra firma and wend through Marghera to the *autostrada,* he flashes blueberry eyes at me, caressing my tears with the back of his hand. Ancient, faraway eyes made of sadness, made of mischief. It was the eyes I loved first. The eyes and the shy Peter Sellers grin. *Unexpected* they called it, this story of ours, unexpected, improbable, the stuff of fables. He—no longer young—sits across the tiny room of a wine bar on a stormy Venetian Tuesday and sees a woman—no longer young—who changes something in him, everything in him. This, only days before he begins to change everything in her. A chef, a writer, a journalist paid to trek through Italy and France in search of a perfect thing to eat, to drink, she gathers what she can of her quite lovely, quite lonely life, hugs her two grown and thriving children and goes to live with this stranger on the fringes of the Adriatic Sea. Midst flames of a hundred white candles and musky plumes of frankincense, they marry in a small stone church that looks to the lagoon. They ride the night train to Paris and eat ham sandwiches and chocolate cake in an upper berth. They live this love. They fight and they laugh. They try to learn each other's language, each other's ways, but soon realize there'll never be enough time to know all they want to know, one about the other. There never is.

Summer

I

The Gorgeous Things They're Cooking Are Zucchini Blossoms

The scent of them is enough to send up a short, sharp thrill in a hungry person. Seething hot beauties, they repose in a great unruly pile on the white linen. The yellow of the naked blossoms shows through the gilt sheaths of their crackling skin. Skin thin as Venetian glass, I think. But I'm far away from Venice. We live in Tuscany, now. As of this morning, we live in Tuscany. I say it breezily to myself as though it was all in a day's work. Yesterday, Venice. Today, San Casciano dei Bagni. And six hours after arrival, here I am already in a kitchen: in the small, steamy kitchen of the local bar, watching two white-hatted, blue-smocked cooks preparing antipasti for what seems to have become a village festival.

The gorgeous things they're cooking are zucchini blossoms, fat and velvety, almost as wide and long as lilies. And the frying dance is precise: drag a blossom quickly through the nearly liquid batter, let the excess drain back into the bowl, lay the blossom gently in the wide, low-hipped pot of hot, very hot shimmering oil. Another blossom and another. Twelve at a time in each of four pots. The blossoms are so light that, as a crust forms on one side, they bob about in the oil and turn themselves over and over until a skimmer is slid in to rescue them, to lay them for a moment on thick brown paper. The paper is then used as a sling to transport the blossoms to a linen-lined tray. One of the cooks fills a red glass bottle with warm sea-salted water. She fits a metal sprayer onto the bottle and, holding it at arm's length, spritzes the gold blossoms with the salty water. The hot skins hiss and the perfume of them is whipped up and out into the moist June breeze.

Pan-to-hand-to-mouth food, these are sustenance for the twelve-minute interval before supper, and so when the first hundred are ready, the cook, the one called Bice, hands me the tray and says, "*Vai,* go," without looking up. A kitchen directive from one colleague to another, from one chef to another, she says it with familiarity, as though we've worked together for years. But tonight I'm not the chef. I think I'm a guest—or am I the hostess? I'm not at all sure how this festival got started, but I'm happy it did.

Happy and still unwashed from the morning's journey, from the afternoon's work, I'm salty as the blossoms I offer to people, who take them without ceremony. The same familiarity is at work here as each one smiles or pats me on the shoulder, says, "*Grazie, bella,* thank you, beauty," as if I'd been passing them hot, crisp flowers all my life. I like this. For one moment it occurs that I might run with the basket to some dim corner of the piazza to devour the remaining blossoms myself, eyes half closed in a lusty swoon among the shadows. But I don't. Some can't wait until I reach them but come to me, take a flower while sipping wine or talking over their shoulders. People are collecting about me now, rooks swooping in for the things until nothing is left save errant crumbles, crunchy and still warm, which I press onto my finger and suck.

I move toward the edge of a small group that is complimenting the farmer from whose patch the lovelies were harvested this morning. He's saying he'll have more tomorrow, that he'll drop a bushelful off at Sergio's by seven if anyone desires a few. Here ensue three separate and simultaneous discourses on the best way to cook squash blossoms. To stuff or not to stuff them? To stuff them with mozzarella and a salt anchovy, to stuff them with a tiny slice of *ricotta salata,* to stuff them with fresh ricotta and a few leaves of basil, to blend the batter with beer or white wine, to add olive oil to the batter, to leave the oil out? And the biggest question of all—to fry the blossoms in peanut oil or extra virgin? Distracted by these contentions, I don't hear my name called out from across the short expanse of the piazza.

"Chou-Chou," says Bice, stamping her left foot exasperatedly in the doorway of the bar, her arms stretched out with another tray.

This time, careening through the crowd more nimbly, I dispatch the scorching flowers in record time. Though I've neither actually met nor been introduced to most of these people, all of them seem to know that Fernando and I have just moved into the Lucci place down the hill. This intelligence is but a first whiff of the mastery of the intravillage broadcasting system, activated, no doubt, by the small battalion of San Cascianesi who gathered in our driveway to welcome us earlier in the day. And one thing led to another, but still, how did a thank-you *aperitivo* turn into a supper party, and why am I holding so tightly to this empty tray?

We had left Venice behind in the pale purply hour of first light and followed four Albanians, variously piled into and piloting the big blue Gonrand truck that ported our every material asset. We're moving to Tuscany. Eleven kilometers from our destination, a team of spiffy, high-booted, automatic weapon–toting carabinieri invited our meager convoy to halt on the cusp of Route 321. We were detained and interrogated and searched for nearly two hours. Two of the four Albanians were arrested, aliens without papers. We told the military police that we were intending to move into one of the Luccis' farmhouses and that we needed all of the collected muscle and manpower to do so. They settled themselves in their van and talked on their radio. They stayed a very long time. They got out of the van and parleyed again, roadside.

Some say the carabinieri are selected for their physical beauty, that they represent the glory of the Italian state. Surely these do it honor, their dark brows and pale eyes an aesthetic diversion during the wait. At last one of the booted gentlemen said, "Fine, but it's our duty to accompany you." A much grander colonnade now, we inspired intrigue in the trickle of farm traffic we passed along the way until the big blue truck and the police van came to rest behind our old BMW in the back garden of the house. Let's get to work.

There had been a well-defined agreement with Signora Lucci that the house would be clean and that it would be empty. Neither is the case. As the clandestine Albanians begin to carry in our goods, I requisition the carabinieri to help me carry out the signora's tokens of welcome, all in the form of irrefutable junk. There are armoires with crushed-in doors and tables and chairs that, in order to stay upright, are cunningly leaned up against each other. There are six sets of bunk beds. We heave it all into the barn. In our bedroom, I'm dusting a handsome print of a cypress-lined lane framed in hammered copper. It swings on its wire hanger and behind it I find a wall safe. This house, this barely restored stable of a house, which has no central heating and no telephone and electrical wiring sufficient for a blind hermit, has a safe. Not the little hotel-room sort of safe, this is a grand, official-looking thing with two levels of knobs and a clock, and I call Fernando to come look at it.

"It's obviously new, something the Luccis installed during the renovation. I don't think it's meant for our use," says Fernando.

"But why would they need a safe here? Wouldn't one in their villa suffice? I think it must be for tenant use. Let's see if we can open it."

We fiddle with it, twirl and push at the knobs, until Fernando says, "It's locked, and without the combination, we'd never gain access. If we want to use it, we'll have to ask for the coordinates. Besides, what would we possibly put in it?" We each think for half a minute and begin laughing at our dearth of riches: documents tucked inside a whiskey-colored leather portfolio, a rosary that belonged to Fernando's grandmother, his father's pocket watch, my son's and daughter's birth bracelets, a few jewels.

"I'd put chocolate in it. Not just any kind of chocolate, but my stash of ninety-percent cacao. And my fifty-year-old balsamic vinegar," I say, but my plan is interrupted by one of the Albanians, the one who keeps moving boxes from room to room, seemingly at will. Once again, I tell him about the numbering system and then go back downstairs to see how the rest of the crew is faring. One of the carabinieri seems to be without a job, so I ask him to help me move an undesired sofa out to the barn. Fernando shoots me evil looks that say you can't just tell an Italian military policeman to hoist up one end of a molding brown velvet sofa that weighs two hundred kilos and pull it backward down a narrow, curving staircase while you push the other end with all your might, causing him to totter and lurch on the heels of his shiny black boots.

I remember my first sight of Fernando's apartment on the Lido. Scoured of all vanities, it was the lair of an ascetic, the mean hut of an acolyte. Savonarola could have lived there, all of it bespeaking reverence for a medieval patina, undisturbed by the passing of time or someone's riffling about with a dust cloth. This is already much easier.

By now, a small, trawling knot of townspeople has gathered in the garden, hands behind their backs or folded across their chests. After greeting them and introducing myself, saying how happy we are to be new San Cascianesi, I approach the only woman with hands on her hips. She looks ready to pitch in. I ask if she might recommend someone who would have time today to give us a hand. "*Buongiorno, signora. Sono molto lieta di conoscerla.* Good day, madam. I'm very honored to know you," I say, extending my hand to her.

"*Il piacere è mio. Mi chiamo Floriana.* The pleasure is mine. My name is Floriana."

"*Ci serve un pò di aiuto.* We could use a little help."

"*Ci mancherebbe altro.* It's the least we can do," she says, as though helping us was already her plan.

We have two new brooms, a plastic bucket, a squeeze mop, and at least one specimen of every gel and foam and spray and wax that promises pine-scented refuge from household dirt. This is a pittance. Our neighbors disappear and soon return with their own arms. Liter-size plastic bottles of pink alcohol, plastic bags full of what seem to be filthy rags, industrial-size mops and brooms.

Soon there are three window washers, a sweeper on each floor, with moppers at the ready. The restoration of the house had been completed less than a month before and the disorder is mostly cosmetic. In less than four hours, things have definitely improved. Windows sparkle, floors are somewhat cleaner, appliances are scrubbed, walls dusted, bathrooms shine. The carefully numbered boxes are piled in their correct rooms. Floriana snaps fresh, lace-trimmed burgundy sheets into place on our pale yellow wooden *baldacchino,* lately assembled by Fernando and the two carabinieri. And all the squad has had to sustain it were paper cups of warm Ferrarelle, imported from Venice.

Fernando and I conference and, since it's nearly six, we invite the crew to join us in the village at Bar Centrale for *aperitivi*. By this time, the policemen are in it for the long haul, demonstrating not a whit of rush to depart. Only the Albanians seem furtive, signaling escape routes with their eyes. The now-mellowed policemen let this play out, having already decided they'll be looking the other way when the crew drives off. We trudge up the hill into town, some of us walking, some of us riding, all of us exhausted and satisfied, each in his own way. We've had a barn raising, a quilting bee, and we've all earned our thirst and hunger.

Campari and soda gives way to white wine after which someone begins pouring red. And what better after bowls full of fleshy, salty black olives than a great heap of *bruschette*—bread roasted over wood, drenched in fine local oil, dusted in sea salt and devoured out of hand? Still, no one seems ready to say *arrivederci*.

More conferencing ensues, this time among Fernando and I and the two cooks, Bice and Monica, who work at the bar's restaurant. Our numbers have grown to seventeen. Can they feed us all? Rather than giving a simple yes or no, Monica reminds us that each of these seventeen people is related to at least one other person, and that all of them are expected home to either sup or cook within the next half hour. But I needn't have worried. Floriana, formerly with hands on hips, has taken over here just as she did back at the house. Some women scatter. Others move out onto the little terrace, push tables together and spread plastic cloths, set plates and silverware and glasses, plunk down great jugs of wine. More tables are unearthed from the cellars of the nearby city hall and soon the whole piazza is transformed into an alfresco dining room.

The *fornaio,* the baker, had been summoned and, like some sweat-glistened centaur, peaked white hat floured, bare knees poking up from his aproned lap, he pumps his bike up the hill into the village, alternately ringing his bell and blowing his horn. I watch him and the others and I think how so simple an affair can inspire their happiness.

He unloads rounds of bread big as wagon wheels from his saddle baskets, lays them on the table, stands back to admire them, telling us one was meant for the *osteria* in Piazze and the others for the folks in the castle up in Fighine. "Let them eat yesterday's bread," he says remounting, yelling over his shoulder to save three places for him at table. After brief raids on their own kitchens, fetching whatever it was they had prepared for their family supper, the scattered women reconverge at the bar. Their mothers and children and husbands in tow, they come toting pots and platters under an arm, a free hand tucking drifting wisps of hair under their kerchiefs. Like a gaggle of small birds, their high-pitched patter pierces the soft ending of the day. Flowered aprons tied—at all times of the day or evening, I would learn—over navy tube skirts, their feet slippered in pink terry-cloth, they move easily between their private spaces and the public domain of the piazza. Both belong to them.

A man they call Barlozzo appears to be the village chieftain, walking as he does up and down the tables, setting down plates, pouring wine, patting shoulders. Somewhere beyond seventy, Barlozzo is long and lean, his eyes so black they flicker up shards of silver. Gritty, he seems. Mesmeric. Much later I see the way those eyes soften to gray in the doom just before a storm, be it an act of God or some more personal tempest. His thick smooth hair is white and blond and announces that he is at once very young and very old. And for as long as I will know him, I will never be certain if time is pulling him backward or beckoning him ahead. A chronicler, a raconteur, a ghost. A *mago* is Barlozzo. He will become my muse, this old man, my *animatore*, the soul of things for me.

FRESH FROM THEIR triumph of the squash blossoms, now Bice and Monica come back laden with platters of prosciutto and *salame—cose nostre,* our things, they say, a phrase signifying that their families raise and butcher pigs, that they artisinally fashion every part of the animal's flesh and skin and fat into one sort or other of sausage or ham. There are crostini, tiny rounds of bread, toasted on one side, the other side dipped in warm broth and smeared thickly with a salve of chicken livers, capers, and the thinly scraped zest of lemon. Again from the kitchen, two large, deep bowls of *pici,* thick, rough, hand-rolled ropes of pasta, are brought forth, each one tucked in the crook of Bice's elbows. The *pici* are sauced simply with raw crushed green tomatoes, minced garlic, olive oil, and basil. Wonderful.

Many of the women have brought a soup of some sort, soup, more often than pasta, being the traditional *primo,* opening plate, of a Tuscan lunch or supper. No one seems concerned that the soups sit on the table while we work at devouring the *pici*. Soups are most often served at room temperature with a thread of oil and a dusting of pecorino, ewe's milk cheese. "There's more intensity of flavor *quando la minestra è servita tiepida,* when the soup is served tepid," says Floriana to me across the table, in a voice both pedantic and patient. "People who insist on drinking soup hot burn their palates so they must have it always hotter yet, as they search to taste something, anything at all," she says as though too-hot soup was the cause of all human suffering.

There is a potion made of *farro,* an ancient wheatlike grain, and rice; one of hard bread softened in water and scented with garlic, oil, rosemary and just-ground black pepper; another one of fat white beans flavored with sage and tomato and one of new peas in broth with a few shreds of field greens.

The second courses are equally humble. Floriana uncovers an oval cast iron pan to display a *polpettone,* a hybrid meat loaf/paté. "A piece of veal, one of chicken, one of pork, a thick slice of mortadella are hand ground at least three times until the meat is a soft paste. Then add eggs, Parmigiano, garlic, and parsley before patting the paste out into a rectangle, laying it with slices of *salame* and hard-boiled eggs, then turning it over and over on itself, jelly-roll fashion. Bake it, seam side down, until the scent makes you hungry. You know, until it smells done." Floriana offers this information without my asking, talking about the *polpettone* as though it was some local architectural wonder, looking down at it with her head cocked in quiet admiration.

Her whole creation couldn't weigh more than a pound or so, and I am preparing myself for a loaves-and-fishes event when two of the other women uncover their own version of *polpettone*. Each slices hers thin as leaves, then passes the plates around. Still, we are thirty at table. But soon enough other dishes are introduced.

Faraona, guinea hen roasted with black and green olives, is offered by the baker's wife. There is an *arista,* a loin of pork stuffed with herbs and roasted on branches of wild fennel, a casserole of tripe, its cover still sealed, which had been set to bake with tomatoes and onions and white wine in a slow oven the whole day long. There are all manner of little stews and braises, each of a moderate portion, a dose meant to sustain two, perhaps three, restrained appetites. Yet the crowd ogles and groans and protests.

"*Ma chi può mangiare tutta questa roba? Che spettacolo.* But who could eat all these things? What a spectacle."

Each person eats a bite or two from the dish that is closest to him, takes a slice or a morsel of whatever is passed before him. Chewing and mopping at jots of sauce with their bread, sipping wine, arms in *allegro* postures of discourse—I wonder if this is a Tuscan reading of *The Emperor's New Clothes.* Are they truly convinced this collection of their suppers to be *la grande bouffe?* How careful they are to pass the plates and dishes, how they ask, check, ask again who would like some more. Many here seem beyond fifty, some twenty or thirty years more. Those who are younger echo their elders' kindnesses and somehow seem older than their years. There is less distinction among the generations. A girl of perhaps seventeen gets up to fix a plate for her grandmother, telling her to watch for the bones in the rabbit stew, asks her if she's taken her pills. A boy, not more then ten, slices the bread, telling his younger brother to stay clear of his work, that he should never play where someone is using a knife. A suggestion of calm and small graces wash the tableau in long ago. 1920? 1820? How is this evening different from an evening in June when the oldest man here was young, I wonder. I ask the question of Floriana, who is of a certain age, though hardly old. She's quiet for a bit before she puts the question to the table. People answer but more to themselves than to the assembly.

Up from the din, Barlozzo says, "No one's going to bed without his supper tonight." Shifting the great bony length of himself to sit sideways in his chair, he crosses his legs, lights a cigarette. The laughter that follows is thin and sounds like memories.

Wearing a rumpled face and a stiffly starched shirt, one bumptious man redeems the mood, "Whoever cooked the lamb stew is the woman I'll take for my next bride." Now the laughter is refreshed and Floriana looks at me, nods toward the rumpled face, "He's ninety-three and has buried four wives. There's no one left who'll take a chance with him. The last one was only sixty-three when she died. She was a bit fat but in perfect health. One day Ilario, here, went mushroom gathering, came home and cooked a frittata for his wife's lunch. She was dead in an hour. Some say it was her heart, but we all know it was the mushrooms."

"Did Ilario eat the frittata, too?" I want to know.

"Only one alive who knows the answer to that is Ilario, and he's not talking."

I sit breaking my bread into pieces, dipping them into my wine. I notice three people. I look at Fernando sitting across and halfway down the table from me, smiling, holding court, it seems, among the men and women around him. They are comparing dialects, the Tuscans trying to mimic Fernando's slippery Venetian cant but managing only what sounds like an underwater lisp. They applaud and laugh with each new phrase he offers. His voice is in symphony with his face, which is beautiful, pink-cheeked from the wine. Floriana stands up, putters about the table, adjusting things, sweeping crumbs with the side of her hand, scolding, teasing as she goes. I catch her eye or she catches mine and she nearly whispers, as though there are only two of us, "*Tutto andrà bene, Chou-Chou, tutto andrà molto bene. Vedrai*. All will go well. All will go very well. You'll see."

Barlozzo stands behind Floriana now, smoking and sipping wine as though his watch is finished for the evening, as though, now, he can stay a little apart from things. From everything and everyone except Floriana, that is. Nowhere has he fixed his eyes but on her for more than a few minutes at a time all evening. A discreet chatelaine? A gallant lover? Surely he'd heard Floriana's affirmation to me. Surely he never misses a beat. I look at him. I watch him. And he doesn't miss that either.

Bice sets down a small plate in front of me, a fine-looking *panna cotta*, cooked cream, unmolded and sitting in pool of crushed strawberries. I'm about to excavate it with my spoon when a man who introduces himself as Pioggia, Rain, comes to sit by me and asks if I've yet met Assunta.

"No, I don't think so," I tell him, looking about.

"Well, she's Piero's"—he points to a burly, youngish man in jeans and a T-shirt—"finest cow. And she's blue-eyed. Assunta is the only blue-eyed cow I've ever seen," he says.

He reads my open-mouthed stare as disbelief and so he softens the story of Assunta's astounding loveliness.

"Well, her eyes aren't exactly blue, but they're not brown either. They're gray and brown with little blue spots in them and they're wonderful. So after I milked her this morning, I brought the milk directly up here to Bice. I do that only with some of Assunta's milk, all the rest of it goes to the co-op to get pasteurized and ruined. Can't make a decent *panna cotta* with pasteurized milk. At least that's what Bice tells me, and so I bring her a six-liter jar of Assunta's morning milk at least three times a week, whenever she tells me she needs it. *Prova, prova*. Try it," he urges.

I shrink for a moment under this revelation of Assunta's most private ministrations. From her teats to my spoon with only Pioggia's jar and Bice's pot in between. These facts redraw my concept of "fresh." And so I eat blue-eyed Assunta's milk, coaxed from her by a man called Rain, and it's delectable. I lick both sides of my spoon and scrape the empty bowl, and Piogga beams.

Una crostata, a tart, sits within reach, but Pioggia is watching me and, if I touch it, I fear he will somehow anthropomorphize the apricots that sit, crowded in their own treacly juices, on a palette of crust. I just know this fruit will have been plucked from the only tree in Tuscany where druids live.

• • •

As we're saying *buona notte,* we notice the carabinieri bending over maps with flashlights, giving the Albanians directions back to Venice. The Albanians are going back to Venice. But we're not.

Over these past three years that Fernando and I have been together, our journeys have always ended with our coming back over the water to our funny little house by the sea. But there's no more beach house waiting for us now. We've exchanged a beach house for a stable. And though the warm welcome offered us this evening seems a fine forecast of life in these hills, what could truly measure up to those last thousand days we lived in Venice? It's still unclear to me *why* we let go of the Princess's skirts, *why* we left behind her glories for a leap onto dry land to dice with yet another beginning.

I know this launch is different. This time our collective stakes have been pulled. We have neither a home nor jobs, and no more than the sheerest notion of how we'll whittle out the next era. Much about this new life suggests a reassertion of our vows—"for better, for worse, for richer, for poorer." Fernando remains giddy with anticipation and unmanaged expectations. He's a child who's run away from home, a man who's run away from disenchantment, from the torpors of an unexamined life and from old, still tortuous pain.

As we climb the steep stone stairs to our new front door, I am quiet, taking in his joy but resonating little of my own, save a giggle every once in a while when I think of Assunta. I delight in Fernando's pleasure at this fresh new gambol, yet I wonder about the Homeric me. Can I kindle her another time? Is she still supple, will she fit lissomly into her old mettle?

I stay outside alone for a moment playing games with my longing for Venice. I tell myself, "Look at that Tuscan landscape. This is where everyone in the world would like to live. There are no cypress trees in Venice. And no olive trees in Venice, either, no vines, no sheep, no meadows, no fields of wheat, no sunflowers, not even one poppy field. Nor a thatch of lavender high enough in which to hide." I try not to think about the sea and the rosy light and the beauty of Venice that, not for a day, failed to astonish me. This starting place is good, this place among two hundred souls, they and it and now us, lost in time. They and it and now us clinging to a patch of ancient earth where Tuscany and Umbria and Lazio collide. I hear Fernando rummaging about, tripping over what remains of the packing crates. He's singing, and his sounds are so sweet.

I head indoors and directly to the puce-tiled bath to fill the tub. As we sit there in the vanilla bubbles, I want to know, "Is it possible to *paint* ceramic tile?"

"Cristo," says Fernando. "We've just arrived and you want to paint over brand-new tiles. What *is* this fire in you to always be changing things?"

"I don't like puce," I tell him.

"*Che cos'è* puce? What is puce?"

"It's the color of these tiles. Puce is brown and green and purple. And I hate brown and green and purple all stewed together. Actually we could just take the tiles down and replace them with some sort of deep, toasty terra cotta. Or we could do a reprise of our black and white in Venice. That's what we'll do. Tell me true, you ended up loving that bathroom, didn't you? Come on. It will make us feel more at home here. Say yes. We can put up the baroque mirrors and sconces, hang the small lantern that was in the entry, and, with baskets of beautiful towels and soaps and candles, this could be luscious." But my voice already sounds of defeat.

"Why must a bathroom be luscious? Luscious is for cakes with cream. Luscious is for beautiful women," he says, pulling hard with both hands at the damp hair about my temples.

The bed doesn't feel right. It seems crooked, as though the canopy frame is higher on one side. But the sheets and my husband both feel cool and smooth. How delicious it is to rest after such a day. To lay down blood and bones in a place, almost any place, where someone waits to hold what's young of you and what's old of you. What's just happened to you and that which has happened so long ago to you. All of you.

While Fernando sleeps, I lie there and think of our little dawn hegira, which already seems part of another lifetime. Was it only this morning? I miss the sea. I wish for a single blue velvet caress of thick salt air. And for a walk, a half-loping run over damp sand at land's end, icy seafoam purling round my ankles. It's no use. I can't sleep. I get up, pull on Fernando's robe, and go to sit on the terrace.

Even the sky is different here, I think. The lagoon sky is a cupola, softly hung and barely out of reach. This one is farther away, as though the night roof was raised a million miles. A boat horn's wail was my Venetian lullaby. Now it's made of newborn lambs bleating.

The village church bells ring quarter past midnight. My first Tuscan friend is a bell who will make himself heard four times an hour, every hour. Loyalty. And what else is there in my thin store of assets? Besides the bells and the sheep and the big sky, I have my own history. I have the love of my children, as they have mine. The man whom I love with my whole heart is inside sleeping in the yellow wooden bed. I have my two hands, which are older than I am. And I have that quiet frisson. An undine's hissing near my ear, part threat, part invitation, it penetrates me with some unclassifiable hunger. A thistle fallen back somewhere in my mind, gently, urgently rasping, it keeps me curious, keeps me new. These are the things I can count on. These are my comforts. My charms.

Deep-Fried Flowers, Vegetables, and Herbs

1½ cups all purpose flour
2 cups beer
½ cup cold water
2 teaspoons fine sea salt
3 ice cubes

Peanut oil or extra virgin olive oil for frying

Zucchini blossoms, nasturtium flowers, and borage flowers, rinsed, dried, and stems trimmed
Celery leaves cut in branches, rinsed, and dried
Whole sage leaves, rinsed and dried
Tiny spring onions or scallions, stems trimmed to about 4 inches in length, rinsed and dried

Warm sea-salted water in a sprayer

In a large bowl, beat together with a fork the flour, beer, water, and sea salt to form a thin batter. Let the batter rest for an hour or so, covered and at room temperature. Stir in the ice cubes and let the batter rest for an additional half-hour. Stir the batter again. It should now be smooth and have the texture of heavy cream. If it's too thick, add cold water by the tablespoonful until the "heavy cream" texture is achieved.

Over a medium flame, heat the oil in a deep fryer or a heavy pan to a depth of 3". The more slowly the oil heats, the more evenly it will heat, helping you to avoid hot and cold spots and unevenly fried foods. Test the oil by dropping in a cube of bread. If it sizzles and turns golden in a few seconds, the oil is ready.

Drag the flowers, herbs, and spring onions through the batter, shaking off the excess. Place them into the hot oil and let them bob about for half a minute or so, allowing them to take on a good, dark crust. Turn them with tongs, to finish frying, then remove them with a slotted spoon to absorbent paper towels. Using a virgin plant sprayer, spray each batch immediately with warm sea-salted water and keep them in a 100-degree oven while you fry the next batch. Better, gather people around the stove and eat the things pan to hand to mouth. A very informal first course.

2

Figs and Apples Threaded on Strings

It's the next morning but I've only just fallen asleep. And now someone is forcefully leaning on what must be our doorbell. I open my eyes to a slice of pink sun insisting itself between the two panels of Signora Lucci's lace curtains, stippling our tangled legs in new light. I pull myself upright and into the the old green robe. I like the coolness of the stone floor under my feet as I walk from the bedroom through the hallway to the front door. Opening it a chink, I find a muddy plastic carrying case spilling over with squash blossoms, bouquets of them, each tied with kitchen string. There is no note. A visit from the Welcome Wagon, I wonder? I look for the courier, but no one is nearby. Now, I am certain the gift is Barlozzo's. I carry the bounty downstairs to the kitchen, where sitting on the drainboard, the flowers look like a giant's garden thrust inside a doll's house. The proportion is wrong, and yet it appeals. Fernando and I pass on the stairs. I hear his "*ma guarda che roba,* but will you look at this," when he sees the flowers and then his tinkering search for the espresso pot while I'm pulling on shorts and sandals, shouting down, "Why don't we just run up the hill for *cappuccini?*"

Up at the Centrale, some of last evening's guests stand just where we left them. Save their less festive costumes, they seem not to have gone home at all. Crowded three or four deep at the bar, they're quaffing 7:30 a.m. red wine, throwing back *caffè corretto,* greeting us, welcoming us back to the stomping ground. We say no, thank you, to the wine and the grappa-spiked coffee, standing firm for hot foamy milk and a shot of espresso, and they bewail our feebleness.

Wanting to pay our bill for the portions of last evening's supper provided by the bar, we ask to see the owner. A woman called Vera, small and square with pale, rheumy oyster-colored eyes, invites us to the back table near the kitchen door and to settle ourselves across from her while she tallies. Working from a fistful of scraps—one of which reads *due chili di pomodori*, two kilos of tomatoes, another *affettati,* sliced, cured meats, the others I fail to read slant-eyed—she counts aloud, does the addition, scratches out her errors, counts aloud again, before finally asking Fernando to add the numbers. He writes the final figure and passes it over to her. "*Ma è così tanto?* But is it that much?" she asks, astounded. "*Contiamoci un'altra volta.* Let's count again." Fernando assures her that the sum is correct and reaches for his wallet. The oyster eyes are troubled, they look despisingly at the scribbles. "*Senti, puoi pagare un pò ogni mese.* Listen, you can pay a little each month," she tells us.

The bill for the *aperitivi, bruschette,* at least a hundred-and-fifty fried flowers, *salame* and prosciutto, what must have been two kilos of *pici,* and a river of red wine is lighter than a quick lunch à deux at Harry's Bar. There is a great cost-of-living divide between a country mouse and a city mouse. Fernando and I try to ease Vera from her gloom. Enter Barlozzo.

There's something of Gary Cooper in him, and I will learn that it's always high noon when Barlozzo arrives. No niceties, not even a *buongiorno,* he asks if I'd put the flowers in a cool place. And he wants to know how I'm planning to cook them. I tell him I'll probably make a frittata and then fry the rest as Bice and Monica did last night. The bar crowd quiets, shuffles position. My casually stated culinary intentions cause provocation. One by one they ease themselves over to the table where we sit across from the now less-troubled oyster eyes.

"*Ma perchè non un condimento per la pasta?* But, why not a condiment for pasta?" asks a man whose blue satin suspenders arch valiantly over the great girth of his pure white T-shirt before disappearing into the gully under his belly.

"*Oppure una bella schiacciata?* Or a beautiful flatbread?"

"*No, no, no. Oggi ci vogliono i fiori crudi con un mazzo di rucola, due foglie di basilico, un pomodoro, ancora caldo dai raggi del sole, un goccio d'olio. Basta.* No, no, no. Today you want the flowers raw with a handful of arugula, two leaves of basil, a tomato still warm from the sun, and a drop of oil. Enough."

All this passion over a handful of blossoms. But I, too, am captivated by these lithe yellow flowers, having grown them over the years, sometimes begging space in friends' gardens when I didn't have my own, becoming familiar with their whims as plants, how their gentle savor can refine and ornament other foods as well as please on its own. All species of *zucca,* squash, sprout flowers in the first phases of growth, but it's the flower of the *zucchine* which is hardiest. One must harvest the flowers when the squash is still small and slender, not more than eight to ten inches in length, plucking the flower along with the the squash so a new flower and a new squash can bud in its place on the vine. Blossoms grow from both the feminine and masculine zucchini, but the feminine flowers grow more broadly and bell-shaped. I'd noticed that nearly all the blossoms Barlozzo brought this morning were decidedly feminine. "*Come mai quasi tutti i fiori in questa zona sono femminili?* How is it that almost all the flowers in this area are feminine?"

The question brings on a bawdy laugh all around and it's the blue suspenders who answers it. "Because we're fortunate."

Foolishly, I begin to banter with them, as though I were really a part of the discussion, saying that we must shop for the fundamentals to stock our pantry, that we have few provisions at hand and so something simple will do very nicely today, but they are off on a roll, reciting formulas, whispering gastronomic lore like vespers. Our squash blossom opportunities have stimulated an hour's worth of appetizing talk, and it is evident that it matters not at all if we are there or gone away in the meantime. We say unheard good-byes and leave with Barlozzo close behind us. "They all know the truth, that there are only three subjects worth talking about. At least here in these parts," he says. "The weather, which, as they're farmers, affects everything else. Dying and birthing, of both people and animals. And what we eat—this last item comprising what we ate the day before and what we're planning to eat tomorrow. And all three of these major subjects encompass, in one way or another, philosophy, psychology, sociology, anthropology, the physical sciences, history, art, literature, and religion. We get around to sparring about all that counts in a life but we usually do it while we're talking about food, it being a subject inseparable from every other subject. It's the table and the bed that count in life. And everything else we do, we do so we can get back to the table, back to the bed."

We thank Barlozzo for the flowers, ask him to come by and join us for our premier lunch, but he refuses, proposing instead to come by at four to see if we need help with the rest of the unpacking, with getting settled. He says this as though it is his job. He can tell us whatever we want to know about the house. This he says in a very quiet voice.

On the high curve of the piazza sits Sergio's fruit and vegetable shop, so we look about for things to enhance our blossom-lunch menu. Sergio suggests a *fritto misto,* a mixed fry, of vegetables and herbs. He pulls out a handful of sage leaves, each one long and soft as a rabbit's ear, whacks the leaves and small stems from a head of celery, picks through a basket of skinny green beans and adds some to our pile. He asks if we like potatoes but doesn't wait for us to answer before digging into a cardboard carton of yellow-skinned ones, still covered in dirt, each no bigger than a cherry.

Four steps away up toward the church and the city hall is a *gastronomia* where we buy flour and sea salt, a bottle of beer for the batter and peanut oil for frying. I ask for eggs and the man cocks his head, looks pityingly at me, and says all I need do is stop at the hen house just down the hill from our place. *"Può prendere da sola, signora, direttamente là,"* he says in a snuffy tone as though egg gathering in a henhouse was a daily Tuscan sacrament.

Across from the *gastronomia* sits an *enoteca,* a wine shop, where we choose a Vernaccia and a bottle of tourist oil, as Barlozzo later calls it—a pretty, one-liter bottle filled with third-rate oil that costs more than do five liters of the best stuff, straight from the mill. There is much to learn. The butcher, a jeweler, an *antichità,* the antiques shop, two other general grocers whose spaces are big as walk-in closets complete the shopping potential of the *centro storico*. It will take another long, sugarless day before we discover a *pasticceria* in town, tucked up and out of sight behind the church, and another bread baker on the slope that leads out of town toward the other side of the sheepfold.

I have never before gathered eggs from under a hen. Fernando has never before seen a hen. We bend low into the shed where perch a dozen or so fat lady birds. There's no shrieking or fluttering at all. I approach one and ask her if she has an egg or two. Nothing. I ask in Italian. Still nothing. I ask Fernando to pick her up but he's already outside the shed smoking and pacing, telling me he really doesn't like eggs at all and he especially doesn't like frittata. Both bold-faced lies. I start to move the hen and she plumps down from her perch quite voluntarily, uncovering the place where two lovely brown eggs sit. I take them, one at a time, bend down and nestle them in my sack. I want two more. I peruse the room. I choose the hen who sits next to the docile one. I pick her up and she pecks me so hard on my wrist that I drop her. I see there is nothing in her nest and apologize for my insensitivity, thinking her nastiness must have been caused by embarrassment. I move on to another hen and this time find a single, paler brown-shelled beauty, still warm and stuck all over with bits of straw. I take it and leave with an unfamiliar thrill. This is my first full day in Tuscany and I've robbed a henhouse before lunch.

Back home in the kitchen I beat the eggs, the yolks of which are orange as pumpkin, with a few grindings of sea salt, a few more of pepper, adding a tablespoon or so of white wine and a handful of Parmigiano. I dig for my flat broad frying pan, twirl it to coat its floor with a few drops of my tourist oil, and let it warm over a quiet flame. I drop in the rinsed and dried blossoms whole, flatten them a bit so they stay put, and leave them for a minute or so while I tear a few basil leaves, give the eggs another stroke or two. I throw a few fennel seeds into the pan to scent the oil, where the blossoms are now beginning to take color on their bottom sides. Time to liven up the flame and add the egg batter. I perform the lift-and-tilt motions necessary to cook the frittata without disturbing the blossoms, which are now ensnared in the creamy embrace of the eggs. Next, I run the lush little cake under a hot grill to form a gold blistery skin on top before sliding it onto a plate, strewing it with torn basil. The heat of the eggs warms the herbs so they give up a double-strength perfume. Now I drop a thread of fine old *balsamico* over it. And, finally, let it rest.

Fernando and I batter and fry the sage leaves and celery tops, eating them right from the draining paper while standing in front of the stove, daring to move only our upper bodies and even those parts with the skill of second-story men who samba. The kitchen is smaller than the one in Venice, smaller than any kitchen that doesn't come in a kit. We fry only a few of the blossoms and all of the tiny potatoes and green beans and carry them out to the terrace with two glasses of Vernaccia and the frittata.

I ask Fernando, "How does it all seem to you—at this early point, I mean?"

"I'm feeling some of everything, I guess. There's fear. And lots of excitement. I can't yet believe it's true that there's no more bank, no more house on the Lido. I mean, it's all precisely as I'd wanted it to be and, yet, it's still too *untried* to seem real. And the house is, well, it's so different from any house I've ever seen, let alone lived in. I know some of the rooms are cut up strangely, but all in all, it's so big." Fernando has lived his whole life in a succession of two small apartments, one less than a kilometer from the other, and so his impression of this strange old dwelling—half stable, half farmhouse—is predictable. Yet to me, the great eccentric space is intriguing.

"I like that it rambles. It's feels more a refuge than a house, and I like it because it *is* so primitive, so rough. It's the right house for a beginning. The outside looks so forlorn, though, almost scorned somehow, sitting on the edge of the road. Like there's suffering clenched between its stones."

Fernando moves from his chair to sit on the terrace floor, leaning his back against the house, sipping at his wine. "Certainly it's not the Cà d'Oro but it doesn't look suffered to me as much as it does *eroica,* heroic. It looks like a place that endures."

"No central heating, no telephone, no television—we're going to be short on comforts."

"True. But we're inventive," he tells me, from out of his tenderest Peter Sellers grin. Three years ago, when I left America to come to live in Italy, it was neither Venice nor the house on the beach that lured me. Rather it was this man, this Fernando. It's quite the same thing now. We've hardly come to Tuscany for a house.

Having found each other, now it's innocence we've chased over the sea and all the way here to these pink-sand slopes. We've come here to make a life scrubbed clean of clutter, a life that follows the rhythms and rituals of this rural culture. A life, as they say here, that's made *a misura d'uomo,* to the measure of man. We're hoping this is a place that still remembers real life, the once-upon-a-time life, the hard parts and the joyful ones. *Dolce e salata,* sweet and salty. Like fasting before a feast, each side of life dignifying the other. It may be that everywhere in the world there is the possibility to live with this balance, but it's here, right here, where we've come to look for it. And so we packed up the fickle stretches of time and gleams of light we think might remain for us and we ran hard and fast to this place. We've come because we think it might be here where we can learn which way progress runs. Our suspicion is strong that there is a greater peace in going backward. We'll see. What we know already is that life is a mayfly, flitting. We'll caress each day into its simplest form, keeping the illusions thin if not altogether absent. We've just broken down the structure of one life and so the immediate building up of another would be only backlash. Especially before we've given ourselves the chance to determine what we truly desire from and believe we can accomplish by raising up new structure.

We won't be like a prisoner, emotional or physical, faltering before the wide-open door of his claustral cell, timid and not at all certain he wants to leave. What will he do without the walls? he asks himself, and so he sets out to build new ones, to draw fresh limits to his freedom—to commit the same crime, to marry the same person, to take the same train, to find the same job, write the same letter, the same book. People who search for change, new beginnings, another kind of life, sometimes imagine they'll find it all set up and ready for them simply because they've changed address, gone to live in some other geography. But a change of address—no matter how far away, how exotic—is nothing more than a "transfer." And at the first moment they look about them, they see everything they thought to leave behind has arrived with them. Everything. And so, if we have a plan at this early point, it's to invigorate our lives, to reshape them rather than to repeat them.

We wander about our new home, room to room, up the stairs and back down again. Fernando says it's great and I, too, say it's great if we want to live in an *agriturismo* or a sanitorium for consumptive Berliners.

"Some paint. Some fabric. A few wonderful old pieces of furniture." I shrug the words in falsetto, oiling them in indifference, and yet I don't fool my husband. Only a few days after I'd come to live with him in Venice, he left the comfort of his dust-crusted beach house one morning, returning nine hours later to a pasha's lair—marble floors burnished, white brocade flung at every surface, the delicate preen of cinnamon candles chasing twenty years of cigarette smoke.

"*Cristo.*"

BARLOZZO ARRIVES AT four bells. Unsmiling and at ease with silence, his Tuscan reserve clashes with my piffling chatter and my Donna Reed–twirling about him, patting a cushion where he might sit, telling him how happy we are to have our first visitor, coming at him with a wine glass full of water, which he refuses, saying, "*Acqua fa ruggine,* water makes rust." Once I've exchanged his water for wine, he drains half the glass and, without preamble, reveals that he was born in this house. "Upstairs in the little room that looks west. Down here is where the animals lived. Dairy cows and a mule slept here," he says sweeping his hands about our *salotto,* living room, "and the manger was in there, in the space that's your kitchen."

This fact enchants me, soothes the earlier jilt I'd felt about its stingy space. Now I think my kitchen is a beatific snug. I'm so sure that Donna Reed never cooked in a manger. "Four generations of Barlozzo men sharecropped Lucci lands. I would have been the fifth but, after the war, everything changed. My father was too sick to work, and so I did odd jobs for the Luccis to earn our keep. I was more valuable to them as a handyman than a farmer. They have eight properties that sit between Piazze and Celle and I just moved from one to the other, patching roofs, building up walls, trying to rescue things from neglect, from the shame the war left behind."

At ease with silence. Until he wants to talk. As though he's been saving stories, his is a soliliquy, an old monk's soft chanting. He tells us that when his parents passed on he stayed alone here for a few years before he rented a postwar apartment in the new town, a kilometer or so down the road. He was the last person to have lived in this house full-time, its having since been used for storage and sometimes to house the extra hands the Luccis hired during the olive and grape harvests. He hasn't worked for the Luccis or even set foot in the house for more than thirty years. What he doesn't say is as eloquent as his spoken story. He rests between phrases, leaving time for us to listen to the silent parts.

"Would you like to see how it's been restructured upstairs?" I ask him.

He walks the rooms with us. Barlozzo's family kitchen was where our bedroom is now. He runs his hand over the new drywall where the fireplace once was. The two other bedrooms were a pantry—*la dispensa,* he calls it—where, from great oak beams, his father set the wine-washed hind legs of his pigs to swing in the cool, dry breezes of a winter and a spring until the haunches shriveled into the sweet, rosy flesh of prosciutto.

"We hung all sorts of things from these beams," he says, "figs and apples threaded on strings, whole salami, tomatoes and chiles dried on their stems, braids of garlic and onions. There was always a pyramid built up of round, green winter squash, each one piled on the other, stem-side down, and they'd last that way from September til April. The walls were lined with wide board shelves sagging with the weight of peaches and cherries and apricots preserved in jars, *sotto spirito,* under spirits. When things were good, that is."

Having understood him to say *"Santo Spirito,"* I tell him I'd surely like to have the Holy Ghost's formula for putting up cherries, and it's the first time I hear him laugh.

We show him the two bathrooms and he just shakes his head,

mumbling something about how shabbily the Luccis put things together. He talks about claw-foot tubs and exposed brick walls. He laments that the Luccis ignored the mountains of old handmade terra cotta floor tiles that sit in their sheds and cellars all over the valley, opting for the sheen of factory-made ones. The distinctiveness of the old farmhouse has been disgraced.

"*È una tristezza,*" he says, "*proprio squallido come lavoro.* It's a sadness, an absolutely squalid work. The Luccis did everything as cheaply as they could with the state's allotment."

Though we don't understand the meaning of this last sentence, Barlozzo's facial expression and the bold period he'd placed at its end make it clear this is not the moment to seek further. His cruelly honest take on the house smarts, and yet I share it with him. I remind myself that we didn't come to Tuscany for a house.

THE SUN HAS gone to wash the other side of the sky and the light is blue over the garden when we go out to sit on the terrace. It's just past seven and Barlozzo is still in soliloquy mode, talking now about the history of the village. Like all good teachers, he begins with an overview of his subject. "The last of the hill towns on the southern verges of Tuscany as it gives way to Lazio and Umbria, San Casciano is *precisamente,* precisely, 582 meters above sea level, built on the crest of a hill that divides the valleys of the river Paglia and the river Chiana." It's thrilling to be sitting in the midst of what he describes, and I want to tell him this, but so deep is his own captivity in the story that I stay quiet. "Old as Etruria and likely older yet, the village grew up under the Romans. It was the baths, the healing, theraputic waters that sprung from the rich argillaceous soil of the place that attracted the upper-bracket Romans, put the village on the map." And when the Empire built the Via Cassia—a most grandiose feat of construction that connected Rome with Gaul—San Casciano dei Bagni, San Casciano of the Baths, now more accessible to travelers, became the watering hole of such personages as Horace and Ottaviano Augustus.

"Toward the medieval epoch, baths gave way to wars and invasions between the Guelfs and Ghibellines in all the territories from Siena clear to Orvieto. And so it wasn't until 1559, when the village entered under the protectorate of the Grand Duchy of Tuscany, commanded by Cosimo dei Medici of Florence, that the baths of San Casciano returned to fame, attracting all of crowned Europe and their courts. This royal traffic inspired some of the more ornate constructions in and surrounding the village." All that history right outside our door. Though I still look at Barlozzo as he proceeds, my mind flits about, needing to rest from his docent's lessons. It's enough for now to just imagine that we can bathe in the same warm spring where an Augustus once did.

Each morning, we walk early, while the sun is still rising. We find the Roman springs, which gurgle up soothing and very warm waters in which we soak our feet or, when we like, much more of us. The still cool air and the hot water are delicious taken together before breakfast. There are few paths among the meadows and moors and so walking becomes a swashbuckling causing my thighs to burn as they did during my first Venetian days among the footbridges. A rogue breeze ripples up every now and then, intruding upon the stillness. Sometimes it becomes a wind, announcing the rain, which soon blows down in sultry sheets against us, the force of it carving tiny rills in the warm earth. We take off our boots, then, and squish in the mud like the two children we never were but can be now.

When we can't bear to wait for breakfast any longer we move fast as we can through the brush, over the fields, back up to the house, arriving breathless, hearts pounding, bodies sweating out the juicy scents of grass and thyme. I feel as though we are living in a summer camp directed by obliging absentee counselors who look smilingly and from afar upon genteel eroticisms. We bathe and dress and head up to the village.

Within a few days, we are setting rituals. As we pass the baker's, he, or sometimes his wife, meets us on the road in front of their shop with still-warm cuts of *pizza bianca* wrapped in thick gray paper.

Made from bread dough stretched thin, swathed in olive oil, dusted with sea salt then heaved into the oven beside his bread, it bakes in a minute or two. He pulls it out on his old wooden peel, slashes at it with a thin knife, and sets the thing, peel and all, on a table by the door. The whole village wakes to its perfumes. We devour the pizza, the first course of breakfast, during the thirty-meter trek up to the Centrale. Once installed at the bar, our *cappuccini—caldissimi e con cacao,* very hot and with a sprinkle of bitter chocolate—are set before us, the tray of croissants slid within reach. There will never be a substitute for Pasticceria Maggion's warm, crisp cornets fat with apricot marmalade with which I'd buttered my hands and chin daily for three years on the Lido. But these will do. And I feel that I will, too. I was mistaken about the adventuress. The mettle, the suppleness. All my parts arrived from Venice to Tuscany, entire. I still savor things. A kiss. A breeze. The trust is still at work here. And just as it happened in Venice, an exciting sense of place rescues me from nostalgia.

Here, right here, along this road where I gather wild fennel stalks, passed the Roman legions. It is the ancient Via Cassia, now Strada Statale Numero 2, and right here beside it, in this field where we've made love and drunk our sunset wine, the Romans surely laid fires among the Etrurian stones and cooked their porridge of *farro* and slept a cheerless sleep. We seem to be always in a dazzle. We drive to Urbino and say, That house is where Rafaello's mother was born. In Città della Pieve, we say, That church is where Il Perugino worked. We wander about in Spoleto and say, This is the gate at which Hannibal was stayed by the *spoletini* tribes. In the woods just beyond our own garden, we say, That band of Sunday stalkers will take two wild boar this morning, practicing the same rites and rituals of medieval hunters.

In nearly each village and commune and fraction of a *borgo*, there will be one ruin to redeem its humbleness, one fragment of a wall, one painting, one chapel, one grand church, a tower, a castle, a lone and everlasting umbrella pine defending a georgic hill, a half a meter's worth of a tenth-century fresco still discernable from among the millennia of transformations surrounding it. Preserved, revered, now it is a bit of frostwork ornamenting a pharmacy, a chocolate maker's kitchen. Passages, imprints, traces that, like us, ache to be touched and never forgotten.

We learn a little each day. We stop along every roadside *frantoio* and taste olive oil until we find one we like enough to fill our twenty-liter spigoted terra-cotta vase, called a *giara*. At the usage rate of one liter a week, the supply will serve until December, when the new oil will be pressed. We haul the oil vase in through the stable door and set it in a dark, cool corner.

This is the land of *Chianti Geografico.* Though the wine here is built from the same grape varietals and with much the same methodology as it is in the Chianti itself, these vines lie outside the designated Chianti regions and must bear a different classification. We set out over the hills, our supply of just-scrubbed and sparkling five-liter bottles clinking about in the trunk, and knock on every vineyard keeper's door on which there is the invitation *degustazione, vino sfuso,* tasting, barrel wines. We swirl and sip our way through the afternoons and finally settle on one from Palazzone to be our official house red.

From Sergio and several other garden farmers, we shop for each day's vegetables, herbs, fruit. Our egg supply is secured. We buy bread flour in ten-kilo paper sacks, buckwheat and whole wheat flour in two-kilo sacks from the miller in town. We are still deciding who will become our *macellaio di fiducia,* butcher of confidence, though the tall young man in Piazze who wears a cleaver slung from his Dolce e Gabbana belt appears to be winning us over. There's a cooperative in Querce al Pino where other necessaries wait. And for help beyond the table, the local *lavanderia* is much more than a laundry. The services include dry cleaning and dressmaking; a fabric shop and a knitting factory sit under the same busy roof. The proprietress also sells her famous cordials and tonics, rustic poteens elicited from a still that often purls along beside the steam presser. Her husband is the village shoemaker, her son the auto mechanic, her son's wife the hairdresser, and all their enterprises are neatly clustered about the modest square footage of their yard. Thus we have achieved essential maintenance. This is good. This is how I'd wished it would be.

One morning on our way up to the bar, we catch Barlozzo breakfasting outside the henhouse. We watch as he cracks an egg into his mouth, takes a modest swig from a bottle of red, wipes his mouth with his handkerchief, places the wine back in his sack and is about to head up the hill. We yell to him to wait for us and, once up at the bar, he swallows another wine chaser while we sip *cappuccini*. He tells us all that milk we drink is going to kill us.

Dispensing with invitations and acceptances, Barlozzo simply takes on the habit of visiting each afternoon at four. And we take on the habit of waiting for him. Between us, Fernando and I call him *il duca,* the duke, yet we never use that name with him directly. But in his honor, we've christened the house Palazzo Barlozzo, and each time we call it that, his face ruddies like a boy's. I'm never sure if it's in pleasure or discomfort.

Barlozzo and Fernando are easy together, as one might expect Gary Cooper and Peter Sellers to be easy together. Barlozzo instructs Fernando on how to care for the olive seedlings he'd planted a few months earlier when we'd first decided to rent the house. They discuss a vegetable plot, but Barlozzo says most of the land assigned to the house slopes down toward the sheepfolds and that the patch that was his mother's kitchen garden is where the Luccis put up the ugly cement-block structure they refer to as "the barn." He says what's left of the garden is just too small to do much other than plant some flowers. But when Fernando tells him I've been begging him to construct a wood-burning oven out there, Barlozzo, the thin set of his Tuscan lips taking on a slight upward pitch, says, "I'll take you to see a friend of mine in Ponticelli. He'll cast the *canna fumaria e la volta,* the chimney and the vault. And there's plenty of old brick around that we can use to line the oven chamber and to build up a hearth wall all around it. We'll use clay and sand to insulate and . . ."

He proceeds, touched, I think, by the fascination he's causing in Fernando's eyes. Has my husband found a hero? Like two nine-year-olds, as nine-year-olds once were, they call for paper and pens and sit cross-legged on the floor scratching out primitive designs not so different from the ones an Egyptian might have drawn for the first ovens a few thousand years ago.

We tell Barlozzo about our hunts for communal ovens all over the north of Italy when I was researching my first cookbook. Our favorites were the communal ovens in some of the smaller villages of the Friuli, ovens that are still lit at midnight each Friday with vine cuttings and huge oak logs so the Saturday bake can begin at dawn. We tell him about the official *maestro del forno,* the oven master, a man whose social and political position is second only to the mayor. The oven master maintains the oven and schedules the baking times, which begin at sunrise and end just before supper. Each household has its own crest of sorts to identify its bread — a rough cross, or some configuration of hearts or arrows slashed into the risen loaves just before they're slid onto the oven floor. And then, so as not to squander the waning heat after the last bake, people arrive toting terra-cotta dishes and iron pots full of vegetables and herbs bathed in wine, a leg of lamb, once in a while, or hefts of pork with small violet-skinned onions and rough-cut stalks of wild fennel to braise in the embers all through the night and then to rest awhile in the spent oven, breathing in the lingering aromas of wood smoke. On Sunday morning before mass, the older children in each family come to fetch Sunday's lunch, some of them wrapping their prizes in linen, carting them to church for a priest's blessing.

Now the upward pitch of the Tuscan mouth has nearly reached into a smile, so I ask Barlozzo about the communal oven in San Casciano. "Actually, there were two village ovens once. One of them was in the meadow, which is now the soccer field, and the other is still sitting behind the tractor repair shop on the road to Celle. But there hasn't been a communal oven in use since before the second great war. And the smaller ovens most of us built in our yards are mostly squirrel dens now, or pigeon nests, or rests for tools and flowerpots," he says, as though he can't quite recall why or when that became so.

Barlozzo suggests that we three work on the oven every morning, beginning at ten, breaking at one for lunch and avoiding the afternoon heat. This is good, because it's exploration we want to do in the early mornings. But I suspect Barlozzo already knows this and thus has set the plan to accomodate us.

As we work one morning, I ask him why this can't be the new communal oven, why we can't fire it up on Saturday mornings and invite the San Cascianesi to bake their bread. "Because the San Cascianesi don't bake their bread. No one bakes bread anymore. Neither inside the house nor outside. Almost no one. We've got two perfectly fine village bakers who keep us supplied. People just have other things to do these days. All that's part of the past," he says.

This sounds like a reprise of Fernando's early tirades in our Venice kitchen when I wanted to bake bread or roll out my own pasta or construct some six-storied confection slathered in butter creams. He'd tried to cool my desires with the same arguments, saying that no one bakes bread or desserts or makes pasta at home. Even grandmothers and maiden aunts queue in the shops, then sit in the cafés with their *cappucini* all morning, he'd assured me back then. Was that the same man who, now, can't wait to get his hands into the bread dough?

"And so why are you helping us with this oven if all this is only 'part of the past'?" I want to know.

"I'm helping because you need help," he says. "Because from everything I'm learning about you two, it appears that what you want most is the 'past.' I'm hoping all this isn't just some folkloric interlude for you two. I'm hoping you've got your feet securely on the ground. What I mean is, you've come here from another life and yet you seem to expect to step into this one just as it used to be in the nineteenth century. As though it were waiting for you, as though it were Utopia. Or worse, as though it were Sybaris. Well, there is no Utopia here, never has been. And you must know what happened to Sybaris? The past here was sometimes brutal and tragic, just like the present can be."

The swiftness of his exit leaves a chill behind in the burning light of noon.

I am startled neither that the old duke knows Greek history nor that he would finally get round to digging into our souls. He cuts off all receiving channels, except to bid us "*buon pranzo,* good lunch" over his shoulder as he takes the shortcut through the back meadow up toward town. Barlozzo's questions were both oblique and semantic. He can be sharp as a scimitar, even though I don't believe he means to cut. We watch him for a while and then look at each other, both of us a bit mystified. We've trespassed upon Barlozzo. Though it's been he who has pursued us in his often vulpine manner, he who loves to talk and preach, to plumb his history before such a new and eager audience as we are, he will not suffer our sidling up too close to him or upon his memories. Barlozzo is a man with boundaries, confines unsusceptible to our pressing for even the smallest part of him that lies beyond them.

THOUGH DISAPPOINTED, NEITHER of us is surprised at 4:00 when no knock sounds on the stable door. Fernando says the duke is staying away for the sake of showmanship—*un colpo di teatro,* a theatrical move. We pretend not to notice when the afternoon becomes evening without sign from him. A long time to keep his audience waiting, I think. We're out on the terrace, changing our shoes and just about to start up to the bar for apperitivi, when the duke rounds the back of the stable.

"*Avete benzina per la machina?* Do you have gas in your car?"

"*Certo,*" Fernando tells him. "*Ma, perchè?* But why?"

"Because I'm inviting you out to supper."

We drive south through the nearby villages of Piazze and Palazzone. Twenty minutes later, Barlozzo, navigating from the backseat, says "*eccoci qua*" as we round a curve on which sits a curious structure.

Half hut, half rambling shed, its haphazardness is surrounded by grand magnolia bushes whose shiny leaves are strung with many-colored lights, their winking and shimmering making the only noise in the dark, silent night. Tomatoes and garlic are moving about together over some nearby quiet flame and the scents curl up to and mingle with the char of slow-burning wood. Leaving the car on the edge of a ditch and alongside a truck that Barlozzo says belongs to the cook, we push our way inside the place through a curtain of red plastic beads.

Pinball machines, wine casks, a small bar, and the strangled air of fifty thousand smoked cigarettes fill the first room. There is no one about. A second red bead curtain leads to a larger room set with long refectory tables, each one covered in a different pattern of oilcloth. Announcing himself with "*permesso,*" Barlozzo walks through a small door at the end of the room, letting loose the steamy breath of a good kitchen. He motions us to follow.

Slowly, rhythmically rolling a sheet of pasta on a thick wooden table is the truck-driving cook—a petite woman of perhaps seventy, her violently red hair pinned up under a white paper cap. She is called Pupa, Doll.

We are interrupting the final scene of *The Good, the Bad, and the Ugly,* which creaks out from a wall-hung television set. As though he were at mass, Barlozzo seems to know to wait for the film's finish before speaking and so we stand, equally hushed, behind him. As Clint lopes out into the Maremma, Pupa—never once having broken her rolling stride—turns only her head to us and, rolling still, bids us good evening. "*C'è solo una porzione di pollo con i peperoni, pappa al pomodoro, cicoria da saltare, e la panzanella. Come carne c'è bistecca di vitella e agnello impanato da friggere.* There's only one portion of chicken with peppers, there's tomato porridge, chickory to sauté, and bread salad," she tells us without being asked what's for supper.

"*E la pasta?* And the pasta?" Barlozzo wants to know, nodding toward the thin yellow sheet she's been rolling.

"*Eh, no. Questa è per domani, per il pranzo di Benedetto.* No, this is for tomorrow, for Benedetto's lunch," she tells him, slowly unfolding her torso from the rolling posture.

"We'll take a little of everything, then," he tells her, and realizing he'd forgotten us, he says, "*Scusatemi, siete i nuovi inquilini di Lucci.* Excuse me, they are the Luccis' new tenants."

Back out in the dining room, we wander about looking at the wall art—a serious collection of *Daredevil* comics covers, each one framed in bright blue enamel—while Barlozzo fills a ceramic pitcher from the spigot on a barrel of red and pours it into tumblers.

"*Aspetta, aspetta, faccio io,*" says a voice from the other side of the red beads. It belongs to a young man of twenty or so who seems to have sprung from somewhere beyond the magnolia bushes, engulfed in Armani, jet hair gelled into curly Caesar bangs and giving up the scent of limes. Barlozzo introduces him as Giangiacomo, grandson of Pupa, and official waiter.

He shakes our hands, welcomes us, gives Barlozzo a three-kiss greeting, seats us, pours wine, tells us the lamb is divine, and all of a sudden, here in the Tuscan wilderness, we could be tucked in at Spago. Even though this is a trattoria without a menu, a place where one dines on whatever it is grandmother has cooked that day, Giangiacomo insists on taking orders, writing them down scrupulously in a slow, labored hand, recounting each person's wishes aloud several times, then racing off to the kitchen, carrying the news like hot coals.

"He wants to be a waiter in Rome and he's practicing here for a while before heading off to find his way," says Barlozzo, as though waiting tables in Rome were the same as selling postcards in Sodom. Barlozzo tells us that hunters bring their quarry here for Pupa to clean and hang and then cook for them. One of the hunters is her *amoroso,* boyfriend, and during the season, he calls her on his *telefonino* from his truck each morning to give her a report on his bird pursuit. According to Barlozzo, Pupa says it's *carina,* sweet, when he calls her from the road. She says she gets dressed, fixes her hair, sprays herself with perfume, and waits for the phone to ring. Then again, Pupa is always in a twitter over something. Anyway, she and her *amoroso* settle on a point of rendezvous and she drives to meet him so he can hand over his bag of birds, which she'll cook for lunch, and so she can pass him a pair of *panini* stuffed with mortadella, an eight o'clock snack before he gets to work in his garden.

"During hunting season, there are more wild hare and boar and deer, pheasant, woodcock, thrush inside her kitchen than are left in the woods. All the hunters bring their booty here and then take turns ordering big feasts for their family and friends, for each other, but it's always Pupa who does the cooking. This is the sort of place where one can phone in the morning and order a fried rabbit and a dish of stewed beans for his supper," Barlozzo says as though it's his own habit he's talking about.

"When a man finds himself alone, through death or some other interference, he simply joins the ranks here at lunch and supper. Even the widows come, but mostly they stay in the kitchen helping Pupa before they all eat together and watch *Beautiful*. Then they walk in the hills, gathering wild grasses for salad and telling their own stories. Until it's time to start cooking again," he says.

Barlozzo is proprietary, as if we are sitting at his own table. There is a great wedge of bread, which he tears at, passing crusty chunks of it to us before serving himself. This is how I've always served bread at my table, but it's the first time anyone has ever served it to me this way. We begin with that last portion of chicken with red peppers, which, once Giangiacomo sets it on the table, he spritzes with a few drops of the same white wine in which it was braised. There are just two or three lush bites for each of us. Now Giangiacomo brings out a bowl of bread salad. It's a wonderful Bordeaux color, very different from the usual look of *panzanella*. Here, lost bread, rather than being moistened in water, has been doused with red wine, then mixed with chopped tomatoes, shreds of cucumber and tiny green onion, whole leaves of basil, tossed about with oil, and set to rest while each perfect element becomes acquainted with the others. There are small dishes of fresh tomato soup, thick with more bread and gratings of sharp pecorino, before a platter of the thinnest lamb chops, breaded and fried, is served with leaves of wild lettuces. There are charcoaled veal steaks set down with wedges of lemon, a bottle of oil, a pepper grinder, a dish of sea salt. Pupa herself rushes out with an oval copper pan of bitter greens sauteed with garlic and chile.

To finish, there is *ricotta di pecora,* ewe's milk ricotta, served in tea cups. Pupa goes around the table pouring espresso over the ricotta from a little pot she's just brewed. She sets down a sugar bowl and a shaker of cocoa. We watch as Barlozzo mixes in a little of this and some of that, stirring the potion in his cup and eating it like pudding. We do the same, and I want to ask for more, but I fear Pupa will think me gluttonous. Soon enough she'll know it's true.

While we dine, the room fills with several other small parties. I notice how Pupa has been fretting over them, apologizing that there's nothing much left in the kitchen at this hour but bread and *salame* and prosciutto, some cheese and honey, a little salad. Of course none of them seems to mind—one couple with Florentine accents, which can sound almost Castilian as they say certain words, and another couple, decidedly English in their smart, perfectly wrinkled linens. Each couple has a child: the Florentines a daughter, probably not yet four, the English, a boy of six or seven. The handsome blond boy seems to have caught the eye of *la fiorentina.* Walking sideways across the room toward the English table, hands stuffed deep into the pockets of her white dress for courage, she stops in front of the blond boy's chair. *"Come ti chami? Io mi chiamo Stella."*

Sufficiently embarrassed by her brazen presence, the boy is doubly befuddled, since he hasn't understood her. His dad rescues by saying, "She wants to know your name. She's called Stella. Answer her in English."

"My name is Joe," he says without enthusiasm.

Now it's Stella's turn not to understand. Or is it? In any case, I think it's difficult to perplex a Florentine. Dispensing with all other preliminaries, she says, "*Allora, baciami. Dai, baciami, Joe. Forza. Un bacetto piccolo.* Well then, kiss me. Come on, kiss me, Joe. Try. Just a small kiss." Stella has learned young to ask for what she wants.

The Holy Ghost's Cherries

Choose fruit that is glossy, ripe but not overripe. A mix of cherry varieties also works nicely—those that are dark and sweet as well as those that are scarlet and sour.

Two pounds cherries, unpitted, rinsed, and dried with paper towels; stems trimmed or left long
1 quart of kirschwasser (cherry-flavored eau-de-vie) or a fine-quality grappa (one from Nonino in the Friuli, for example, which is widely exported to the United States)
1¼ cups granulated sugar

Wash, rinse, and thoroughly dry two 1-quart jars. Place half the prepared cherries in each jar. Mix the kirschwasser or grappa with the sugar, stirring well to dissolve the sugar. Pour half the mixture into each jar, over the cherries. Cover the jars tightly and store in a pantry or a dark, cool place. Shake the jars vigorously once a day for two weeks and then let them rest, undisturbed, for another two weeks. At this point the fruit can be stored for as long as a year before using, but once the jars are opened, store the remaining fruit in the refrigerator.

The same procedure can be used with other small stone fruits, such as apricots and plums. Raspberries, blueberries, and gooseberries are delicious preserved in this way. Experiment with other flavors of eau-de-vie, such as framboise with raspberries, or *mirabelle* with plums.

Wonderful as these are when used as a garnish for gelato or any creamy dessert, they are astonishingly good served with roasted or grilled meats. My favorite use of them is to accompany fresh or pungent cheeses. In this last case, serve a tiny glass of the preserving liquors alongside.

3

The Valley Is Safe, and We Will Bake Bread

A ten o'clock breeze is sending up the greenish scents of new wheat and Fernando croons out over the meadows, "*Ogni giorno la vita è una grande corrida, ma la notte, no.* Every day life is a grand battle, but the night, ah, the night." I swear the sheep listen to him, so still are they during his morning Neopolitan concerts. I listen, too. And I sing with him. "*Già il mattino è un po grigio se non c'è il dentifricio, ma la notte, no.* Already the morning is a bit gray if there's no toothpaste but, the night, ah, the night."

Barlozzo is late for work, but after less than a week of his patient instruction, Fernando is sailing through the cement mixing–spreading-troweling-leveling–brick laying maneuvers of building up the wall that will eventually enclose the wood-burning oven. Some days, he doesn't come at all, and it's clear that his absence is calculated, that he senses Fernando's possessiveness about this, the first truly artisinal project of his life. Proof: I'm hardly welcome on the building site, my participation having been relegated to fetching and hostessing while my husband discovers his hands and how beautifully they can create. Lovely for him, I think, but I grow weary of standing or crouching, waiting for the next command for lemonade or paper towels. And so I gift myself these hours each day to spend on my own.

First thing I'll do is to shed my Tuscan uniform. Since we'd arrived, I've worn nothing but work boots, khaki shorts, and my daughter's abandoned Cocteau Twins T-shirts. Though I am flourishing in this country life, it's not country clothes that suit me. I am Private Benjamin longing for sandals and a lunch date. Better, I want my bustier and a skirt that rustles. My summer closet looks like Mimi's wardrobe for *La Boheme*. Taffeta and lace and tulle, crinolines, a blue linen jacket with a peplum, the same one done in chocolate silk, hats to pull down tight over my too-thick hair. A romantic collection mostly from Romeo Gigli, the delicateness of these things is balanced by some forties-style vintage pieces from Norma Kamali. My few token civilian dresses I choose to overlook. Venice animates all appetites, not the least an impulse for costume. It felt right there to wander through a shadowy *calle* in a ruffled lace skirt, its baroque fullness tempered by a skinny, high-necked sweater, my hair tamed into a tight chignon and pinned low on the nape of my neck. And on the deck of a boat, plunging the starlit waters of a midnight, past marble palaces sprung, tottering, from a lagoon, a woman can feel delicious in a velvet cloak with a hood that flutters in a cold black wind. Shimmying up to the bar here at the Centrale in that same velvet cloak could only rouse scandal and feel like Halloween. Yet the straight, polyester, just-below-the-knee skirt, square overblouse and sling-back pumps of my feminine neighbors is not a *mise* I can adopt. Nor will I spend my country life safely packed into jeans, accommodating other people's comfort.

From my closet, I choose a thin silk dress, a little print thing scribbled all over in orange and pink roses. Bias-cut, clinging gently to the derrière, its skirt widens below the knees and stops midcalf. I like how it moves as I do, as though it's part of my body. I decide I'll wear it with the old work boots, mostly because I desire to preserve my ankle bones on these hills but also because I like contrast. In the mornings, I'll grab a cardigan and a big straw hat, my old Chanel dark glasses. Later on I'll wrap myself in a long white apron for cooking and baking. In the evening, I'll tie up my hair, add a necklace and Opium. And before getting ready for bed, I'll slip the dress over my head, liking the smell of the sun and how it mixes with my own, and toss it in the bathroom sink, rinsing it like lingerie, in a drop of musk-scented bath soap, pressing the water from it and draping it on the last of my satin hangers. It will always be dry by morning. I like the idea of not having to think about what I'll wear, knowing that the dress with the roses is the best dress of all for me during these summer days.

The next entry on my private agenda asks for a work plan. As much as we want to bolt the stable door on such imperatives and mandates as those which tortured Fernando's life as a banker, I must submit to some sort of discipline. It's my turn to work now for a while so that he can luxuriate in his fresh status as a pensioner. My first book, written in Venice, is a volume of memoirs and recipes, scenes from my travels through ten of Italy's northern regions. Since it's buried in the production process, due to be published in late autumn, there's nothing more I can do to help it along right now. Meanwhile I have a contract to write a second book, this one with much the same format but focusing on eight regions of Italy's south. The eighteen months I've been given to research and write seem to stretch out like forever before me, yet I know what a trickster time is. It's now that I must begin writing outlines, planning the journeys.

I look forward to the whole process, yet, at least for this moment, I'd rather tuck it all under the yellow wooden bed and just live this Tuscan life. But I can't. Even though I want to be true to our rebellion against structure, there are also several monthly assignments from clients still clinging from the states—a newsletter for a small group of California restaurants, some menu and recipe development for another, and, most recently, concept and development for a start-up project in Los Angeles. The deeper-down truth is that I luxuriate in all this, am grateful for these opportunities that will sustain us, keep our hands out of our own thin pockets.

I begin setting up an office of sorts in a space across from the fireplace in the stable. And like a hound on the scent of a hare, Barlozzo angles his bony self halfway inside the door. "*Ti serve un mano?* Do you need a hand?" he wants to know, looking at the great snarl of computer wires in my hands. The duke already understands I submit to only the smallest doses of the twenty-first century. "I thought you'd be writing your books and stories with a quill on sheepskin," he tells me as he takes over.

"I use the computer as a word processor. *Only* a word processor. Its more complex wiles, I leave to Fernando. But how do you know so much about such things?" I ask.

"I'm not so sure I do, but I must know more than you do," he says. "Besides, all the instructions are in Italian and I do read. You just go on with your work as a *tappezziera,* upholsterer. There must be something left in the house that's not yet been draped or swaddled."

Why must he stick fast to this sham scoundrel's behavior? Shaking my head and muffling a laugh at his nearly constant need to hide his kindness behind that Tartar face and voice of his, I pull curtains out of a trunk. Of heavy yellow brocade, they'd once hung in some theater or chapel, according to the merchant from whom I'd bought them at the fair in Arezzo. I push them onto the black iron rod with the wooden filials carved like pineapples that fits across the top of the stable doors. The fabric glides into place. Three panels, each about six feet wide, twice again as long, the lush length of them pours down into great buttery puddles over the stone floor. I fix one panel off to the side with a long piece of red satin cord, tying it into a perfect Savoy knot. The thick cloth restrains the sun but still the sun exalts its color, drenching the little room in gold. The duke hasn't said a word through all this, and even now, sitting back on his haunches looking at the effect, only his smile tells me he thinks it's lovely.

As THE CONSTRUCTION of it proceeds, there is much daily pacing round and round the oven site by the village men. There are mutterings and whistles, some saying it's *formidabile*. The ones who pull their hair and screech "*madonnina*" say we'll blow up the whole damn valley the first time we light the thing. As Fernando nears the finish—rallied now by technical contingents both official and voluntary—people from nearby villages drive by in the evenings, leave their cars roadside and come to visit the oven like a shrine. Our wayward humor prompts us to call it Santa Giovanna, St. Joan. Nearly everyone who comes wants to talk about the oven of their childhood, what auntie roasted on Sundays, what never-to-be-forgotten loaves mama baked. Part baptismal font, part beehive, it's so large I won't be able to heave anything into its chamber without standing on the wooden box Barlozzo has fortified with a slate top for the purpose of elevating me.

In his neolithic way, Barlozzo has made our tools by hand. He slowly sands a meter-and-a-half length of oak into a handle, attaches it to a metal sheet he's pounded into thinness with a rock. This is our peel. An oven broom he makes from a clutch of dried olive twigs tied in a braid of weed stems. With an evil instrument that might have been some form of Neanderthal-ish pincers, he evenly pierces two other sheets of metal, stacking them, separating them with cuts from the oak handle. Our cooling rack.

Fernando and I discuss what bread we'll make first. "Something with cornmeal or buckwheat? Or flatbreads with fistfuls of rosemary?"

Fernando wants dried black olives and roasted walnuts and nothing with buckwheat.

The duke has yet to look up from his metal piercing. He knows our talk is idle. He knows the first loaves—and if we're wise as he hopes, every loaf we'll bake thereafter—will be pure Tuscan saltless loaves with thick hard crusts and a chewy, sour crumb. We make a new *biga*—a pinch of yeast, a handful of flour, some water, all mixed together, then left to roil and gather force—to add to the one we brought from Venice. This will be a cross-cultural starter to build a Tuscan bread with Venetian memories.

It's on a Sunday that the oven is finished, and we make a pact that the first bake will be on the next Saturday morning, the last one of this July. After the bread, we'll braise a *coscia di maiale al chianti*. Maybe two haunches if enough people want to join us. We leave invitations at the bar, tell everyone we see about the inauguration supper, tell them they're welcome to bring up their bread dough in the morning and bake with us if they'd like.

"*Senz'altro, ci vediamo, ci sentiamo prima.* Without fail, we'll see you, we'll talk before," said so many of them.

OUT IN THE garden ahead of the sun, we arrange the wood and kindling as Barlozzo recommended, only with greater precision. We create a still-life of oak branches and vine cuttings, a great faggot of dried wild fennel stalks piled on top for fragrance. For luck. Fernando lays a match on the fennel, another on the kindling under it, igniting a roar through which flames leap and thick muffles of smoke push out the chamber door, concealing us even from each other. We run from the wreckage until we see the choking gust is contained and beginning to climb the chimney walls before the black runic plume of it bursts through the aperature. Coughing, screaming, we are triumphant. The valley is safe, and we will bake bread.

In two wrought-iron chairs pulled up close in front of the oven, we are midwives who wait. The meadows beyond are green, barely green, like crushed sage and celery run through with mascarpone, the olive trees glint silver messages up to a flight of scolding birds and the wheat stumps in farther-off fields are roasted to a crackle, brittle as caramel gone cold. I'm living the life I've always imagined. I want what I already have. When I tell this to Fernando, he says, "It's time to move the wood about." Perhaps we are saying the same thing.

Sliding his hand into the leather strap of his long, homemade baker's pole, he riddles the red-hot pile, shooting sparks and smudging the air all over again. It won't be long now, so I go inside to shape my half-kilo *pagnotte,* rounds of dough, let them rise for an hour. Using the pole again, Fernando shoves the coals to one side while I climb up onto my box, give the peel a good shake, slapping the loaves onto the oven floor, heaving the chamber door closed with my hip, sending them to glory. It's nearly 9:30 and we thought someone would have come to join us by now. No one yet.

And no one later during the morning. While the second batch bakes, we pull a fresh leg of pork out of its red wine bath, making incisions in its purpled flesh, stuffing the holes with a paste of garlic and rosemary and cloves, rubbing it all over with oil, then pouring the marinating wine back over it. The oven is cooling as we set down the sealed pot, banking it with the white ash, hoping for the best. We breakfast on our first bread, lunch on it, too, laying it with prosciutto and munching it hungrily out of hand between pulls of cool *trebbiano.*

It's nearly nine in the evening now and, in the aftermath of a fierce, short storm, a languishing sun reappears, bids a flitting good night. We're setting the table for supper out on the terrace as we look up to see Florì shuffling reluctantly down the hill, holding a bowl to her chest as though it were a rifle she was carrying over a river. Twenty meters behind her is the duke, swinging a five-liter bottle of red in a straw basket. There will be a celebration supper after all.

I run down to meet Floriana who is breathless from her hike. She stops in the road, the last light at her back. Prickles of rain cling to her unkerchiefed, loosened hair, capturing her in the flickering russet frame of it. Topaz almonds are her eyes, lit tonight from some new, old place, from some exquisitely secret oubliette, which she must often forget she possesses. We talk for a minute and Barlozzo passes us by like a boy too shy to speak to two girls at once.

"*Belle donne, buona sera.* Beautiful ladies, good evening," he says without breaking stride.

Our guests are polite, pleasant, yet, even if lightly, they seem to wear some weight of obligation. But the pork is tender as fresh cheese, its sauce is like thick, black mulled wine. The bread tastes of scorched wood and of the ages. And soon they begin to talk more between themselves than to us, and we know that what they're also tasting is a greater ease in our company. I try not to stare at them, but they're really quite wonderful together, each of them taking care of the other without making a show of it. I don't think I've ever seen them touch or even look at each other directly and yet there's a sense about them of great love, the first-love-in-the-world kind of love. Officially, they are not a couple, or at least not in any way either of them has shown us in all these weeks. Each has his own home, her own life, and goes about it it all quite separately. But there must be more. There has to be more.

"So do you know the derivation of the word *compagna,* companion?" Barlozzo asks as he takes a new loaf and tears it down its center. "From the Latin. *Com* is 'con,' with, *pan* is '*pane,*' bread. A companion is the one with whom we break bread."

Each of us raises his glass, each of us passes the loaf to the next, all of us skate pieces of the bread over the last of the sauce. Amen.

After supper, the gentlemen want to sit and smoke and snort their *grappa*. Florì and I decide to trek down to the thermal springs where Fernando and I go to bathe most mornings. We stuff handfuls of biscotti into a paper sack and put it in a shopping bag with a small blanket and an old towel to dry our feet; we check the batteries in two flashlights, kick off our sandals, and slide on mismatched emergency Wellies we find in the barn. Covered in our shawls, we take leave of Fernando and the duke.

The night is cooling quickly, and we giggle and shiver and agree "*siamo due matte*, we're two crazy women" to be setting off like this so late. I sense her joy in this delicately savage escapade and hers enlarges mine. As we walk, she begins to talk about *Adventures of Huckleberry Finn.* I like the notion of this sixty-something-year-old Tuscan woman with a head full of pre-Raphaelite curls reading this quintessentially American adventure story. "You know, Chou, I've always wanted to build that very raft and float down that very river—the biggest river in the world—and pull into some lonely bank at the edge of a forest, light a fire, cook bacon, and eat it straight out of the pan. *Come si dice* pancetta *in Inglese?* How do you say *pancetta* in English? Ah, *bahcone. Certo. Sarebbe bellissimo.* It would be beautiful."

Once down at the springs, we arc the flashlights, looking for the right place to sit, kick off our boots, and plunge our feet into the warm, percolating water. But now that our feet are warm, the rest of us is colder, and Florì reaches for the blanket. Wrapping ourselves about the shoulders with it, we sit there talking about the books of our lives. Despite her love for *Huckleberry Finn,* Florì says her favorite "foreign" books are *Madame Bovary, David Copperfield,* and *Anna Karenina.* Especially *Anna Karenina*. "Ah, how I wanted to know a man like

Vronsky. Someone *dangerous* like him. Dangerous in that there could never be anyone *but* him. Do you know what I mean?"

"I think so," I say, knowing that I do. Still wrapped in the blanket, flashlights spent, we lie back now, flattening the weeds and the prickly stalks of thyme, making little nests for ourselves, our faces tilted at the moon. Thrust by the winds, clouds swim fast about it, so fast it feels as if we're swimming, too, backstroking across the sky. Free.

Florì sits up and takes her feet out of the pool, then crouches by the springs, running her hands in the water, still gazing at the moon. Déjà vu rushes up from some long-ago place. "I knew a woman once who looked like you," I say to her.

"Do you mean to say that I look like an American?" Florì asks shyly, turning only partway around to look at me.

"Not exactly. I saw this woman just once. I was eight or nine, I think, visiting friends or distant relatives of my grandmother who lived on the coast of Liguria, near Genova. I don't think I was too happy about being there. Anyway, I went wandering on the beach near their house one day and I saw a woman who was roasting potatoes over a driftwood fire. She wore several layers of long skirts and was all wrapped in shawls and scarves. She smiled at me and I sat down on the sand next to her, watching her. Pulling a silver flask from her pocket, she reached out and turned my palm upward, poured out a few drops of thick, dark green stuff into it, lifting my palm to my lips. She poured some out deftly onto the wrinkled heel of her own hand

and sucked at it, closing her eyes and smiling. I did the same. At first I though it was awful, like medicine for a stomachache, but as I swallowed it, really tasted it, I smiled, too. My introduction to olive oil."

Florì stays crouched by the water and, while I talk, it's to her closed-eye profile. Opening her eyes now, she turns to me, pokes her legs out in front of her, arranges her skirts. Lips compressed in an endearing smile, she stays still. "Please don't stop. Tell me more."

"Well, the Potato Lady crouched down on the sand just as you were a moment ago, her thick rubber boots jutting out from under her skirts. She would stare at the fire or stand up and heave a stone or a hunk of wood out to sea, and as the potatoes blistered golden, she turned them, anointing them with the oil. She threw on a fistful of salt pulled from some other place in her magic stores, urging great, leaping flames from the fire. Finally she speared two or three pieces of potato onto a twig and offered it to me. By then I was fairly shaking with hunger for them, and I ate them, burning my mouth and tasting them and the moment with some new appetite. I wanted to be her. I wanted to be that woman on the beach. I wanted her skirts and her scarves, her shawls, her silver flask. I wanted to make a potato taste better than a chocolate pie. As much as anyone ever has, she let me see myself. Sometimes I think the Potato Lady must have been a dream or a red-wrapped specter come to pass on the great secret that living in the moment and being content with one's portion makes for the best of all lives. But she was real, Florì. And as I think about her now, she likely had her miseries. It was how she seemed to stand apart from misery, though, how she pulled the beauty out of that afternoon as skillfully as she pulled the flask from her pocket. That was her gift to me. She made happiness seem like a choice."

"Do you think it's true? Is happiness a choice?"

"Most times I think it is. At least much more often than many of us understand or believe it is."

The village bells ring midnight and, Cinderella-like, we scurry about, packing up our things, pulling on our boots. Laughing all the way, we climb the slippery hillside, tugging each other up the steep. We find the men sitting on the terrace floor, facing each other, the duke giving an astronomy lesson to a sleeping Fernando.

"I see all's well here, so I'm going up the hill to bed." Florì laughs her little girl's laugh while the duke unscrambles the length of him to follow her, their *buona notte, notte ragazzi, notte tesori* chiming through the blackness and the breeze. Arms crossed over my chest, hands trying to rub warmth into my shoulders, I stand there thinking about how much alike human hungers are, about camping along the Mississippi and splashing in Etruscan pools and bacon frying and the perfume that can come from a potato and a weed set together over the smoke of a fire, about the smell of a wild sea and the hoarse moaning of water rasping on stone, of the waves as they push farther and farther onto the sand, searching for the end of the earth. A place to rest. And how we do, too.

Schiacciata Toscana

Tuscan Flatbread (or "Squashed" Breads)

Two 15-inch flatbreads

1 tablespoon active dry yeast or 1 ½ small cakes of fresh yeast

1 scant teaspoon of dark brown sugar

2 ¾ cups tepid water

½ cup extra virgin olive oil

3 teaspoons fine sea salt

6 ½ cups all-purpose flour

1 cup finely ground yellow cornmeal

2 tablespoons fresh rosemary leaves, minced to a powder

coarse sea salt (optional)

additional extra virgin olive oil for baking pans, drizzling, and final glossing

In a large bowl, mix the yeast and the sugar into the tepid water, stirring until the grains of sugar are dissolved. Cover with plastic wrap and let the yeast activate for 10 minutes. Stir the oil and salt together and pour it into the yeast mixture. Begin adding the flour, a cup at a time, stirring well after each dose. Add the cornmeal all at once and mix to form a soft, dry dough. Add additional flour—a tablespoon at a time—if the dough feels sticky. Turn the dough out onto a lightly floured surface and knead it for 10 minutes. Place the dough into a clean, lightly oiled bowl and cover with plastic wrap. Let the dough rise for an hour, or until its mass doubles.

Release the air in the dough with a firm punch, divide the dough in two, and stretch each piece onto the surface of a lightly oiled 12-inch baking pan sprinkled with cornmeal. The dough will fight a bit, but don't be tempted to use a rolling pin. Using your fingertips, push the dough to the edges of the tin and let it rest. Go back to it in a few minutes and stretch it to the edges once again. The dough will have relaxed sufficiently by this time and should behave quite nicely under your hands. Cover the prepared *schiacciate* with clean kitchen towels and let them rise for half an hour. Meanwhile, preheat the oven to 450°.

After the second rise, press your fists, knuckles down, all over the breads, "squashing" them and creating indentations. Drizzle the tops of the *schiacciate* with oil, which will be captured in the indentations, and sprinkle over the rosemary and the sea salt, if using. Bake the *schiacciate* for 20–25 minutes, or until they are deeply golden. Transfer the baked breads from their tins to wire racks to cool. Using a pastry brush, paint the hot, just-baked breads with a few drops of oil.

Serve warm or at room temperature. Traditionally, rather than being cut into slices, *schiacciate* are torn and passed around the table, hand to hand.

4

Are You Making a Mattress Stuffed with Rosemary?

The left. Always the left. A reflection of political sentiment in this part of Tuscany and of the hand Barlozzo uses, skillfully as a maestro before his orchestra, to punctuate his speech.

"*Siamo un pò rossi qui*. We're a little red here," says Barlozzo one evening as we walk up to the bar for *aperitivi*.

His reference is to communism. Red politics took root here after the First World War, when the *contadini,* the farmers, came home to Tuscany to less than they had when they left it. The gulf between the haves and the have-nots had grown wider and deeper until poverty was savage as plague. People died of hunger just as though the war still raged. The political factions that sprung from that poverty demanded the right to work and eat, not unlike similar factions were doing in Russia. That's what being red meant here. Still does.

After the First World War, the state legislated and relegislated, inventing glorious-sounding systems, some of which were even brought to light, functioned, carried relief. But the momentum was too weak, too ill conceived against what remained an essentially medieval serfdom for those who would still work the land. The nobles continued to write contracts with their illiterate farmers declaring that 75, even 80 percent of the yields would be surrendered, the lords knowing full well these portions would keep the farmers hungry. Education for the farmers' children was forbidden, not only because even the youngest hands could work, but because unstimulated minds insured another generation of servitude. As they'd been doing for seven or eight centuries, in handsome coats cut from rich cloth, riding high in the saddles on their cosseted Crimean hunters, the lords bought more land with their profits. Always more land, without a thought to better tools or the renovation of the houses where their serfs lived with the animals. And so in the short peace that interrupted the two wars, there'd been time only to tinker with reconstruction. But afterward, the leftist factions gathered force.

The nobles remained noble, but local legislation firmly inspired their reform. The farmers' shares were increased, the more hideous edges of their squalor eased. Too little, too late; many country people were long gone, having taken flight north, feverish for an encounter with an industrialized misery. Wages that could buy food and pay rent, if barely, seemed a grand benevolence, and they hardly looked back.

Sitting on the stone wall in the piazza, a pitcher of wine nearby, we three have been talking politics through the sunset. The duke brings the subject to the present. "There is always happiness in a new set of problems. And because that's true, there's another kind of flight going on right here and now in the village." Curls of smoke wreathe his blond-white head. "The crusade of *i progressisti.*"

The more clamorous of the two distinct San Cascienesi social sects, *i progressisti,* are chomping to leap into the future, pounding their fists and shrieking *basta,* calling for progress like another round of gin. In voices more wistful, the other sect, *i tradizionalisti,* court the rituals, saying that the only true progress waits a few steps back into the past.

I progressisti who live in the village want to sell their crumbling red-roofed houses, heaped up along the tiny, winding streets. Fernando and I think these houses—defiant, bewitched in an eternal rakish slant—quite beautiful and wish we could buy one. But the villagers prefer a condominium or an apartment in one of the pink and yellow cement-block palaces that wait in the lower town. No more carrying wood up the stairs and ashes back down the stairs. Just the diligent, passionless flames of a nice gas fire. They're longing for built-in, plastic-finished closets rather than those cherry-wood armoires, big and deep as caves. They want stainless-steel sinks rather than some marble tub worn to silk from matriarchal scrubbing; they want great, fake suns swaying from the ceilings instead of the rough, hand-wrought iron lanterns Biagiotti's grandfather forged for the whole village a hundred years ago.

As for *i progressisti* who still live in the countryside and farm the nobles' lands, they ache to leave behind their rent-free, meter-thick-walled, freezing-eight-months-of-the-year houses, where once three and four generations of families lived together, each one doing for the others. But there are no more of these epic families. With the old ones dying and the young ones escaping, only the ones too old to escape and too young to die, only they, in that tethered, frozen range, remain.

For some time now there's been a paycheck every month for working the land, along with a very fair portion of the yields. So *i progressisti* say that surely they're rich enough to buy their own piece of one of the pink and yellow palaces where their cell phones will have clear signals and where there are more outlets for television sets and fewer windows to wash. But it's not just this lust for electronic amusement and straight, smooth walls that goads the progressives. The chafe is ancestral. "*È la scoria della mezzadria.* It's the sludge left from the shareholding system," Barlozzo is saying as Florì enters the piazza carrying a plate covered with a kitchen towel.

She approaches us, tiptoeing, mouthing *"scusatemi"* as though she's come late to the second act of *Madame Butterfly.* Barlozzo acknowledges her arrival by rising, taking the plate from her and putting it down on the stone wall beside our wine, kissing her hand, giving her his chair. Hardly missing a beat, he picks up with:

"Ashamed they still sharecrop a nobleman's fields, ashamed they still pay homage to him, take off their hats to him, they are resigned rather than proud to leave baskets of the best porcini and the fattest truffles by his great polished doors. A paycheck is too thin a gloss to paint over the history of a serf."

Knowing something wonderful waits under the towel, Fernando uncovers the plate, revealing what looks like a sweet but what turns out to be a round of salty, crusty pecorino bread. He cuts thin, very thin slices of the bread with the small knife Florì placed on the rim of the plate. She has paper napkins in her sweater pocket. Without taking her eyes from the duke, she pulls out the napkins, places one under each slice of bread as Fernando cuts it, passes it to each of us. This quiet diminishing of the bread by Fernando and his even softer distribution of it continues at well-paced intervals.

"*I tradizionalisti* shake their heads. Some live in the village, some on the land, but not one of them will go to live in the pink and yellow palaces. They say life was better when it was harder. They say food tasted better laid down over hunger and that there's nothing more wonderful than watching every sunrise and every sunset. They say that working to the sweat, eating your share, sleeping a child's sleep, is what life was meant to be. They say they don't understand this avid bent to accumulate things you can't eat or drink or wear or use to keep you warm. They remember when accumulation still meant gathering three sacks of chestnuts instead of two. They say their neighbors have lost the capacity to imagine and to feel—some of them, the capacity to love. They say since we all have everything and we all have nothing, our only task is to keep searching to understand the rhythm of things. Light, dark. The seasons. Live gracefully in plenty and live gracefully in need. Embrace them both or swindle yourself out of half a life. They say that everyone who's gone to live in the pink and yellow palaces is waiting to die and, in the meantime, they watch one more degenerate television transmission introduced by dancing girls and a man with a bad toupee, calling the experience *leisure*. Ease and plenty seep together to form a single sentiment that comes out looking a good deal like nonchalance. All that ease, all that plenty. What can one expect of them but nonchalance?"

Barlozzo's word for nonchalance is *sprezzatura*. A hard word, a hard concept. The translation is "the state of effortlessness." It means the mastering of something—an art, a life—without really working at it, with the result being nonchalance.

"*Traditionalisti, progressisti. Bah.* Maybe the only thing that matters is to make our lives last as long as we do. You know, to make a life last until it ends, to make all the parts come out even, like when you rub the last piece of bread in the last drop of oil on your plate and eat it with the last sip of wine in your glass," Florì says.

The duke gets up and walks over to Fernando, on whose shoulders he rests his hands. He looks from me to Florì and back to me again. "You and Florì are two of a kind, Chou. But you're even more like my mother. Life was hard for her, too."

"But I don't think life is hard."

"Of course not. Not now, anyway. Not with all the 'adjustments' you've made over time. My mother made similar adjustments. For her, life was too garishly lit, too big and too distant, and so she screwed up her eyelids and shortened the foreground. Like an impressionist painter, she rubbed the juts smooth, created her own diffusion, her own translucence. She saw life as if by the light of a candle. Nearly always she seemed to be wandering about in an elegant sort of defiance. Holding tight to her secrets. Like you do. And she thought everything could be solved with a loaf of bread. Like you do."

"It's true, she sees things in her own way." Fernando tells a story about Erich and me. About a morning I was driving him to school along the Rio Americano highway in Sacramento. We knew every turn and twist in the road and all the buildings and landmarks along the way, so that one morning when, about a hundred yards ahead, I spotted a new sign, I nudged Erich and said, "Look, honey, a new French bakery." *Pain,* bread, is what I read in the four bright red letters.

"Mom, that sign says *pain*. Pain, like in hurt. It's a clinic, mom," he told me.

Never one to spoil a good story by sticking to the truth, Fernando decorates the events, raising up a hand-slapping between him and the duke. I wait until they're quieted down and my embarrassment softens a little before I ask Barlozzo, "What do you know about my secrets?"

"If I knew something about them they wouldn't be secrets, would they? All I can say is that mysterious people usually recognize other mysterious people."

"So if you recognize that I have secrets, that means you have them, too. Right?" I say.

Florì raises her head, quickly recovering her surprise by reaching for the dish, empty now except for crumbs and the old silver knife.

"Right. And let's just leave it at that for now."

"OK. But as for my trying to solve things with bread, well, all I think is that along with everything else there is or isn't, a good loaf of bread can't hurt. Speaking of bread, I'm out of rosemary again. Will you bring some to me?"

"Are you making a mattress stuffed with rosemary? I've never known a person so fixed on this damn weed as you are," he tells me.

"Maybe it's because I miss the sea. *Rosmarino.* Rose of the sea. The patch up by the old spa is almost as good as the salt-crusted bushes that grow along the Mediterranean."

"I'll get you enough rosemary to stuff a dozen mattresses and I'll happily sit through any number of your exotic suppers. But will you always make me my own personal loaf of normal, daily bread? And will you pour me a glass of wine and put a pitcher of oil on the table? I think it's time for me to do what Florì does, to practice making the parts come out even, the bread and oil and wine."

5

Sit the Chicken in a Roasting Pan on a Pretty Bed of Turnips and Potatoes and Onions, Leeks and Carrots . . .

Some mornings we abandon our walks down to the thermal springs and trudge up behind the village to the site of the original *terme,* spa. The very word *spa* is a Latin acronym for *salus per acquum,* health through water. Peeking into the derelict halls where the the Medici once came to soak, we're wondering if what village intelligence touts is true. A grand reconstruction of the spa by a Florentine corporation would surely change the color of the village, a seduction for the chic and the stressed who would come to be revived by warm waters and kneading hands across their aching backs. The sleepy little village would be awakened, but not necessarily by a handsome prince. I steal a look at my own handsome prince as we walk without talking, each of us wandering inside his own reverie. But what is this? What is this long, slow shudder in me? Could it be caused by the tizzy of the winds, trying to push away the summer? Is it from the strength of my husband's hand on my hip as we walk? My face is burning where he held it a moment ago as he kissed me, and I like the taste of him that stays on my mouth and mixes with the tastes of coffee and milk and bread, the grains of undissolved sugar on his lips. Like a good buttery *kuglehopf,* he tastes. How can he do this to me? How can he make me giddy? Maybe it's not him at all. It's high blood pressure. Why didn't I think of that? I'm sure of it. High blood pressure is causing the quiver. Or is it a hormone rushing away, then rushing back again, just for fun? Maybe it is Fernando. I decide it's him, but it's horrid not being sure. More horrid is it that this man can just as skillfully send up a shudder in me of a different sort.

I am out in the garden tending to a chicken, fixing it the way Florì told me her mama used to do it for Sunday lunch. I'd done just what she'd said, *sit the chicken in roasting pan on a pretty bed of turnips and potatoes and onions, leeks and carrots . . .*

Her directions had stopped there, so I continue on my own. I fill its belly with a handful of garlic, the cloves crushed but not peeled, then rub its bosom to a glisten with olive oil, finally ornamenting it with a thick branch of wild rosemary. After an hour or so in the wood oven, the skin is bronzed and crisp, the juices running out in little golden streams, and I remove it to a long, deep, heated plate to wait. In the house, I set the roasting pan over a quick flame, scraping the bits of caramelized vegetables and the drippings that cling to the pan, blessing it all with splashes of white wine, finally transforming the juices into a sauce that tastes like Saturday night as much as Sunday noon. I lay trenchers of bread in the sauce, leaving them to soak in it for a few moments while I heat a half cup of *vin santo,* throw in a handful of fat *zibibbi,* raisins from the island of Pantelleria off Sicily. Wild lettuces, all washed and dried and tucked in a kitchen towel, are ready in the refrigerator. I open a sauvignon blanc from Castello della Sala and set it in an ice bucket.

Monet would have loved the terrace table, bejeweled as it is with a jugful of poppies and lavender, candles set in old ships' lanterns against sultry nine-o'-clock winds. I call for Fernando, who is upstairs somewhere. I lay the cool lettuces on a serving plate, drizzle them with more of the sauce, lay the soaked bread on top, strew the warm, winey raisins over the bread and, finally, set the chicken atop the whole creation. I'm starving.

I call up from the bottom of the stairs. "Fernando. *La cena è pronta,* supper is ready."

I pour the wine, stand there on the terrace sipping it, a hand resting on a hip, looking out at the end of the day. Still, no Fernando. I walk out into the garden and call up to the open windows.

"Fernando, will you come down to supper with me?"

Someone who is not Fernando pokes his head out a guest-room window. Even in the dark I recognize him. Perhaps it's more that I *sense* the presence of my old friend, Mr. Quicksilver. The Heaving Breast that inhabited my husband so freely in Venice has found our Tuscan hideaway.

"Non ho fame."

Quicksilver was never hungry. "But why don't you just come to keep me company? The chicken looks wonderful. At least have a glass of wine, a piece of bread. Come and talk to me." I try all the buttons that have worked in the past, but none of them yields.

Master of the dramatic, he gives tension time to build for a few minutes before I hear him schlumping down the stairs. I take a long gulp of wine. One look at him and I see he is a janissary gone to war with his stars. He begins by announcing that his leaving the bank hasn't provided the great washes of peace he'd searched for. He grieves his losses: no security, no position, no title. "There's this hollow place where I thought serenity would be," he says.

I want to tell him that serenity is not geographically dependent, that if he didn't feel serene in Venice, how could he expect to feel serene in Tuscany. Instead, I say nothing. I only look at him in quiet wonder, glorious images from these past weeks and months fluttering through my mind. He tells me he feels robbed. He speaks this indictment while standing very close to me. "And am I the thief?" I want to know. Now, I'm on my feet, too.

"Yes, of course you are. It was you who made it seem possible," he says.

"It was you who made me believe that I could grow to be someone else besides good old Fernando," he says, all ready for the tender mercies he knows are coming.

"Good old Fernando is the most beautiful man I've ever known. Don't leave him behind. Take him with you and be patient. Instead of worrying about who's robbing you of what, worry about how you thieve yourself. You rob time, Fernando. How arrogant you are, taking an evening like this one as though it were some sour cherry, spitting half its flesh into the dirt. Every time you pitch yourself back into the past, you lose time. Have you so much of it to spare, my love?"

Did he expect some Turkish fairy to rake a path for him through the Tuscan forest? Wasn't it his general weariness of being the follower that caused his flight? Fernando cannot, it seems, sustain any emotion, save melancholy. I know this melancholy is an appeal for consolation, yet my ready sympathies are weak against it. His is a peace built up on sticks. The smallest sparring of his visceral forces shatters the falseness of it. Like a seabird's nest riding a wave, it drowns in bitter waters. "Why will you always insist that you're falling off the edge of the world? Haven't you heard? The earth is round, so when you feel yourself falling, tuck and roll and get up again just like all the rest of us have to do." I'm shouting now.

Still he's not hearing me. I pull out André Gide and read, "If one desires to discover new lands, one must consent to stay a very long time at sea."

He says that's rot, yells that's where he's been all his life, at sea. And now he's further out at sea.

"And do you want me to take on the blame for this, when it was you who resigned from your job without even discussing it with me, when it was you who couldn't wait to sell the house and *begin to be a beginner.* Would it just be simpler for you to forget those truths and let me indulge your coltish whinnying? Is that what it costs to be your wife? I don't know if I can pay. I don't know if I want to pay."

I notice that I am speaking these things in pure, hot Italian. And with a fresh, biting eloquence. I am Anna Magnani *and* Sofia Loren. I am stunned as I watch from some safe place inside me while this other woman who is me bites the side of her hand, stamps her feet, tosses her hair. Is that really me screaming oaths? There is some sense of exhilaration in spewing out three years, a hundred years of swallowed thorns. Yes, it's me. Tiny me who just cries when things hurt or smiles, saying something profound and soothing to whomever might be near. I needed another language to release me from my own repression, my good-girl self-censoring. I walk away.

I walk right out the door. It's past ten. The night is still moonless and I'm still hungry. I wish I'd taken the chicken. Though it's hot, I shiver like November inside my dress with the orange and pink roses. I'm hungry and my dress is so thin. I'm not certain why these two facts seem related. At first I head up toward Celle, but change my mind and take a sharp left down the steep, sandy path toward one of the thermal springs. In the darkness, I slide and stumble without my boots. I sit for a while on a rock ledge and feel the tears start but I'm just too angry to let them fall. I use the tufts of dried wild flowers on either side of the path to foist myself back up the sheer side of the hill. I notice how fragile the flowers are, yet I trust them to hold me. I don't have a license to drive in Italy. I have my strong legs, my sandals with the thongs that rub and hurt between my toes. I've forgotten to take my purse. But there's not much money in it anyway. Talk about losses. I feel inside the pocket of my dress and take out a 5,000-lire note. Whatever it is I'll be doing next, this will have to fund it. My steps are fast and heavy as I head down Route 321 toward Piazze. Six kilometers of starlit country road. Saturday night in Tuscany.

Save the few passing cars, I meet only a young gray fox on the way. I walk fast as though I'm heading someplace, but there is no place to go. I know where Barlozzo lives and where Floriana lives, too, but this is not the sort of village where one drops in anywhere at 10:30 on a Saturday night unless stalked by a bear. Except at the bar, that is. I know that's the first place Fernando will look for me, so I've headed in the opposite direction.

Piazze is even smaller than San Casciano, the whole village beginning and ending on a single curve in the road. But there's an *osteria* and as I walk by it I can see the tables full of people still at supper. I walk inside and up to the bar, order an espresso, and try to begin some inane conversation with the *padrona,* but she's all alone to serve and clear and probably cook, too, so she just smiles a *buona serata*. Good evening. Too late for that, I think, as I walk back out onto the road. And then I see the dark blue BMW prowling. I know he's worried. He hasn't seen me yet and I could choose to play with him but I don't. Suddenly, I miss him. I know how hard all this is. I know how hard all this may always be. I step out and pretend to be hitching a ride. He stops and opens the door.

"Whatever else happens, however foolishly I may behave, promise me you'll never do this again," he says.

I promise because it's this that I signed on for. I know that I signed on to indulge the lamenting and the quicksilverishness of him with as bold a signature as I signed on for the goodnesses of him. Still, I'm tired of packing and unpacking my heart. These crises of his, which feel oddly like betrayals, cause desolation in me. And I have to push hard at that desolation so I can remind myself of how he is *made*. All this behavior is an expression of his character, inexorable as bones and blood. Besides that, Fernando is Italian, and he knows what I can't learn. He knows that life is an opera that must be shrieked and lamented and only once in a while laughed. Between acts, he says how much better it is now that he has released himself from his old life's sleep. He tells me he loves being able, finally, to shriek and lament and even laugh. He says he loves most of all that he can cry. He asks me to love him for the difficulty of him more than the ease of him, something a man would never ask of a woman unless he already knew it was so. Still, to pacify him has become a self-indulgence, a vanity of sorts, and I know I must beware of this.

We just sit there in the car, not talking at all, until I speak. "As much as I love you, you can push me away, at least from time to time and for a while. Let me try to tell you how you make me feel sometimes. When I met you, you were tired of being Fernando, that other Fernando who was poorly used in many quarters. You said you'd always been an honorable and patient and sacrificing person and still people handled you ever more brutally. They knew you'd take it. The bank, the family, the friends, they all trusted in your resilience. Do I understand all that correctly?"

"Absolutely correctly," he says quietly.

"And beginning long ago and one by one, each of them was embittered in some way, when you cancelled them from your life. Is that how it happened?"

"That's how it happened."

"Well, then, why are you making me into your Fernando? Don't you see that sometimes you treat me just a little in the way others treated you. It's only once in a while and less often now than it used to be in Venice, but how I wish it was never. I just can't hear you when you scream. And so, in defense, I'm learning to scream, too. And I think I could get very good at it, but then neither one of us will be heard, and there'll be nothing left to do but walk away."

His look speaks of both torment and chafe and I think he doesn't understand at all. I'm too tired to try further, so I surrender to the silence he seems to prefer. I am reminded of my son, of some sting he flinched from years ago, the sort of sting that only a five-year-old knave can raise up upon his four-year-old mate. I remember trying to convince Erich that it wasn't his fate to keep peace at any cost.

Right now all I know is that in love there must be some form of desperation and some form of joy. Both these sensations—along with whatever else the lovers invent or permit—are constants. Lovers are never long without one or the other or both of them. Is the joy fuller through the desperation, as it is to eat when you've been very hungry, to sleep when you've been awake too long? And if it is, shouldn't we welcome the despair as much as the joy? The giving, the getting, the taking, the nurturing, I have begun to understand that we take turns signing on for one or another of these as though they were daily jobs. We continue to assume jobs until all of them are filled, until all the roles established. The dynamic part of love lies within each of these jobs but rarely beyond it. Consider, too, that love transforms the lovers.

As though matter is recast, nothing can ever be as it was before the love. As you were with each other at the beginning of love, how you moved through the days and nights together, that is how you'll move always. It was at the beginning when you learned to dance together. Notice that even now you dance together in the same way. Music, no music. A languid glide before an abrupt, explosive half-twist before a full turn. Two beats of stillness, awaiting further consideration. Fast, slow, quiet, sweet, angry. Love is a very personal tango. And every once in a while, just so we won't forget it, the old truth comes to visit, the one that reminds us that we can grow but we can't change.

NEITHER OF US wants to go home just yet. We head up into Camporsevoli, lay the car quilt on a hillside in a stand of pines. We talk. I lie on my stomach, a hot cheek pressed to the earth's coolness seeping through the quilt. The pine boughs make a thick curtain over our heads through which moonlight prickles. He lies so close, nearly covering me with himself, as though to protect me. I love the weight of him. This thought makes me smile and I say the word, *irony,* out loud. Fernando says "Hi, honey" back to me. He is perplexed at my laugh. We sleep this way. We wake and talk some more, sleep some more until we smell, then see the somber violet breath of first light, trembling, blowing out the stars. Just a few at a time, a contained overture, until *ecco, Apollo,* shrieks good morning to the night, exploding what's left of the darkness, firing up the sky in great hallelujahs of amber and orange and the fierce pink of a pomegranate's heart.

Fall

6

Vendemmiamo—Let's Pick Those Grapes

As we approach Palazzo Barlozzo it's just seven, a touch early even for the duke to be paying us a call, and yet there he is coming round the back of the house, looking like Ichabod Crane. We walk up to meet him and, as a worried old papa who finally sees the objects of his concern all safe and sound might do, his dread slides into a scowl before it settles into peevishness.

"*Buongiorno, ragazzi. Sono venuto a dirvi che la vendemmia a Palazzone comincerà domani all'alba. Io verrò a prendervi alle cinque.* Good morning, kids. I came to tell you that the harvest in Palazzone will begin tommorow at sunrise. I'll be here at 5:00. Be ready."

"Great, perfect, wonderful. Of course, we'll be ready," we tell him brightly but shamefaced, trying to slur the edges of our mischief. It's clear he knows we'd had a bout of trouble, and I think

Fernando is about to explain some of it to him, when the duke says, "Listen, Chou, the next time you want to let off some steam, take the road to Celle. It's less dangerous. In trying to find your own tranquility, you're disturbing the local peace."

Without warning, this man who's yet to shake my hand is taking me, hard, by the shoulders, kissing each cheek, saying he'll see us both in the morning. It's stunning not only that he knows we've spent an unusual night but that he can scold and soothe and threaten with a few words and a single gesture.

"*Adesso, io vado a fare colazione in santa calma.* And now I'm going to have my breakfast in sainted calm," he says through wintry lips and assassin's eyes, loping his way to the henhouse.

We try not to laugh until one of us begins to laugh anyway and when he hears us, he turns back and he's laughing, too.

"*Vi voglio un sacco di bene, ragazzi.* I want your happiness, kids," he yells out into the faint plash of a September rain.

We had begun back in June to ask Barlozzo where he thought we could help pick grapes. In my journalist life, I'd traveled much of Europe to participate in one *vendemmia* or another—in Bandol in southern France, on the island of Madiera, and once, farther up north in Tuscany, in the Chianti—to collect information and impressions for my stories. Each time, the farmer in me was inspired. I couldn't imagine *living* here and not being part of it. And more ardent even than my yearning for it, Fernando's was fixed. One way or another, the banker was going to pick. But Barlozzo had been restrained about the idea. Did we realize it was *un lavoro massacrante,* a murderous work, that began each morning as soon as the dew was dry and lasted until sunset? He said that neighbors gathered on one farm, picked it clean, moved together to the next to do the same. He said that there were often six or seven or more small harvests in each of these circles bound by friendship and a mutual need for the simple wine that was food to them.

"Whose grapes do you help pick?" I'd asked, hoping the directness of the question would stave off more scenes of Armageddon under the still-cruel September sun.

"Usually I go to help my cousins in Palazzone, though now they've got so many children and in-laws swarming the vines, they hardly need me," he'd said.

"Well, is there other work we can do to help? Can we cook?"

"What you're not understanding is that the harvest is 'family' work, open to neither the curious nor the admiring. But we'll see. I'll ask around."

After his clearly stated cultural lesson, I'd just let the subject sit. And the first we'd heard that we were invited to pick was this morning's announcement that he'd be waiting for us at dawn tomorrow.

La vendemmia, the grape harvest, is anticipated, celebrated more than any other seasonal event in the life of Tuscan farmers. The oldest cultivated crop on the Italian peninsula is the vine, the tendrils of its history wound about and grafted into rites pagan and sacred, into life itself.

Almost everyone has vines, either his own or his landowners', either a hundred or so scraggly plants grown up among blackberry bushes or set between rows of feed corn or hectares and hectares of luxuriant and photogenic vines nurtured by masterful hands. Or, as it is with Barlozzo's cousins, some configuration in between. Most often, except on the great parcels of land where mechanical means are sometimes employed, the grapes are cut, cluster by cluster, the clicking of the secateurs meting out an ancient, pastoral rhythm.

A strange sort of flat twig basket is hung from the vine where the harvester works, freeing his hands to clip the clusters and drop the fruit into it in a smooth two-step motion. When the basket is full, the fruit is turned out into larger plastic tubs, which are then carried to the small trucks or wagons that wait here and there among the vines to port the grapes down the road to the crusher. When I lived in California, I found that the innocent pleasures of wine were too often diminished by prodigies—real or self-imagined—bent on deep-reading a glass of grape juice. There is no such blundering here. These farmers make their wine in the vineyard rather than in the laboratory the way commercial winemakers do. The fruit—undisguised, unmanipulated, and just as the gods send it—is the stuff of their wine. That and their passion for it. And this congress is all the alchemy there is. Rough, lean, muscled wines, wines to chew, thick rubescent elixirs that transfuse a tired, thirsty body like blood are these. No fragrance of violets or vanilla, not a single jammy whiff nor one of English leather, these wines are the crushed juices of the grape, enchanted in a barrel. As we tumble out of Barlozzo's truck on the vineyard road, we see what must be thirty people standing and sitting near a small mountain of baskets and bins. To a person, their hair is tied in some form of bandanna or kerchief. Hat brims buck up against the vines and inhibit the work of picking. This other form of headgear holds back sweat, if not the sun's violence. I decide to put my Holly Golightly straw hat back in the truck, hoping not too many of the harvesters have noticed the two-foot diameter flounce of its offensive brim. As I come back to join the group, Barlozzo hands me a neatly ironed blue-and-white bandanna, boycotting my eyes, the better for me to feel his scorn. I want to ask him why he just didn't remind me of my inappropriate hat while we were driving to the site, but I don't. Fernando is loathe to surrender his black Harley baseball cap and receives the duke's tacit approval.

The other thing that separates us from the pack is that we have not come with shears attached to our belts. Suddenly I feel like a chef with no knives, a plumber who must borrow a wrench. But there are others without arms, and soon the *vinaiolo,* the winemaker, is distributing weapons and errant gloves to us as though we were on a breadline and had asked for toast.

The spirit of festival is thin among the vines and under the wakening sun as the *vinaiolo* assigns territory, demonstrates technique to the few first-timers. I can't help remembering the California harvests I'd witnessed. The estate manager and the winemaker mill about the vineyard, variously nodding and shaking their heads, touching, smelling the fruit, writing in notebooks, racing with the grapes into the lab to test the Brix. Would there be a harvest today, or would we wait for tomorrow and the further concentration of the fruit's sugar? Here it's another story: when the moon is waning and the grapes are fat and black, dusted in a thick white bloom and sun-dried of dew—the residual moisture of which might dilute the purity of the juice—the *vinaiolo* snaps off a bunch of grapes, rubs one or two on his shirt sleeve, tosses them into his mouth, chews, swallows, smiles and says, *Vendemmiamo,* Let's pick.

The work is beginning, but I have to use the bathroom. Two women in pinafores and corrective shoes with the backs cut out flutter about my needs, show me the way, ask after my comfort. I'm the last one to slip into the leafy avenues of the vines. My partners are a man called Antonio, thirtyish and swaggering, and another called Federico, seventyish, chivalrous as a count. When they see that I know how to use my secateurs, holding the curved handles easily in my fist, that I can burrow deep into the vines to clip and drop the fruit into my basket almost as rhythmically as do they, Holly Golightly is redeemed. "*Non è la tua prima vendemmia. Sei brava, signora.* This is not your first harvest, my lady. You're good."

Less than two hours have passed and, drenched in sweat and rouged in grape juice, I am febrile, weak as a babe as I step out from the humid enclosure of the vines and into the light of the fiendish sun. It is the first collective rest of the morning and I can't remember if I've ever been this tired. My legs feel just-foaled, not quite able to hold me as I try to stand. My body is seared but somehow exquisitely exalted and the all-absorbing sensation is not unlike a postcoital one. I look about for Fernando, who must be on the other side of the hill that separates the two fields. There he is, waving me toward him. Because they're so beautiful, I can't resist limping among the vines rather than along the sandy path beside them. Here and there among the green, succulent leaves, one or two are tarnished gold by the sun, crisped and beginning to curl. A symptom of autumn.

We go to join the rest who've collected about iceless tubs of mineral water set in the shade between two old oaks. There are barrels of wine. There is no one actually swallowing the water, except the errant splashes of it that land in the mouth as they pour it over their heads and shoulders, chests, arms. They bathe in the water and drink the wine, and it all makes sense. I do what they do. There is a basketful of panini—thick cuts of bread stuffed with prosciutto or mortadella —and I eat one hungrily while Federico refills my tumbler with wine. I drain it like a true spawn of Enotria. I feel faint.

I manage to recall enough strength to return to the bending and clipping until I hear an accordian whooshing and voices singing. Only sun-inflamed I think I am and that the pleasant fit will pass until Antonio says, "*È ora di pranzo.* It's time for lunch."

Merciful lunch and a serenade. I find Fernando, unfolded flat between the vines he was picking when lunch was announced. He's laughing, saying he'll never move again. We follow the others to the place under the same oaks, if a little deeper into their shade, where a long, narrow table is laid with a green and blue cloth and set with great, round loaves of bread, bowls of *panzanella,* wheels of pecorino and a whole *finocchiona*—the typical Tuscan *salame,* big around as a dinner plate and scented with wild fennel. There are flat baskets piled with crostini smeared with a paste of *fegatini,* chicken livers. Someone taps into another demijohn of wine and people stand in line with pitchers while some let the stuff fizz directly from the spout into their glasses. Sitting on the packed earth among our colleagues, we and the sky and the sun are stitched together in a primitive agragrian motif.

On a far hillside there are women on ladders pulling fruit from a stand of fig trees. They seem painted, a Sapphic bevy at work. Glass breaking under velvet is their laughter, riding the air like a shiver. They carry the fruit back to us in the skirts of their pinafores, letting the figs drop softly onto the table. I take one and it's hot from the sun. I bite it, piercing its honey juices, rolling them about in my still wine-wet mouth. I bring one to Fernando and he eats it whole with his eyes closed. Everyone is quiet for half an hour, sleeping, half-sleeping. The accordianist sings alone.

THE *VINAIOLO* MANOEUVERS through the vines, saying, "*Per oggi, basta, ragazzi*. For today, that's enough, kids."

It's only just after five in the afternoon, nearly two hours earlier than the usual quitting hour, and there's a buzzing among the harvesters wanting to know why. The drift that circulates says it's because we've stripped more than half the vines in record time and that the crusher, even though it will be fed all through the night, simply can't accommodate more fruit than we've already picked. A great cheering rises up and the men strut about, hugging and kissing each other like a band of Latin desperadoes fresh from a raid. Grappa is offered all around midst the rush for autos or trucks and the milder spoils of a bath and a bed. The *vinaiolo* stands at the end of the drive where all our vehicles are parked and shakes hands with each of us, looks us straight in the eye and says thank you fervently, as if we'd snuffed the fires of hell. And I think how artistic is the Italian's glissade from mood to mood. Perhaps it's all the olive oil.

We harvest with the same champion group in four different vineyards for nine successive days until all the grapes are in. The weather stays warm, energy and good humors prevail. Riding back home with Barlozzo in the truck on the last day, I tell Fernando my thighs have grown strong and firm, and he tells me he's certain now that working the land is what he's meant to do. Barlozzo says we're once again lulling ourselves into the quaint thinking of the middle-aged in crisis. He says all we did was help our neighbors to pick a few grapes. The duke's nimble restoration of equilibrium. I squeeze my Titian thigh and think maybe it's not so taut after all. To heal his trounce, I suppose, he asks if we're ready for the evening's festival.

We can't wait, we tell him. And as we're jumping down from the truck, Fernando says, "*Tutti al bar per gli aperitivi alla sette mezza, va bene?* Everyone at the bar for *aperitivi* at seven-thirty, OK?" Even though the ritual of *aperitivi* is sacred, one of us always reminds the others.

THE HARVEST SUPPER is staged in a vineyard we'd picked a few days before. It is the smallest one we worked but I think the most beautiful, sitting in a pine-hemmed field and sharing its estate with an olive grove. Long and slender tables, built of boards laid over barrels, are covered with starched white linens and set among the stripped vines. Makeshift benches flank either side of them. All the light is fire. Torches have been pummeled into the red earth. In a space enclosed by a low wall of piled stones, a great wood fire burns. Candles are set down the whole the length of the tables, and yet more candles in paper sacks mark the pathways up to the farmhouse. Scents of new bread and new wine intoxicate the twilight and a dawdling piece of moon climbs the sky.

I want to help in some way, but our thirty-person picking troops have burgeoned into a sixty, perhaps seventy. And so I watch. Our supper site is the home of my older picking partner Federico, who comes to greet me. He steers me up to the widely flung doors of the kitchen, where his wife and daughters direct the spectacle. I count nine women, but they all move so swiftly there are probably more. They sing as they cook, naturally separated into sopranos who ask lyrical questions of the altos, who answer the sopranos and then ask questions of their own. An operetta among the flour and the steam.

At one table women are stretching bread dough into flat rounds, laying them with grapes. They tell me the story of their bread, that the first cluster of grapes cut by the *vinaiolo* from each family's vineyard are taken together in a basket to the church to be blessed by the priest. The grapes are then placed in a bowl to loll about in extra virgin oil perfumed with rosemary and crushed wild fennel. The bathed grapes are then laid, one by one or in tiny bunches, over the dough. The women heave fistfuls of sugar—white and dark brown mixed together—over the grapes and grind on pepper with a violent hand.

They slide the breads, then, into the wood oven at the back of the cavernous kitchen.

"*Schiacciate con l'uva.* Grape flatbreads," says one of the women as Federico appears again, hoisting a large reproduction Etruscan urn. He runs his finger over its decoration and points out the disclike objects held high by the women parading round the curves of it. "*Vedi. Sicuramente anche gli Etruschi hanno fatto le schiacciate durante la vendemmia. Questo pane è una cosa antichissima.* See. Surely the Etruscans also made this bread during the harvest. It's an ancient thing," he says.

The breads bake in no time and soon Federico recoups them from the oven, setting them on a battered wooden door perched on the kitchen table. When all of the breads are baked, four kerchiefed, pinafored women, each with a hand on her hip, their faces flushed as brides', raise up the door and carry it out and down the candlelit path into the vineyard. People make way for them, shout "*brave, bravissime,*" and, in poses and movements eerily like those of the Etruscan priestesses on Federico's urn, they pass the sugar-crusted beauties, two or three to each table. The crowd applauds.

Federico hurries me on to the next glory. Under the ashes of last evening's fire in a hearth wide and deep as a small room, he'd set fat white beans to braise in bulbous-bottomed wine bottles, most of them remnants from his grandfather's winemaking days, he says. He'd mixed the beans with water, sage, garlic and rosemary, sea salt, just-cracked pepper and a dose of extra virgin oil. He'd stopped the bottles with pieces of wet flannel so the steam would hiss away without exploding the glass and left the beans to cook all night long. *Fagioli al fiasco sotto le cenere,* beans in a flask braised under ash. Now he's pouring the cooled, herb-scented beans from all the flasks into a huge white bowl, drizzling on more oil and tossing them. When everyone is seated he and his wife will carry the bowl together, passing the creamy-fleshed beans table to table, person to person, just like his grandparents used to do.

There's so much happening at once, so many people trying to show me something, I'm twirling about from oven to table to fireplace, forkfuls and spoonfuls of one thing or another offered, urged, imposed, whipping my hunger for more. More.

One of the women is crushing a bowlful of grapes with a potato masher, saying she'll press them over her face and leave them to dry overnight, says the facial refines the grain of her skin, leaves her pink, glowing. She's not more than twenty-five; I decide she's likely to be pink and glowing in any case, but I thank her for the advice.

There are yet *more* grapes, just washed and being plucked from their stems and nestled on top of and between fat sausages in a thick, huge copper pan. A thread of oil is dropped by one woman, another's hands move under it, massaging the grapes and the sausages to a shine. Another copper and then another is prepared for the oven in the same way. All three of them onto the oven floor, the metal door slammed shut.

"*Quaranta minuti e saremo pronti, ma adesso venite tutti per il battesimo.*

Forty minutes and we'll be ready, but now everyone come for the baptism," says Federico. The crowd has moved to stand near the fence of a kitchen garden, fallow save great orange pumpkins snarled in their vines. The leaping fire in the stone ring backlights the pageant. A young, blond man in jeans and pink T-shirt is holding a very tiny baby, his son, barely evident among the soft folds of a white blanket. There is a wooden tub sitting on a small table, also draped in white. The thrall is thick as the jasmined night. A woman comes forth, adjusting the father's arm to better cradle the baby's head; another one, surely the baby's mother, presses her hands to her cheeks in a gesture both anguished and thrilled. An intake of breath. The hush. The father says a prayer of thanksgiving for the harvest, for the health and the well-being the wine will provide, for the love and friendship of his neighbors, for the birth of his beautiful baby boy who is called Filippone, Big Philip. A quick flourish, the blanket is unfurled, dropped to the ground and, holding the baby's head in one hand, his other hand supporting the baby's back, the father immerses Big Philip, just-born scion of this tribe bound by the land, into a tub of just-born wine. The symmetry of this impresses me. The bath lasts a flicker and the father holds up his placid, naked, grape-washed, six-day-old baby high over his head to the shouts of the crowd, "*Eviva Filippone, eviva Filippone,* long life to Big Philip.' "

A tiny son of Bacchus. In a few days, he'll be taken to church and washed clean of original sin. Heathen rites, Christian rites. Big Philip will be unassailable on all fronts.

Everyone settles in at table then, passing platters and trays and baskets. There is the inevitable pouring of wine. And no supper truly Tuscan begins without the thin slices of cured meats, the crostini of chicken livers, the roasted bread smeared in oil. This night will be no exception. Federico's white beans and the sausages, charred now and crisped, spooned out with the thick, winey juices of the heat-swollen grapes, are eaten with the *schiacciate* and chunks of black-blistered, roasted pumpkin, the flesh caramelized to sweetness, their only condiment a whispering of salt. The harmony of these foods taken on this night and among these people is one of the most delicious of my life.

Just as the supper seems to be ending, the last of the plates cleared, the cloths brushed clean of crumbs, the kitchen troupe appears with yet more baskets, this time overflowing with biscotti or piled with *crostate*. Bottles of *vin santo* are passed down the table and everyone sets to the work of softening the brittle cookies in the wine, eating them between sips of the ambered stuff while the jam tarts are broken, pieces of them eaten out of hand.

"*Aspettate, aspettate, ragazzi, c'è anche la saba.* Wait, wait, kids, there's also *saba,*" warns Federico, trailing the perpetually bowl-toting women. *La saba* is the fresh must, the unfermented juice of wine grapes, distilled over a quiet flame into a haunting, tawny syrup, sensual as a smoky old Port. Ancient as winemaking is this sweet, and bottles of *saba* are hoarded in the *dispensa,* guarded like relics. Tonight, threads of *saba* have been folded into tubs of mascarpone. Offered in espresso cups with small spoons, *la saba* is the festival's cold and silky good night, and yet no one moves from his place. We are all quiet, though, each one of us gone back into himself. Fernando seems to have nodded off, his head heavy on my shoulder. Everything having been said for the night, tales told, laughter laughed, there is only a sweet peace under the milky radiance of the shrinking moon, smudged, now and then, by the racing of a cloud. Fireflies ricochet off the sheared vines, someone caresses the strings of a mandolin. My husband's snuffling is sibilant on the breeze. And Big Philip is somewhere near, suckling.

Winemaker's Sausages Roasted with Grapes

Serves 6

⅔ cup extra virgin olive oil
2 tablespoons fresh rosemary leaves, finely minced
2 teaspoons anise seed
2 teaspoons fennel seed
pepper from the mill

2 pounds artisanal pork sausages made without garlic or chile (Aidelle's pork, duck, or rabbit sausage are a good choice)
A mix of 2 pounds red and white and black table grapes, rinsed, dried, and relieved of their stems
1 cup red wine

In a small saucepan over a low flame, heat the oil—taking care to not let it reach the boil—and add the herbs, seeds, and generous grindings of pepper. Stir and cover the pan, permitting the oil to infuse for 15 minutes. Meanwhile, pierce the sausages with the tip of a knife, one or two pricks each, place them in a large kettle, and barely cover them with cold water. Bring the kettle just to the simmer; cover it, leaving the lid askew, and poach the sausages for five minutes. Meanwhile, preheat the oven to 400°.

Drain the poached sausages and place them in an ovenproof roasting pan. Pour the infused oil over the sausages, add the grapes, and toss everything together, coating the sausages and the grapes with the perfumed oil. Place the pan in the preheated oven and roast the sausages and grapes for 25 minutes, turning them so the sausages will crust and the grapes become plump, their skins bursting with juices. With a slotted spoon, remove the sausages and grapes from the roasting pan and keep them warm.

Add the red wine to the pan and stir over a medium flame, scraping up any bits and pieces that cling to the pan. Raise the flame to high and let the wine reduce almost to a syrup. Pour the reduced wine over the reserved sausages and grapes and spoon them quickly onto warmed plates. A purée of potatoes and leeks or a ladleful of polenta makes a wonderful sop for the juicy sausages and grapes. Alternatively or in addition, pass chunks of crusty bread.

Fagioli al Fiasco sotto le Cenere

Beans Braised in a Bottle under the Cinders

So passionate are Tuscans about their beans, Italians from other regions often refer to them as *mangiafagioli,* bean eaters. The most ancient, most succulent method of cooking beans is *al fiasco,* in a bulbous-bottomed wine bottle. The parboiled white beans are mixed with water or wine, olive oil, a branch of rosemary, a few cloves of garlic, and a handful of sage leaves and poured into the bottle. The neck of the bottle is gently stoppered with a moistened cloth, set loosely enough to permit steam to escape, and then the whole is buried under the ash of a dying fire. The beans cook through the night and are ready next morning (or afternoon or evening) to pour out into deep bowls over crusts of yesterday's bread, the lush juices drenching and softening the bread. A final thread of oil, a few turns of the pepper grinder, a flask of red wine nearby, and a Tuscan is safe for another day.

Serves 8–10 (or 4 Tuscans)

1 pound of dried white cannellini beans, soaked overnight
2 teaspoons coarse sea salt
1 cup extra virgin olive oil
1½ cups water
1 ½ cups dry white wine
1 large branch of rosemary
3 or 4 fat cloves of garlic, peeled and crushed
a good handful of sage leaves
2 teaspoons fine sea salt

Drain the soaked beans and place them in a kettle, covering them with cold water. Add the coarse sea salt and bring the beans to the boil over a high flame. Lower the flame and cook the beans for an hour. Drain them and pour them into a round-bottomed 2-liter Chianti bottle or some similarly shaped vessel. Add the oil, water, wine, rosemary, garlic, sage, and fine sea salt. Shake the bottle to distribute the ingredients. Stop the bottle with a strip of wet cloth, bury the bottle in the ashes of the fireplace, and go to bed. Alternatively, to cook the beans on top of the stove, braise them over a quiet flame in a heavy kettle for two hours, or until they are creamy but not collapsing.

7

Dolce e Salata, Sweet and Salty—Because That's How Life Tastes to Me

"Because things are different now, that's why," Floriana fairly snarls at me over the crashing timbres of October.

"It's been twenty years or more since I've bothered with all that. Do you know how many tons of peaches and plums and tomatoes and green beans and red peppers I've picked and cleaned and jarred and boiled and put away in my lifetime? And now you want me to do it all over again?

"*Neanche per sogno.* Not even in a dream," she says as we collect the last of the black plums from the trees in my yard, racing with the tempest threatening at our backs.

"Well, what I'd had in mind was only to save these," I tell her, sweeping my hands across the crop piled into baskets all around us. "We can't possibly eat them all before they rot, and then I went and bought two bushels of tomatoes in Cetona this morning and I thought we could just spend a few hours together so you could show me how to handle them. Then I could do the rest by myself. All I need is a start," I say, knowing I've asked too much.

As we walk back up toward the house, she says, "It never works that way. Canning is like kissing. One thing leads to another, and before you know it we'll be surrounded by hundreds of jars and bottles with no place to put them and, in my case, no one to eat all the beautiful stuff that's inside them. Like so many other things we used to do to survive, canning just doesn't make all that much sense now."

I stay quiet, just looking up at her from the seat I've taken on the terrace steps, thinking how little I still know of her. How little she's willing to have me know and yet how it seems enough. She's been a widow for more than twenty years, she has no children, she's a housekeeper and a cook, working four days a week for a family in Città della Pieve. Her home is a small and handsome apartment—*una mansarda,* a rooftop space—in a small palazzo near the church. Born, bred, and having lived all her life right here in the village, she is warm and indulgent with her neighbors, yet often seems apart from them, a red-haired stranger embraced in sympathy by a benevolent flock. A Rafaello madonna, she is perhaps the most beautiful woman I've ever seen. An oval of moonstone for a face, the skin of her is translucent as a butterfly's, blushing easily in deep patches of scarlet that make her seem a girl. From the bantering I've heard between her and Barlozzo, she must be nearly ten years younger than he, perhaps somewhere in her sixties. He always refers to her as *una ragazzina,* a little girl, and she calls him *vecio mio,* dialect for, my old one.

From the first day we arrived, when Floriana stood here in the garden with her hands on her hips, offering to help us move in, there's been something lovely between us. Something made of contentment. I think often to that piece of a July evening we spent with our feet in the thermal springs, eating biscotti by moonlight. Since then, on some of her days off she comes to visit in the late morning, giving me a hand with whatever I'm cooking or baking, or she stays outdoors to help Fernando rake or sweep. She must always be doing something. Earning her way through life, moment by moment. While Fernando and I are puttering about with one thing or another, sometimes she sits upstairs in the small room off the front hall and does her mending by the window. There, against one wall, is a large table filled with dozens of photos of my children, our wedding, our travels. She says she'd like to know my children and always looks at their photos for a long time, picking up one, then another and another, smiling and clucking. She says Lisa looks like Audrey Hepburn, that she should forget the university and just go to Hollywood. She loves Erich's eyes, says, "*Lui è troppo tenero da vivere tra i volpi.* He's too tender to live among the foxes." Fernando says that's her way of saying he looks kind. She is particularly fond of one of our wedding photos, one in which my back is to the camera as Fernando helps me step up from a gondola onto a landing stage. She takes it over to the window where she can see the detail better. She always looks at that photo for a very long time.

Florì never stays very long, an hour or so, and won't hear of sitting down to lunch with us or eating or drinking a thing. I think she just wants to be here. Once in a while we walk together in the early evening, meeting by calculated chance more than design along the road to Celle. Not a talker, Florì is comforted more by smiles than words, by linking her arm through mine as we walk. We put our faces to the weather, both of us liking it in all its forms. One evening, I'll have a sack of licorice drops, two ripe pears, or an orange, but most often Florì has her sweater pockets filled with tiny chocolates wrapped in blue foil. We divvy them like diamonds. I take on her ways, not feeling much of a need for words myself. If we never knew anything more about each other than what we'd gleaned from that first day, I think we would still be friends. Yet both of us can be politely curious about the other, and sometimes we ask questions freely enough. She wants to know about America, specifically about San Francisco, where I worked for many years, says she wants to walk along the Golden Gate Bridge one day and to ride the ferry to

Sausalito, to stand outside on the deck in the fogs as she saw an actress do in a film.

She likes the story of how Fernando and I met and wants me to tell it to her over and always asks me to repeat some part or another of it. Once I asked her about Barlozzo, about how long they'd been a couple, and she answered that they'd really never been a couple in the sentimental sense, that they'd been friends all their lives, always would be. Another time, she said she was *impazzita,* crazed, about him when she was still a girl, but that he never took much notice of her. She says he was always *un lupo solitario,* a lone wolf. I understand that when her answers are less than large, it's not because a question offends her but more, I think, that it confuses her because even she doesn't know the answer. Lit by sun, quickly hidden by shadows, I can see her but then I can't. A trick we all use. Or perhaps there's no trick at all with her. Perhaps it's only that Florì is Tuscan.

"Oh, Chou. I'm not some depository of tradition you can tap into the way you do with Barlozzo. He'll never tell you so, but he's truly fond of taking you both by the hand and strolling backward. In one way or another he tries to do the same with as many of us who'll let him. But with you two, and especially with Fernando, he seems to think he's bequeathing his legacy, passing on the stories and somehow assuring the significance of his life. You three are complicit. And complicity is a kind of love, don't you think? In some ways, he *is* behaving like a man in love. He's just been around all the rest of us for so long. The ones of us who are older than he think he still has so much to learn, and those of us who're younger think we want something more—or is it less?—than the past. Older or younger, though, all of us are tired in our own way. It's the freshness of you two that's turning his head."

Pulling away from her musing, she turns sly, saying, "It's too bad you can't ask *him* to help you with the plums and the tomatoes. Conserving is probably the single food art in which he's not an expert. He can stick a pig and butcher it, saw the haunch bones just right so the prosciutto dries firm and sweet. He can make *salame* and blood pudding and head cheese, he can pickle the ears and the tail and boil down the fat to make cracklings. I've seen him skewer its heart on a branch with sage leaves, roast the thing over a fire and then gnaw at it, calling it supper. *Lui qualche volta è una bestia, altre volte, un principe.* He's a beast sometimes, other times, a prince. But he's always good, Chou. *Barlozzo è buono come il pane.* Barlozzo is good as bread."

She's doing her best to distract me, but it's not working. All this publicity about Barlozzo's talents and virtues is redundant, wasted on me. I'm already convinced he's a fallen angel with neolithic, Roman, medieval, and Edwardian pasts. I know he knows everything. Except how to can plums and tomatoes.

"*Ciao tesoruccio, devo andare. Ma, sai di che cosa hai bisogno? Un congelatore, bello grande. Così puoi conservare tutto quello che vuoi, anche tutte le prugne toscane. Ciao,* little darling, I must go. But do you know what you need? A freezer, a great big one. With that you can save all the plums in Tuscany."

For a moment I think she's serious and I'm about to condemn her blasphemy, but I see she's having herself a fine laugh, so I do, too. Walking down the hill, she is a lonely figure who's left me standing in a squall amidst the molding fruit.

BARLOZZO AND FERNANDO are sitting at the dining table, drawing. Inspired by the one in Federico's garden on the evening of the harvest supper, this time it's a firewall they'll build. All the project needs are stones and a flat, isolated earth space where the flames won't threaten the trees. It will be a primitive barbecue pit over which we can grill and, with one of Barlozzo's contraptions, hang a pot and braise everything from birds to beans, he tells us. An alternative to the wood oven, the fire ring is practical not only for cooking but also for our own bodily warmth. "Otherwise you'll soon be saying it's too cold to stay outside, and you'll miss out on the most beautiful evenings of the whole year. There's a long, deep winter coming on when living by the inside hearth is what you'll *have* to do, but why rush it? And if you're willing to surrender all your linens and candles once in a while, you can sit right down close to the fire, cooking and eating under the stars just like a shepherd," he says. He knew the shepherd image would get to me. He really is in love with us, I think as I listen to him going on about splendid autumn nights and pork chops dripping in garlicky juices. He keeps stumbling over his use of *we,* changing it to *you,* not wanting to impose himself onto these delicious fancies. I wish he'd understand that *we* is most appropriate. Barlozzo has come to matter so much to both of us, but I think he and Fernando are closest, if in their own economical fashion. I think they see themselves in each other. Fernando sees that, as he grew older, he might have become like the part of Barlozzo who is—or is it *was?*—too much alone and always scuffling about on the edges of anger. Barlozzo provided him with a Dickensian visit. The Ghost of Christmas Future. And I think the duke sees his younger self in my husband, most especially when Fernando displays the hard core of his will. That must be the reason he says, six times a day, how wonderful it is that Fernando *scappato dalla banca,* escaped from the bank. I don't know why, but I think Barlozzo wanted to escape something or someone long ago. And because he didn't do it, the duke celebrates all the more Fernando, who did.

THERE'S A *CAVA,* a stone quarry, a few kilometers down the Piazze road. Fernando says we can find enough stones there to raise a coliseum, but Barlozzo tells him someone's sure to see us digging about, wonder what we're building, and then come by to tell us we're doing it all wrong. This is a pleasure, we understand, Barlozzo wishes to keep all to himself. "They'll wander over like they did when we were building the oven and we'll have to listen to thirty opinions about the best way to pile stones. I know a place in Umbria where the Tiber is low at this time of year, and we can take what we need from the river bottom in a few hours. Besides, it's a beautiful ride getting there," he says.

And so on a limpid afternoon we heave our wheelbarrow and a sack of the duke's Stone Age tools into the back of his truck. We're off. Fernando begins his Cole Porter repertoire: "You do something to me, something that simply mystifies me." Sometimes when we sit out in the evenings up at the bar, Fernando and I sing for hours while Barlozzo and his cronies listen, engrossed as though we were a traveling Jacques Brel troupe, applauding and saying "*bravi, bravi*" even when we stop only to think of the next line. The duke has learned a phrase or two and he joins in with Fernando.

"Tell-e mee-eh wh-h-y-ah should eet-ah be-ah, you-ah have-eh the power-r-r-ah to hyp-eh-notize-eh mee-eh?"

I turn to look at him and and he's steely as a hangman, mouthing the words just as he's heard us sing them. A phonetic coup. Pronouncing every vowel and separating every syllable, he's three-and-a-half beats behind Fernando, the Tuscan echo of a Venetian singing American love songs, and the effect is beautiful.

Barlozzo elbows me to sing, too. Our noises seem to propel the old truck, to make it fly over the road all the way to Ponticelli, onto the *autostrada* and then over the snaky trail toward Todi. No matter what song Fernando and I sing, Barlozzo sings his one and only remembered line, fitting the words into the different tunes, always trilling out the last note until his breath gives way. Singing seems to embolden the duke, kindling his curiosity.

"So what do you call that dress you're wearing? *Mi sembra un avanzo del ottocento.* It seems some remnant of the 1800s," he tells me, arching his brows in the direction of my autumn costume, recently assumed in favor of the dress with the pink and orange roses. I wear Wellies and a long, wide black flannel skirt, a Kamali skater's skirt softened over at least fifteen Septembers.

"I guess it's true that both my clothes and I are survivors of some other time."

Barlozzo eases the truck off the road into a swag of soft earth in front of a stand of pines. We take out the tools and the wheelbarrow, cross the road to the riverbank. I leave my boots on the shore. Kilting up my skirt, knotting the bulk of it on my hip, I walk barefoot into the Tiber. The sun is mean on my back, the water ices my feet and, as though I've waded in the Tiber all my life, I'm familiar with it, splashing and kicking at it. As I high-step across the whole eight meters or so of the river to the other shore, a small epiphany roils up in me, and I think once again how much I like this life. It feels purloined in a way, or like a prize. First prize for not waiting. For not waiting to splash in a river, for not promising myself that I would *someday* splash in a river, but for doing it now, right now, before destiny or some other interloper stops by to tell me there's been a change of plans.

The men are loosening stones with crowbars, pulling them up from the shallow, skirling water, laying them in the wheelbarrow. One trip to the truck. Another one. I don't help at all except to sing to them, shout encouragement. I cheer them on with a delectable litany of what we'll cook over the first fire.

Squeezing the river from the edges of my skirt, letting the drops wash my fingers, I go to sit on the bank. Watching them work, then wandering a bit about the woods, cutting orange-berried branches that look something like bittersweet, I am cozy as velvet when they call me, saying it's time to go. We drive up the hill into Todi and stop for *un espresso in piedi,* on the run, stroll for a while before we sit, sipping *prosecco* and agreeing about the grievious state of our hunger. It's only seven, an indecently early hour to contemplate supper and so we head for the truck.

"We can watch the sunset and then go to eat fish at a roadhouse on the way home," says Barlozzo.

We stop at another point by the river's edge, handing each other jackets and sweaters against the gathering breeze. Rinds of golden light wrap apricot clouds and the leaving sun colors the Tiber red as blood, a crimson rift in the heart of the new night. We stumble down to sit by the water, and with no warning I hear myself saying, "I think we're going to look for a place to buy."

"Where?" Barlozzo asks.

Fernando answers, "As close to San Casciano as we can find."

"I thought you were just passing through. I thought this interlude was adventure, amusement. I thought you'd be heading back to Venice at some point, or the States," he says, though he already knows it's not amusement we're seeking. He pushes a tiny spade further into me.

"What are you going to do here? I can understand you wanting a holiday place, just like everyone else in the world seems to want. But most of the folks who buy something here have lives, houses, work. They have a *somewhere else*. Oh, they love it here all right, or at least the parts they bother to get to know, but the best I can say for most of them is that they're straddlers—one foot here, one foot stuck hard back in that somewhere else. In the end they really don't live anywhere. They play it safe. But you two don't seem to be talking about safety. Why would you want to *live* here?"

I don't say a thing but, with my chin, I point to the river and the pines.

"Because of those," I tell him, "and because of what we look at every day back in San Casciano. I want to live there in those pink hills with the sheepfolds and the leaves of the olives twisting in the winds like so much silver and the sound of the bells pounding up through the mists. I want to live there because of all that."

I turn to him, then, and I say, "And because of you."

Bemused now, shadows collect about his eyes.

"I want to live there because of you. I want you to be my teacher. I like that you're passing on to us even a little of what you've seen, what you know, how you've done things. What you feel." Only the river makes a sound until we hear a slow shuffling step coming from a nearby hillside stitched with a few rows of vines. There's just enough light to show us the figure of an ancient, her hair wrapped in a kerchief, a man's cardigan her cape. Likely the *padrona* of the farmhouse upriver, she's come to survey her realm. Her feet spread apart, she stands solidly on her wooden clogs in front of the vines, picking the errant grapes left here and there, unseen by the harvester's shears. As if they were stolen and she was hungry, she eats them from her palm. And still chewing, her hands making sounds like a wounded bird in a bush, she searches in the withered leaves for the next hidden bounty. Venus grown old and artless, she charms me. As though I'd put my eye to a peephole to look at my someday self, she is me. We sit a few yards distant, yet we are unobserved by her.

Or dismissed by her. She knows the truth, that it's all moot, that both calamaties and triumphs are passersby and mostly insignificant. She knows that neither of them is what it seems and that, if there is a difference between the two, it's only that our great feats stale in less time than our injuries are recovered.

"She's craving a burst of sweetness before the light fades. Isn't that what we all want?" asks Barlozzo. "But before I get to that, it's the salty crackle of a great pile of fried fish I want," he says rising, slapping the latest dirt from the back of his already dirty khaki pants.

We eat fried *latterini* at a place called Luciano. Tiny lake fish the size of smelt, a platter of them is delivered to the table. I think it's too much for us, until two other platters of the same dimension arrive and a jug of cold white wine is plunked down. Nothing else. I watch the duke. Picking up one and putting a part of it in his mouth, he does a sort of folding motion and the whole diminutive structure is dispatched in two chews and a swallow. I do the same and taste the suggestion of hot, crisped, sweet flesh, but I need two or three more, taken faster, then faster yet, before I can get the full, rich taste of them to fill my mouth. I sip the cold wine and rest.

The stone ring is built up in a day, and over the smoldering ash of our first fire, we roast a meter's worth of fat sausages made by the butcher with the hachet that swings from his Dolce e Gabbana belt. We turn them until they're bursting, laying them, then, on trenchers of good bread and eating them between long, hard pulls of wine, sitting right there on the red Sienese earth like Barlozzo said we would. We feed the fire again, watching the flames burn holes in the dark, feeling the night roll in and over us like a silent sapphrine wave.

"Why do you insist on sitting so close to the fire? Do you desire to become a burnt offering?" Fernando asks me.

"I have to find the right position. I like being close to the edge. Not too close but not too far away, either. Though I guess I prefer to be too close than to be too far," I say.

"You don't trust comfort any more than I do, Chou," says Barlozzo.

"Because I like to sit close in to a fire?"

"No. Not just because you like to sit close in to a fire. That's only a symbol of the fact that you don't trust comfort. You trust risk more than comfort. I've always been afraid of comfort, too. Bring on the pain, because during those moments when I can neither see it nor feel pain, when it's quiet, I know it isn't really quiet at all but only gathering force. Better that pain stays where I can keep an eye on it. There's risk in comfort. There's comfort in risk. Risk, risqué. It adds piquancy, that's what risk does. Repress the appetite. Give in to the appetite. Stay close to the edge. Stay away from the edge."

"Which is it?"

"It's all of them. All of them in judicious doses, taken at judicious moments. Finesse is what life asks. Otherwise one rots before his time."

The duke is grisly this evening. Fernando stares at him, abashed, I think, that his simple warning to me to sit back from the fire has unleashed discourse about the risk comfort poses, about judicious doses of finesse and a faster rotting. We both know there's nothing to do about it and so we listen.

"*Cominciamo dal fondo*. Let's begin at the beginning. St. Augustine said it most clearly, *We are, every one of us, going to die.* Rotting is the way of all things. A tree, a cheese, a heart, a whole human chassis. Now, knowing that, understanding that, living begins to seem less important than living the way you'd like to live. Do you agree with that?"

I look at Fernando, we nod yes to each other, he nods yes again to Barlozzo.

"So, life, by definition, is impermanent. All the energy we spend in trying to fix it, secure it, save it, protect it, leaves damn little time for living it. Pain or death or any other pestilence doesn't pass over us because we're careful or because we have insurance or, God forbid, because we have *enough* money. All right. So how does one come to understand exactly *how* one wants to live? How one wants to use up his time?"

Fernando seems to be holding up under the irascibly delivered monologue, but I'm caught back somewhere between St. Augustine and the rotting cheese. Yet I understand that, for Barlozzo, the shortest distance between two points is a convolution, so it's not surprising when he says, "If you want, I'll help you to look for that house."

Floriana was right. We three are complicit.

THOUGH IT'S FELT like another room in our house since that first night we spent in San Casciano, as time goes by, Bar Centrale becomes more like a whole other home. Rosealba, Paolo, Tonino, Signora Vera, the whole family of patrons who oversee the bar takes us in, makes life better for us. There's a telephone on the wall in the corner by the pinball machines. When we call Lisa or Erich or my agent in New York or editors in California, Signora Vera shushes the clamor of the children, telling them we're talking to Bill Clinton. After having lived for years under the gelato maker, an old fax machine is dusted, cleaned affectionately with cotton dampened in alcohol, and set upon a small table behind the bar that has so recently become the international communications center *and* bar, truly *Centrale*.

Three, four, sometimes more times throughout the day and evening find us there, at a table on the little terrace, leaning into the bar in the morning with hands wrapped around our *cappuccini,* screaming into the phone in the late afternoons. Wiping the coffee drips and the wine stains off the day's fax receipts, the Centrale is the great convergence. It's Hollywood and Vine, it's Wall Street, the Champs Élysée. It's the juncture at which all news, even the undistorted, is revealed. It's where fortunes are punted, mostly at cards, and where, when thirsts are tamed, peace is restored. It is our office, tea salon, war room, inner sanctum, refuge, and pied-à-terre. Is there anyone who really needs more than this? I begin to understand why some Italians will tell you they'd rather choose their bar than their neighborhood, that it's better to settle for an apartment short of their dreams as long as the local bar feels right. Some will even tell you that their bar is what the neighborhood church was to its parishioners long ago—a place for comfort.

And constant as are true Centrale's pleasures, so, too, is Barlozzo's desire to provide delight. Or his idea of it. A giver, he is. A giver from far away, most often. He leaves things by the door or, yet more removed, piles up his gifts on our habitual path through the woods—a purple-stained sack of blackberries propped up with an armload of white flowers, a small, neat stack of split wood tied up in a weed. When we thank him he says he knows nothing at all about wildflowers or a wood stack. Hoof-up, wiry black hairs standing stiff and straight and stuffed in a plastic sack, the haunch of a beast is one morning's gift. Screaming, slamming the door shut on the piece of a beast, the fracas brings a naked, half-sleeping Fernando running down the stairs. "*Cosa c'è?* What is it?"

My back tight against the door, I tell him with my eyes and a slight lean of my head that something evil lurks behind me.

He takes on the silent mode of communication now, mouthing his questions. "*Che cosa è sucesso, chi è?* What happened, who is it?"

"*Guarda*. You look," I dare him.

Barely cracking the door, placing an eye to the light, he whispers, "*Non c'è nessuno.* There's no one."

"*Guarda in giù*. Look down."

"*Cristo. È solo una coscia di chingiale.* It's only the leg of a boar," he says, opening the door wide, his slender boy's body bending to retrieve it. What does my Venetian know of wild boar, I wonder as he ports it across to the kitchen, laying it in the sink, removing its wrappings. Another *Cristo* is whispered before a long, slow exhale. "*Caspita che grande.* How huge," he says, hoisting it up by its ankle, turning it, twisting it to inspect it from all angles. "It must weight fifteen kilos or more."

I don't much care how many kilos it weighs. I just don't want it in my kitchen. Adrenalin coursing, I'm about to rush Fernando, to take the thing and heave it somewhere outside, anywhere away from me, when the duke thrusts his grinning face inside the door. "*Buongiorno, ragazzi. È una giornata stupenda, no? Ah, bene, avete trovato quel bel giovane mostro.* Good morning, kids. It's a wonderful day, no? Good, you've found that beautiful young monster."

I notice he is careful to look only at our faces, politely avoiding Fernando's costumelessness yet unastonished by it. *"Permesso,"* he says, walking through the door, turning to shut it, ostensibly giving

Fernando time to head for the stairs and his trousers. But my husband, who concentrates best on only a single thought at a time, has forgotten himself in lieu of the boar. "*Come si pulisce?* How do we clean it?" he's asking.

Hard and fast, I pinch his bum. *"Ah, mi scusi,"* he says, loathing to interrupt the moment.

Still zipping and buckling, he's back before I've had a chance to castigate the duke for the fright he's caused. I just stand there watching them spread newspapers on the terrace, collect knives and the haunch and set to scraping at it. Barlozzo is saying that the boar had been stalked and taken by hunters in Piazze three weeks ago, that the two-year-old male had been cleaned then hung in the village postman's cantina before being butchered and sold off this morning. Long connected to the routings of this group, the duke had put in his bid for the left hind leg. . . . "*È la parte migliore da stufare in vino rosso*. It's the best part to stew in red wine," I hear him telling Fernando while I'm dumping flour into the bread bowl.

Their handiwork complete, they reenter with a much more anonymous mass of flesh and bones. Barlozzo asks me for the largest cooking vessel in my kitchen battery. My old copper *sauteuse* does not satisfy him. "*Torno subito.* I'll be back quickly," he says, and when he returns it's with arms full of wine bottles and a terracotta pot bigger than Pittsburgh. Herbs with their roots and dirt hang from his back pocket. He asks me to heat three bottles of the wine while he lays the herbs on the bottom of the pot, piles in the pieces of boar, salts them, grinds on pepper. He pours over the warm wine, covers the pot and places it out on the terrace. He places three bricks over the cover and says to let it rest for three, four, maybe five days, disturbing it only to turn the flesh once each day. Every morning I watch as Fernando performs the flesh-turning rite with two large forks, fastidiously raising each piece from the bath then submerging it again, pushing it securely into the red depths. He covers the pot, replaces the bricks and stands back, staring at it as if expecting it to move or speak. As dutiful to the cause as is Fernando, Barlozzo comes each afternoon to remove the bricks and the cover, to poke at the flesh, bending his head close to it for a whiff. "*Non ancora.* Not yet," he says on six consecutive afternoons. On the seventh, he says it's ready to cook.

Detemined to begin cooking no matter what the duke said, Fernando had already lit a fire in the outdoor ring after lunch. Now it's burned to nearly the right mix of red and white ash to suit the duke. But first he asks me to bring the boar and its wine to the simmer on the stove. This seems to take forever and, like mechanical toys, we approach and retreat from the kitchen. Finally the first bubbles appear and Barlozzo takes the pot out to the ring. Having banked the ash into a hill, he nestles the pot in it so that the terra-cotta is thickly insulated all around and nearly covered up to its lid. He then lifts the lid, reverses it over the pot, and fills the hollow with more ash. His final instructions are to do nothing until he arrives tomorrow morning. This seems too passive a duty for Fernando, who stands watch over the thing, evening out the ash, sprinkling more of it over the lid, coming back into the stable, making a full turn around the sofa before going back out again to see if there's been some change. I fear the night will be long for him.

When the duke comes to lift the lid next morning, we see that the flesh has braised to a deep mahogany brown, the wine and herbs and juices have concentrated. Its perfumes cause us to swallow hard with longing for it. "Now it has to rest until tomorrow," he says. We're both incredulous that the production is still not finished. Obeisance has its limits. As soon as Barlozzo leaves we spoon the stuff into soup plates, pour wine and, with some of yesterday's bread, sit down to a different kind of breakfast. So tender, we could eat the flesh with a spoon, its flavor both sweeter and more assertive than pork, it leaves a faint taste of hazelnuts on the palate. I pour out some of the copious sauce from the terracotta into a small pan. Adding half a glass of wine to refresh the long-stewed juices, a teaspoon of tomato concentrate, I blend it all over a low flame. A few grains of sea salt and the result is good. We take out a few more pieces of the boar and try it with the adjusted sauce, deciding it will make a fine condiment for pasta.

That's how I serve it to the duke the next day at lunch, before a soup bowl of the boar straight from its braising pot as a second plate. We eat our fill and more, but when I look at what remains, I could swear that the boar has replenished itself. And the plenty inspires another ritual.

We begin to take a supper basket up to the bar on Friday evenings, every Friday evening. A casual thing meant to provide us a form of social life, we share whatever we have with whomever is there. After three weeks of bringing braised boar in one disguise or another, we pack our basket with a mashed-potato tart crusted in pecorino and a little pot of sauce for it made of green olives crushed with leaves of fresh oregano. There's a dish of small red peppers stuffed with fennel sausage and roasted in the bread oven and for later, a plate of crisp cornmeal biscuits rolled in sugar. Vera pours us some wine, brings bread, sets a place for herself at our table, and before five minutes pass it feels as though this is exactly how and where we were meant to spend our Fridays. Vera eats very little, very slowly, and I'm uncertain whether it's the unfamiliar food or just her patrician manners. Still, she seems pleased as she bids us good evening, proceeds upstairs to the family apartments and her television. Tonino takes the night shift. As each person comes in for an espresso or a *digestivo,* he walks out from behind the bar, escorts him or her over to our table, urges a taste, a bite, inviting them to sit with us.

After a few intimate suppers with Vera, we are joined by others until there grows up a quiet fame about Fridays—far less for what we bring to eat than for what the communal suppers recall for the San Cascianesi. Soon they bring their own Friday suppers to the bar, tying up the pots and bowls in white cloths, tucking their stories inside. They tell us how they shared food during the war, they recount every detail of their grandmothers' and great-grandmothers' best dishes and their most cherished sweets. Wanting us to explore friendship free of his tenacious presence, Barlozzo wanders in late, sniffing about for a dessert before calling for his grappa. Sometimes he would portion himself out a plate if anything was left in the pots.

"*Ma perchè i tuoi piatti sono sempre dolce salati?* But why are your dishes always sweet and salty?" he wants to know one evening, racing a heel of bread through the pan juices left from a duck braised with pears in *moscato*.

"Because that's how life tastes to me."

Braised Pork to Taste Like Wild Boar

Serves 6

10 juniper berries, 10 whole cloves, and 10 black peppercorns
2 teaspoons fine sea salt
3 pounds leg or shoulder of pork, trimmed of excess fat and cut into 3-inch chunks

2 tablespoons extra virgin olive oil
3 medium yellow onions, peeled and minced

3 large cloves of garlic, peeled and crushed
1 small dried red chile, crushed
1½ teaspoons fine sea salt
2 bottles sturdy red wine
1 cup thick tomato purée
1 cup red wine

2 large cloves of garlic, peeled, crushed, and finely minced
2 teaspoons good red wine vinegar
1 tablespoon fresh rosemary leaves, minced to a powder

Crush the juniper berries, cloves, and peppercorns to a coarse powder in a mortar and pestle and turn out into a small bowl. Add the sea salt and mix well. Rub this spice mixture over the prepared pork, massaging it onto all surfaces. Place the spiced pork in a nonreactive bowl and cover tightly. Store the pork in the refrigerator for three days, turning the pieces once a day.

Heat the oil in a large, heavy pot over a medium-high flame. Dry the spiced pork carefully with paper towels and add it to the pot—only as many pieces at a time as will fit comfortably without crowding. Permit the pork to take on a crust before turning it, letting it crust on all sides. As the pork is crusted, remove it to a holding plate and continue the process, adding a few more drops of oil as the pan dries, until all the meat is crusted.

Add the onions, garlic, chile, and salt to the pan and stir over a medium flame only until the onion is transparent, taking care not to let it or the garlic color. Add one bottle of the wine and, as it heats, scrape the bits and pieces sticking to the pot. Add the tomato purée and bring the mass just to the simmer. Add the crusted pork and as much of the second bottle of wine as is necessary so that the pork is nearly immersed in it. Heat the mass to the simmer once again, cover the pot, leaving the lid slightly askew, and stew the pork very gently over a low flame. Stir the mass from time to time to keep the meat moist, and continue to stew it for 2 hours. Test the meat for tenderness. Continue the stewing until the meat is extremely soft and falls to shreds at the touch of a fork.

With a slotted spoon, remove the pork to a holding plate; add the last cup of wine to the juices in the pot and bring just to the simmer. Add the garlic, vinegar, and rosemary to refresh the sauce; return the meat to the sauce, stir well, cover, and let rest a few minutes. Serve some of the sauce with pasta as a first course and the meat as a main course, accompanied by only bread, a few leaves of salad, and the same good red wine used to cook it.

8

Now *These* Are Chestnut Trees

"S*ono buoni, proprio una delizia quest'anno.* They're good, absolutely a delicacy this year."

The duke is talking to himself, flailing his cane at the lower branches of one of the chestnut trees that hug the road winding up from the village. He grinds his booted foot over a few nuts, smells the meat of one, chews it. We're returning home from breakfast at the bar and decide to come upon him quietly, intending to give him a good fright. On tiptoe we approach his back, disturbing not a single bronze leaf of the pile in which he stands. "*Domani,* tomorrow," he shouts without turning toward us, knowing all the while we were there. Now shifting toward us, his evil-child grin in full pose, he salutes by touching two fingers to his old blue beret and strides off toward Piazze. Either he talks until we break a sweat or he talks hardly at all. Still, the significance of Barlozzo's *"domani"* is clear. The chestnuts are ready for harvest. He'd been telling us, warning us for days, that as soon as the nuts were ripe, he'd take us into the woods to gather from the oldest, best-yielding trees.

"First order of business in harvesting chestnuts is to prepare the ground under the trees," he tells us next afternoon as we set out.

Walking past all the roadside trees, carrying rakes, a shovel, a tree-swatting device that looks like a carpet beater, a large basket shaped like a cone with leather shoulder straps and three five-kilo jute flour sacks begged from the baker, in single file procession we turn into the woods where the road bends just past La Crocetta. We walk deeper into the woods, still passing by what seem to be perfectly beautiful chestnut trees, until Barlozzo stops short at the entrace to a stand of great, thick-trunked ones and says, soft as a prayer, "Now *these* are chestnut trees."

We unload our weapons and he begins to rake the dross of old leaves and twigs, cleaning and smoothing a wide patch of earth around a tree, keeping the new, just-fallen nuts apart and putting them in one of the sacks. We work together then, doing the same under each tree in the stand. Then Barlozzo hands Fernando the swatter and tells him to whack as high up and firmly as he can to release nuts to the waiting ground.

Fernando is nearly grim as he steps near the tree. Batter up, bottom of the ninth. He concentrates, strikes. And the chestnuts rain down. Repeatedly he strikes, now with war whoops and screeched admonitions for us to stay clear. Observing the monster he's invented, the duke retrieves the swatter, calms his friend, and we begin the harvest.

"Take only the shiniest, fattest nuts," he says, "and leave the smaller ones for the beasts. Too much damn trouble to peel, those little ones. And pick them up one by one, not by the handful. Examine each one and leave behind what doesn't look just right. Don't take what you won't eat. Remember to take enough but don't take too many."

Everything is a life lesson with the duke, I think as I sit on a rock in the leaves, absorbed in studying the size and brilliance of a chestnut. But I've always loved being the student—that is, whenever a teacher instructed up and over and straight into the spleen of the lesson at hand.

"Why don't we put nets or a cloth or something under the tree we're harvesting, so we can just roll it up and funnel the nuts into the bags? That's sort of what's done in some places with the olives, isn't it?"

"Maybe so, but these are not olives, and laying down cloths to catch chestnuts is not what we do here," he says.

There are so many nuts already on the ground, and I'm sifting among these, muttering something in English about the scurrilous duke while Fernando, deprived of his swatter, is climbing trees, plucking the nuts from the highest branches, stuffing his pockets with them, and, when they're full, throwing the rest down to a place on the ground he's designated private territory. I like it when he claims a day of childhood.

It takes no time at all before my hands are numbed with the late October cold, but my gloves are too thick, rendering my fingers clumsy around the nuts. Without words, Barlozzo stands before me, takes off his own strange gloves, the kind with the fingers shortened just above the first knuckle, gives them to me and turns back to what he was doing before. I'd rarely seen him without the things. He'd worn a canvas version of these woolen ones in high summer.

I tug my hands into the duke's gloves, still warm from him. Though they're much too large for me, they feel good. Even with the cutoff fingers they reach beyond the ends of mine and they're anything but clean, caked with mud and who knows what else. Still, I like them. I like them close to me. Maybe they'll enthrall me and I'll become a duke. Or I'll enthrall the gloves and the duke will dance the tango. When our sacks are nearly full, we drag them back out to the road where we've left Barlozzo's truck and head to our house for the unloading. It's beginning to rain and so Fernando lays a fire in the *salotto* rather than out in the fire ring. Barlozzo is out back sharpening tools and I'm scrubbing the duke's chestnut-roasting pan, a heavy, forged-metal beauty with a meter-long handle of olive wood, its bottom pierced all over. At the ready is my chestnut knife—short, evil, and hooked. But Barlozzo has prepared his own knife and demonstrates how to place the nut flat side down on a steady surface and carve a cross into its rounded cheek.

"Never an *X,* he says. Always a cross. An *X* is for canceling. I'll show you how to do that, too, if you want. We all need to know how to cancel, be it a thought or a person or the ghost of a person. But we'll save that for another day. Learning to make a good strong *X* is a rite of passage that takes some time." When the fire is tamed to a steady roar, Barlozzo tells me to throw on some rosemary, saying, "I know it will make you happy, and it won't do the nuts any harm."

Fernando heaves the first batch into the pan and nestles it in a place between the embers and the flames. "Because the nuts are so fresh, they'll cook in minutes. But keep moving the pan, shake it," says Barlozzo. A chef with a *sauteuse,* Barlozzo takes his turn with the pan, holding it by its handle, flicking his wrist, tossing the nuts in the air, catching all but one. He yells for red wine and I hurry to get a glass of it for him, but it's the bottle he wants, and when he has it, he places his thumb over the opening and splashes the nuts, baptizing them, sending up a great spluttering of damp, winey smoke. "To make them tender," he says.

We sit there in front of the fire, two bowls in front of us, one full of just-roasted nuts, the other for the shells and skins, which slide off like a baby's pajamas. We keep on making crosses and roasting and baptizing and peeling and eating and drinking. I'm wrapped round twice in a feather quilt, my head on a pillow set on the hearth step, while Fernando and Barlozzo sit like bookends against either side of the tea table. Barlozzo is telling stories.

"Chestnuts were sometimes the only food people had during the great wars. Lots of other times as well. Around here, until fifty years or so ago, the harvesting of chestnuts was as much a part of rural life as growing grapes and raising pigs. Since medieval times and probably long before that, chestnuts have been a staple food. The leaves were fed to the pigs and chickens, the shells were used as kindling—except in the hardest times, when they were brewed into a drink—and when a tree was sacrificed, woodworkers built primitive furniture from its hard, thick trunk. What do you think your *madia* over there is made from?" he asks pointing to the sixteenth-century chest whose lid opens to the space where I set bread to rise.

"People still talk about when they lived through winters on *pane d'albero,* tree bread. Ground chestnuts and water and a little yeast. It was rock-hard and had to be moistened with water before one could eat it. Some people called it *pane di legno,* wooden bread, and I think that name was better earned.

"My father walked home from the Russian front during the winter of 1943. He walked for three months from the Ukraine to Poland to Germany and Austria back into Italy and finally home here with a chestnut sack tied to his belt—a sack only now and then replenished. By February, he said it was hard to find any chestnuts; most were already gathered, the ones left gone halfway to rot. If the sun shined for a day or two where the snow was thin, a few courageous wild grasses would sprout, and when he found a patch he said he would just sit there, legs splayed, pulling them up and stuffing them in his mouth like they were shreds of life itself.

"Sadder yet is that, when most of these reluctant soldiers, like my father, finally crawled up to their own gates, rather than the succour of home and hearth, what they found were their families sitting about spent fires, just as hungry as they were. No fatted lamb turning on the spit, no bread in the oven. No jugs of warming wine. No hero's welcome. While my father was in the Ukraine searching for chestnuts under the snow, my mother and I were on hands and knees in the forests, digging for them under the leaves, digging just a little too desperately, as I remember. Those days were seared deep into that part of a boy that can't heal. It's still a raw place that screams when I begin to poke about anywhere near it. I remember that as soon as the nuts were ripe we'd make expedition after expedition, filling baskets and sweater pockets, my beret, my mother's apron. Back home, we'd store them in an old *baule,* a trunk in the basement, safe from mice. There were few other animals left scurrying about near the house, let alone in the woods or the fields, most having been sacrificed to a stewpot. We'd rest a little, warm our hands over what was left of the fire, then head back out for another search. We did this for days, for as long as the bounty lasted, finally climbing the trees, shaking the branches against the nuts that clung there, teasing us. And we were always on the lookout for pinecones, too, the great, fat ones that cradled a handful of the tiny, white nuts. *Pinoli*. Those I carried gathered up in my arms, close to my chest, they being the first things I ever thought of as valuable. It was the way I remembered my mother carrying me. As for the chestnuts, some we roasted right away as a reward, splashing them with a few drops of watered wine. Others we boiled and, after peeling away the shells and saving them to dry and grind up and brew like coffee, we'd boil the meat of the nuts in more water, this time with a few field lettuces, an onion, some wild herbs, until the mass was soft and thick as porridge. This we ate hot for supper while we talked about how delicious it would be with just a thread of good oil or even the smallest piece of butter or a few grains of sugar.

"Afterward we'd spread out the rest of the mush onto the kitchen table into a neat rectangle about two inches high, leaving it to harden while we slept. And then, twice each day while it lasted, we'd cut pieces of it with a string and set the little 'cakes' to roast over the fire, sometimes laid between two chestnut leaves, which would curl around the stuff as it roasted, forming a package of sorts we'd eat, hot, from our hand.

"But most of the nuts we'd spread out over the grates in the *essiccatoio,* the drying room. It was an ingenious setup. Halfway up the stairs to the upper level of almost every farmhouse back then, one would create a sort of balcony—a *supalco,* it was called. The part of the balcony near the stairs was constructed of rough floorboards, but the rest was strung with wire netting that swung a few meters above where the wood stove sat. We would place the chestnuts over the netting, the heat and the fumes from the stove rising up and smoking the nuts, slowly drying their flesh before it escaped out the small windows we'd leave opened a crack. The *essiccatoio* in our house, your house, was where the entryway is now. We'd keep the fire going day and night so the nuts would never cool and we'd never risk letting them dry unevenly and spoil.

"It took six weeks or so before the process was complete. The scientific method for determining if they were dried properly was to take two of them, clashing them together like bells. If they rang, they were dry. It's not so different from banging the crust of a just-baked bread, listening for that hollow sound. But when the nuts were dried, that was when the real work began. While they were still warm, we piled them into pillow sacks and pounded them with mallets and stones to free them of their shells and skins. That's when I began to learn how to separate things into parts, understanding what to keep, what to put aside," he says, burrowing his eyes into mine.

"The peeled nuts we'd stuff back into the pillow sacks and then I'd haul the mean bonanza down to Tamburino, the miller, who ground them for us into a rough, brown flour, just as he did for all the families. Back up the hill then, turning for half a second to wave to Tamburino, I'd race to the house, to the front steps where my mother stood, her fists twisted inside her apron. To that juncture, it'd been rugged, this chestnut business. But once we had the flour from them, the rest of our work might have passed for fun.

"Into what had always been our pasta bowl, she'd scoop out two or three portions of the chestnut flour with the metal cup that hung by the sink while I stirred in a thin, steady smirr of water. I knew the recipe well. When the batter was smooth, she'd pour it into a shallow pan. It was my job to strew on as many pine nuts as I was willing to part with from my private store of them. Then she'd place the pan over the coals, set an old pot cover upside down on it, filling its hollow with embers. As though it was for news from the front, the wait for the *castagnaccio* was unquiet, fevered in a way. And when it was almost cooked, my mother would take off the cover, and, rubbing a few dried needles of it between her fingers, she scented our cake with rosemary. She always scented the *castagnaccio* with rosemary. Didn't I already tell you how much you're like her?

"She'd put on her sweater, wrap her head in a scarf and the pan in a clean *straccio,* a kitchen cloth, and head for the bar with me hungry at her heels. And with whomever was there, we ate the thing—part cake, part pudding, still hot—the smokiness of it filling our nostrils and consoling us, feeding us more deeply than any great pot of flesh would forever after that. We were safe for a little longer.

"It was a fairly common thing for people to bring their food to the bar. There were so few of us. A sparse tribe of women and children and men too old to fight. But I think my mother was the one who first began to do it, the one who others followed. But after the wars, all that changed. Everyone stayed to themselves, except during festivals and such, that is, until you began bringing up all your fancy dishes, shaming us out of our laziness and maybe even out of our greed, helping us to remember why we live up here together on this foolish hunk of rock. What made you do such a thing? I mean, what made you bring soup and bread up there to eat with strangers? Was it some sort of memory you had about your childhood?"

"No," I tell him, "at least no memory that's surfaced yet. I guess Fernando and I were a little lonely for company. I guess I just like to cook for as many people as I can gather around me. Mostly I guess it's because every time I sit down at table, I find it exciting—that first sip of wine, that first mouthful of bread—it almost doesn't matter what's on the table, but it's always mattered very much who was on the *chairs*. And since we like you and we like Florì and we like . . ."

Barlozzo's laugh drowns out my homage. His silvery eyes crinkle into shiny slits like starlight.

In bed that evening, Fernando lies with his arms folded under his head, eyes opened but fixed somewhere inside himself. "When Barlozzo tells his stories, he takes me back with him. His words pull me with a force that I can feel afterward in my limbs. And my breath is short, like I've been climbing or running. Do you understand what I mean?"

"Yes. Yes, I think I do. It's not enough for him that we feel what he feels. A part of his power is that he can make us feel what he *felt*."

"I just hope I won't dream of chestnuts tonight," he says, turning toward me, wrapping his legs around mine.

NEXT DAY, I wash the duke's gloves and dry them near the fire, but when I try to give them back to him, he says I've ruined them. I know that he just wants me to keep them, so I do, passing them on to Fernando. He slips one on, pulling at the cuff of it, stretching his fingers through the holes, opening and closing his fist to get the fit just right. Now the other one. "These are wonderful," he says, scrunching his shoulders, then holding his arms out straight in front of him, admiring his gauntled hands, palms up, palms down. "I tell you, I really think I was meant to be a farmer."

On one Friday evening we bring a pumpkin up to the bar for supper. I'd seen the beauty at the market in Acquapendente a week earlier, sitting in the back of a truck with a load of curly cabbages. Not so very big, it was the perfect roundness of it, the tight copper-red of its green-striped skin that intrigued me—a lovely autumn ornament to guard the stable door, I'd thought. But this morning, after baking bread out in the garden, I had nothing ready to use up the waning heat of the oven. I looked at the pumpkin, began to think how I could sacrifice it for supper. In jack-o'-lantern fashion, I cut off its cap, scoop out the innards, discarding the fibers and spreading the seeds out to dry on a baking sheet. A quick perusal of the cupboards and the refrigerator yield onions, bits and pieces of several cheeses, that morning's pair of eggs and half a bottle of white wine. I sauté the onions in some olive oil, mash Gorgonzola, shred a piece of Emmentaler, one of Parmigiano, and blend them together with a tablespoon or so of mascarpone and the eggs. Long scrapings of nutmeg, some white pepper, sea salt, and the wine go in at the last. I stuff the pumpkin with the paste, replace its cap and set it to roast in the wood oven until the pumpkin's flesh is soft and its stuffing is giving off the scents of a good onion soup. I roast the seeds and salt them lightly. We carry the masterpiece up to the bar in the bread bowl to keep it steady, then spoon out the stuffing and some of the pumpkin into soup plates, sprinkle each portion with some of the roasted seeds. With bread and wine, the supper is complete. Except for dessert. I put down a brown-sugared, Cognac-laced chestnut purée forced out through a pastry tube into a hill of thick, smooth strings with barely beaten cream trickling through its crevices and the whole of it dusted in bitter cocoa.

"And what are we calling this, Chou?" Barlozzo asks, as though he'd decided the cocoa was ashes of hemlock and had already disapproved the thing no matter what its name or its savor.

"*Mont Blanc*. A French sweet from the haute cuisine repertoire," I say in my chef's voice.

He tastes it, saying nothing, tastes it again, begins to spoon it up with an almost imperceptibly piqued emotion and yet when he finishes, he says, "That was very nice, but we're not in France and somehow making a thing dainty as this with chestnuts seems a mockery. Like being creative with the recipe for communion bread. It feels like too much forgetting. Next Friday will you bake a *castagnaccio* with pine nuts and rosemary?" asks the Tuscan duke in a half-cracked stammer that might once have been his eleven-year-old voice.

"You know I will. But why must you be so arrogant? You sit there crossing and uncrossing your legs, flinging out damnations like

Mephistopheles. Fernando really loves this dessert and I think condemning it for all of us might be just a bit too absolute."

Fernando is shaking his head in dismay at my outburst. His eyes say "*stai tranquilla,* stay calm"—the constant Italian prayer used to stave off all unpleasantness and secure the sacred state of *bella figura,* good impression. But Barlozzo doesn't seem offended. Like wild mint is the duke. Bruise him and he gives up more sweetness. "*Va bene*, OK, but do I still get the *castagnaccio?* And can we eat it with a spoonful of ricotta and drink a glass of *vin santo?*" His laugh is warmed honey then as he says, "Will you listen to me, rolling out melodies, anticipating all the pieces of my supper just like you do."

OUR CHESTNUT FORAGES continue for weeks, interspersed and sometimes in tandem with porcini hunts. After night rains, in Wellies and wielding viper-discouraging sticks, we follow Barlozzo into thickets of oak woods, stalking wild mushrooms. Fernando and I sing.

"*Must* you provide accompaniment? Please be quiet," he hisses.

He's the only viper in these woods, I think. "Why do we have to be quiet? Who will we wake if we sing?"

"Eventually you'll wake the moldering dead. You disturb concentration. I start listening to you, start trying to learn the words, and I get confounded."

Fernando and I slide our full-voice duet down to a vampy whispering of "I've Got a Crush on You" and trot virtuously behind our conqueror deeper yet into the woods.

Though he was somewhat proprietary about his chestnut trees, Barlozzo is ruthless about guarding and concealing his own muddy haunts where porcini flourish. Sliding his way into gullies, prowling every chine and niche, lifting the camouflage of ancient ferns, the fraud of gnarled roots, he is conspiratorial, silent save his craggy breathing, as he digs the fungi called porcini—the name a titillating allegory to fat, newborn piglets. And while he's at it, Barlozzo grabs a handful of berries from between the branches of a juniper, snatches a pinecone fat with the soft white jewels of his childhood.

We take the haul back to our place, wipe the porcini gently with a soft cloth, cleave them into thick, uneven slices which are ready, then, for the sauté pan. A sprig of *mentuccia,* wild mint, six, only six crushed junipers to a kilo of porcini, garlic, unpeeled, bruised with the thud of a black iron pan, a splash of white wine hissing up the fumes of earth and musk, a fistful of roasted pine nuts, and lunch is ready. Barlozzo is pouring wine, Fernando is tearing into the bread. *Buon appetito*.

"How many kilos of chestnuts do you think we've consumed, you and Barlozzo and me, over this past month?" I ask

Fernando one night in bed, transfixed by the Buddha dome of my chestnut-swollen belly, gleaming up at me in the candlelight. And how many kilos of porcini?" I add, checking myself for mold.

I'm full, plumped from this autumn chestnut/mushroom regime. Though I've rejoiced in their harvesting, rejoiced in the roasting and cooking of them, it's a week of clear, strong broth and bits of beef off the bones from which it seeped that I want now. It's longings for bread and butter and tea that come creeping in the night.

Hoping to trifle what he knows has been pure debauchery, Fernando says, "Not that many. Maybe a half-kilo a day of chestnuts and that much again of the porcini." I watch him ticking off the dishes on his fingers. "Between the ones we roasted and the ones in the soup or the polenta or the pasta, maybe it's more."

I adjust my desires. It will be a week of broth without beef, without bread. Without butter.

I am a day and part of an evening into my *slimming* when Barlozzo suggests a journey. "Let's go to the chestnut fairs on the road to Monte Amiata. Some of the best cooks in Tuscany live up there and it's beautiful country," is his simple seduction.

I am a woman loyal to self-imposed embargo and yet, with the duke's words still hovering, looking for a place to land, I slip my hand, smooth as a lizard, into the waist of my skirt, gauging it might well contain the sins of a few more intemperate days.

"When will we leave?" is all I want to know.

At 1,738 meters, Monte Amiata is the highest peak in Tuscany. A volcano long spent, its earth is fat and fecund, nourished by old eruptions, and over its steep black flanks grow more than 2,000 hectares of cultivated chestnut trees, their collected annual yield sworn to weigh 60 million pounds. That's where we're headed.

Back in the truck and onto the Via Cassia, and then onto the mountain road all the way to the crest where we base ourselves in what's called a *rifugio,* refuge, a log house used mostly by skiers. It's divided into small bedrooms, each one with a camp bed or two and a wood stove. Zero stars. And so for three days and nights, we are pilgrims on a *castagne e porcini* crawl, visiting the villages that cling to Amiata's lower stretches, following the handmade signs to gustatory paradise. Abbadia San Salvatore, Vivo d'Orcia, Campiglia d'Orcia, Bagni San Filippo, Bagnolo, Arcidosso, each one with its characteristic dish—risotto with chestnuts and wild mushrooms; wild mushrooms grilled in chestnut leaves; hand-rolled chestnut pasta with roasted mushrooms; a braise of venison with chestnuts and dried oranges. Of course there are chestnut *gelati* and cornmeal-crusted tarts with chestnut jam and hot, crisp chestnut fritters drizzled with nothing less than chestnut honey.

On the way home, Barlozzo slows down and turns off onto a road not much more than a goat path. We leave the truck and follow him to a ruin set on a hill, its walls thirsty-looking and crumbling down into the weeds. A fetid wind soughs and the droning of faraway sheep grudges through the silence. There is a group of farmers moving about. Like a room in the sky it seems, smoke climbing like clouds out from a chimney and wrapping the little house and the men and women in Elysian mists. We step inside the pageant and find them at work with a great heap of figs. They are preparing to dry them in a *essiccatoio,* just like the one Barlozzo described to us where chestnuts were once set to be parched of their juices. Some of them work at splitting the fruit, stuffing each one with an almond and a few anise and fennel seeds, laying the figs on trays. Another person is ready to carry the laden trays into the house, up the stairs, to slide the fruit onto the net screens that sit above the stove in a shank of wood smoke.

Smooth as jasper beads are some of the figs now, all stuffed and dried and cooled and set before one last pair of hands, which waits with wooden needle and butcher's twine. The hands dart about the fruit, fondling the skin of one or another of them, threading them, cradling a soft new bay leaf between each one and laying the finished necklaces in flat baskets.

Barlozzo, Fernando, and I watch. We begin to talk and they offer us wine and bread, the remnants of their working lunch. The spokesman seems reluctant when we ask if we can buy a few strings of the figs, telling us this is late-harvest fruit, the last of the season and not the best of it. We say they look splendid and he offers us figs from the pile waiting to be strung. I take the fruit from his thick, rough hand, like the paw of a seraph-lion. We chew and close our eyes, saying, "*Quanto buono,* how good."

They all smile as if on cue. The artisan jeweler rises from her bench and, with a three-cheek kiss, places a necklace about each of our shoulders, saying, "*Dio vi benedica,* God bless you."

Fernando is reaching in his pockets for lire but she says, "*Un regalo,* a gift."

I run back to the truck and grab a sack of dried porcini, one of chestnut flour, and the branch of red berries Fernando had cut for me from a roadside bush.

"A gift," I say back to her. We're all laughing, understanding, each of us in our way, that this might be a moment of life as life was meant to be.

9

Do Tuscans Drink Wine at Every Meal?

A slashing November rain loops the olive trees in spangles while it darkles the morning sky. Leaning against the yellow brocade curtains on the long-windowed doors in the stable, I watch my husband climb the hill past the henhouse, past the sheepfolds, and up into our garden. Though the road would have been a drier path, he's chosen the more beautiful way, looking up and around him as he stomps the swollen fields, not caring about the water that drips from his hair, dark and slick now as a beaver's. He's been shopping in the village while I've been writing. His hat must be in his pocket, his umbrella pitched up against a wall at the bar. How I love looking at him, unposed. I can do that more often now, as he remains equally unposed in company these days, this new life on dry land having somewhat loosened the despotic rule of his *bella figura*. He blooms, moves through his own quiet risorgimento. I think even he is beginning to recognize his beauty—the beauty of who he is and not who he might contrive to be.

"*Ciao, bambina*," he says hugging me against him so that we press water from his sweatshirt onto mine. He's full of the morning's stories as he steps out of his boots, works on the fire, warms his hands. He thrashes about the room, alighting for a few seconds on the sofa, darting back to the hearth, kissing my hair or my shoulder each time he passes me as I sit at the computer. He wants to talk.

"I'm just about ready to close up for the morning. Shall I make some tea?" I ask him.

"No, it's too close to lunch. And besides, I've just had two *cappuccini* and an *espresso* for the road. I have something I want to show you," he tells me, opening the armoire with the force to totter a hundred crystal wine glasses. He pulls out a drawer, gathers up the papers he's been working on for the past few evenings.

As a part of our eventual reinvention plan, we've been discussing, for months now, the idea of hosting small groups of travelers on tours through the areas that lie near us. We've talked about it long into many nights, picking up the discourse just where we'd left it as we wake the next morning. Once we'd exhausted many of the glossy guides we'd found in the bookstores of Florence and Rome, it was Barlozzo who took us to visit a gentleman, an academic who lives in Siena, for whom he'd worked years ago when the man still kept a country house near San Casciano, who was willing to lend us texts from his splendid collection of historical works, both culinary and artistic. Since then, Barlozzo, Fernando, and I, and sometimes Florì, have taken turns reading aloud in the evening, the duke being more patient with me than the others when I stumble through a passage or interrupt a narrative when I don't understand the text. Slowly, deliberately, we plow through these books. The most splendid reward for the work is the realization that what we read about lies outside our door. Neither armchair travelers nor those in preparation for a journey to some distant place, we *live* here.

We draw routes, engage ourselves in sessions with winemakers and cooks and artisinal food makers, seeking collaboration. Scouring the tiniest *borgos,* we find treasures. A bread baker who uses wheat ground in an old water mill, a renegade cheesemaker whose son is a shepherd. Out of league with the health department, she must sell her wares from a truck parked behind her village church or, sometimes, pass her soft, buttery kilo wheels wrapped in kitchen cloths down the pews at eleven o'clock mass, small envelopes passed silently back to her. The parish priests look benignly upon the commerce, so content are they with their gratis *marzolino,* fresh ewe's milk cheese.

We haunt the Etruscan museum at Chiusi as well as one in Tarquinia, which lies over the regional border in Lazio, and another in

Orvieto in Umbria. We study the art in the churches, the art in the alleyways, the art that is everywhere, sanctified or, like the remnant tenth-century frescos on a courtyard wall of a dentist's studio, taken for granted as a homely, everyday birthright. We study the offerings of tour guides, visit cooking schools all over the Chianti, rank the beds and breakfasts of small hotels and country houses. What we desire to do is to make a path, both gastronomic and cultural, through rural Tuscany and Umbria. A path for *appassionati* willing to muddy their feet and close their eyes, brave and unphased, as we speed past the Gucci outlet.

We say we'll host no more than six guests for each weeklong journey and that each program will resonate with its season. In September, we'll harvest grapes and sit at the white-clothed tables set between the torch-lit vines in Federico's meadow. In October, we'll follow the Amiata road for chestnuts and porcini, dine with Adele and Isolina, two of Barlozzo's old friends whom we visited during the chestnut crawl, perhaps invite our guests to cook together with us in Adele's kitchen. In December, we'll climb into the crooks of olive trees or search black diamonds armed with truffle-hunting dogs and a flask of grappa in the predawn woods above Norcia. We know how little we know. This truth is soothed by the sight of the books we've yet to read, by our own curiousity, this appetite to learn, by the growing roster of experts we can now count as colleagues. Art history professors from Perugia and Florence and Siena and even from Urbino, which sits over the hills in Le Marche. Museum curators, village chroniclers, church sacristans. Cooks and bakers and winemakers. We are gathering inside the circle of our project those who are *simpatici,* comrades of a sort, each of them intense in his or her own way about the glories of this countryside.

We understand that the study of even the merest jot of these lands and their stories would ask thirty lifetimes. But we've begun. It seems important that we've begun.

I am a sanguine who can walk a sanguine's shoals. If it were only me in this life, perhaps I'd risk writing for my bread. Or set up some sort of rustic *osteria* so I could cook and bake each day for a few locals and pilgrims. But we are two, and Fernando lunches poorly on rainbows. And so this preparation feels good. It feels right. But there are also moments when it seems a bauble, like a Tuscan revival of *The Boxcar Children.* I think back to some of the characters in my life—those who passed through it gently, those who trampled it. To some of the latter group, our plans would be flicked like ashes from the square shoulders of their Zegna suits or drop-kicked by the hand-sewn toe of a Hogan loafer. They would say we are buying lifetime tickets to the threater of the absurd. But that's okay. Meanwhile there's the consulting work, the first cookbook to edit, the second cookbook to write. The banker in Fernando has kept pristine records of every lira we spend and announces, now and then, that life here—life how we live it here—costs not one-fifth of life how we lived it in Venice. If we're not exactly flush, we have enough to buy a little time. "So, show me," I say, perhaps too lightly for him.

"Sit down and concentrate," he chides, spreading his papers.

He traces his fingers along the itineraries he's constructed for three different week-long tours. He has isolated the towns we'll visit, the *trattorie* and *enoteche* and *osterie* where we'll dine, the villas and country houses where we'll lodge. He has considered, measured the distances necessary to travel during each day of the route, he's balanced cultural jaunts with gastronomic ones, composed a harmony between rural and village events, demonstrated where and when we shall rely on our experts. Not waiting any longer for the Turkish fairy to do it, Fernando is carving a path.

As I look at the programs all defined and in contiguous form, the chaff trimmed, the meed of them transparent, revealed as a grape just peeled of its skin, I say, "Bravo, Fernando." I know that's all I need to say. We sit long into the afternoon at the unset table, our lunch still to be cooked. We talk about the canal through which to launch our program. Because we will develop a specific route for each group we host, we know the number of tours must be very limited. Ten weeks a year to begin. But who is our audience, who is it that will be inspired, refreshed by coming here to us? Maybe they are adventures more than travelers, people who've already followed the predictable routes, who now want to *be* in Italy rather than scuttle over it. We'll see.

LATER, WE DRIVE over the mountains to Sarteano. A jaunt to watch the sky change at end of a day. Just beyond the road's peak, I notice a bramble of blackberry bushes, their rain-washed fruit preened in the leaving light.

"Can we stop to pick some?" I ask.

We climb down into a mud trench. There is a miasma of berries. Branches and tendrils wound and woven together and bound up in thorns, the berries overripe and dripping juice at the barest touch. We pick them, carefully at first, placing a berry at a time in the bucket we keep in the trunk for such events until we taste one and it's so sweet, a besotted sweet, sweet like no blackberry before it, and so we scrap the bucket and go directly from hand to mouth, picking faster and faster, damning the barbs of the vines now, laughing so the juice runs out of our mouths, trickles down our chins, and mixes with the blood from our thorn-pricked fingertips.

Thunder. Great ponderous cracks of it. Raindrops. Large, plopping ones, healing ones that feel like tenderness. Climbing up out of the ditch, we head for the car with every chance to outrun the storm. I don't want the dry port of the car. I want the rain. I want to be washed by this water that smells of grass and earth and hope. I want to be drenched in it, made supple in it like a shriveled fruit in warm wine. I want to stand here until I'm sure my body and my heart will remember the privilege of this life. Never minding that we are cold and wet all over, we tramp through the skirring furies of the storm and I think, once again, how much I want what I already have. I shout, "I love you," to Fernando, who's picking over in the next gully, but my voice can't penetrate his falsetto rendering of "Tea for three and three for tea." Though he well knows it's "two," he prefers "three," for the better rhyme.

"*Oggi sono belligerante. Lasciatemi in pace.* Today I am belligerent. Leave me in peace." Inked out in a bold slant on thick white paper pinned to his shirt, this is the message Barlozzo wears one morning up at the bar. Signora Vera shakes her head, the oysters in her eyes sliding upward, nearly out of sight.

"*Preciso come un orologio svizzero, lui ha una crisi due volte all'anno.* Precise as a Swiss watch, he has a crisis twice a year," says Vera. An apology flecked with admiration.

But since this is a duke behavior we've yet to encounter, we stand quietly next to him, sipping, shooting furtive smiles across the divide, longing for one of them to touch down into his exclusive estates. Nothing. I sneak a look at Barlozzo and then look hard at my husband, thinking that this duke behavior is also a Fernando behavior, even if his comes without such a helpful warning label. We shuffle about, order another cappuccino, waiting for the *momentaccio,* the evil moment, to pass, beginning to think it must all be some foolish affectation. But the *momentaccio* doesn't end. As we pass him on the road later that day, his warning notice still intact, he barely brakes his trot. The next day we see him not at all, nor the next after that. Nearly a week passes before he raps a four o'clock knock on the stable door, steps inside. Tattered, broken he seems and I want to hug him and feed him. I want to wash him. He sits at the table and I set a tiny glass of brandy before him, stand nearby. Not even a sigh has one of us spoken.

"People, especially people who live in small clutches like we do, tend to be a chorus of sorts, everybody singing the same song, if in different keys. Everyone endorses the thoughts of everyone else here. And this, in most part, thwarts any hope one man has of meeting up with himself, let alone with the peace it takes to nourish one or two of his particular hungers. Being on intimate terms with the cause of one's own sufferance is the only way to kill it off, to choke its haunting. It's the hardest work of all. And each one of us must do it for himself. Most of the pain in life is caused by our insistence that there is none. There are times when I just have to be alone, when I can't tolerate another minute of anyone else's chattering, much less their pontificating," he says, himself in his own pontifical fever and worrying the week's stubble on his face.

Barlozzo paints when he talks. He prepares the canvas, splashes on the color, and throwing down his brushes sometimes, he opts for the thicker texture gained from a pallette knife. This is one of those times. "These past few days I've just been walking down the past like it was a country road, squinting at my own history, piece by piece."

"And so?"

"And so here I am all fragile and naked as though I'd misplaced my sack of tricks, as though I've awakened from some long dream. But I think the dream was my life. It's like I'd been sleeping on a train and suddenly arrived at my destination having seen nothing of the route. There's all this howling going on inside me but I'm not sure if I still *feel* anything. Do you think I'm a crazy old man?"

"Yes, of course you're an old crazy man, one who's suffering from his autumn crisis just like Vera said you were. You're a crazy old man and a duke and a teacher and a child and a satyr. Why would you want to be one thing less than you are?"

He doesn't answer. Barlozzo never answers unless he likes the question. He shifts his bones as though the new position will make him less visible to me. He knows I feel, even see, that he has more to tell. But he wants to be finished more than he wants to continue. He sips the brandy.

I look outside and watch as the day consigns itself to the night in a last great heap of fire. The sight goads my courage. I risk invasion.

"What else is troubling you right now?"

"It's not what, it's *who*. Time. He's a blackguard, Chou. I didn't even notice how old I'd grown until we began staging our little renaissance of the past. When you all pick up and leave—and you will pick up and leave—will I go back to spending my afternoons playing cards with the Brazilian shepherd on the hood of his Saab? It's been years since I'd remembered how good a *castagnaccio* can taste, longer even since I'd sat in the fields and really looked at a night sky. I didn't know I'd surrendered all of my mystery and damn near all of my defiance. Did you know it's defiance that keeps a man optimistic? Without his secrets, his rebellions, his little vendettas against another man or against the same wild hare who eludes him three days in a row, against hunger, against time itself—if he loses these, he loses his voice. I'm faded, spent, yet I'm young and eager. Or is that only memory? I was born for, built for, a certain life that no longer exists. Oh, I don't mean that all of it's gone. Some of the appetites for life as it used to be still survive but it's not the same. Can't be the same. There's an emptiness that comes with plenty. It's that same sprezzatura, that nonchalance we've talked about before. I feel hollow and dulled most of the time, as though it's only in the past where I can find myself. I'm my own ancestor. I'm full of history but

I have no present. I feel like I've lasted too long, while others didn't last long enough."

I'm not sure who these others are who didn't last long enough. But I know he needed to say all this, to take it out of the fusty hole inside him and bring it to the light, if even for a minute. Still, he's holding fast to some part of it, the hardest part. The duke is sitting on something just like a Sard sits on a stone laid over the firepit where his supper cooks. I understand that the argument is closed for now.

"What's happened since I last saw you? Have you redrawn the boundaries of Tuscany?" he asks with a wide, fake smile.

Fernando brings out his portfolio of the programs and hands one to Barlozzo, who reads them slowly and without comment, placing them neatly back into the folder. He closes the folder. He looks at Fernando and then at me, back at Fernando. He's smiling from his eyes now, shaking his head, still saying not a word.

"*Allora*, well?" asks Fernando.

He doesn't like that question either. I take another shot.

"Listen, would you like to come with us next week up into the Val d'Orcia? We're going to evaluate one of the programs, go through it day by day, see how it all fits."

"Not if I have to wear the same white sneakers Americans wear. I've called Pupa and she's roasting pheasants. I'm really hungry. Aren't you so very hungry, kids?" he asks as though bread and wine and the flesh of a bird can fill up emptiness. "*Aperitivi* at the bar? 7:30?"

Feeling more upholstered than dressed this evening, I'm wearing a new skirt, one I've made with leftover lengths of drapery fabric from my house in California. The skirt is red, an amaranthine red, velvet and dark and like burgundy before it goes brown. There were only eighteen-inch widths of it from where I'd trimmed the hems of the too-long drapes in my bedroom, so it's a tiered skirt I've put together—wide, overlapping ruffles of velvet attached to a taffeta lining. It's heavy and warm and nice with a thin rusty-colored sweater. Boots and a shawl and Opium complete my winter costume, and here we are at one of Pupa's long tables, shoulder to shoulder with a party of Hollanders. They tell us they've been renting the same nearby farmhouse in Palazzone each November for twenty years, but even without that introduction I think we would all be easy together. We make our way through a heap of *bruschette* and then a great tureen of *acquacotta,* cooked water—a beautiful soup built of porcini and tomatoes and wild herbs that Giangiacomo ladles into each person's dish over roasted bread and a perfectly poached egg. Up through the fine porcini steam and the fumes of honest red comes the thick Hun-ish accent of one of the Hollanders asking, "Do Tuscans drink wine at every meal?"

Just then, holding aloft two giant platters, Giangiacomo enters, followed close behind by Pupa, cheeks pink with triumph, screaming oaths that she'll cut short her grandson's life should he spill even a jot of sauce. The crowd screams. And so we scream, too, get to our feet and applaud just as they do while the duke stays seated, laughing, but just a little. The Dutch are a fine culinary audience and ask Pupa all about the preparation of the pheasants. She says she roasted the birds wrapped in cabbage leaves, each one of them bound round its middle with a thick rasher of pancetta, and glossed them with nothing more than their own scant, rich juices. But underneath the pheasants we find apples, roasted and still whole, their skins bursting, the aromas from the soft meat of them enchanting the air.

"The cabbage and the apple," Pupa explains, "keep the dry flesh of the birds moist during the roasting. *È un vecchio trucco,* an old trick for roasting rabbits and quail and other wild birds. The gamy flavor of the flesh is enhanced by the sweet juices of the apples on which they sit while the smokiness of the bacon seeps in from the top. *Buono, no?*"

"Buono, si," say the Hollanders in a single voice. And as the table sets to work on the pheasant, Barlozzo, with an appetite for distraction more than for wild birds, repeats the question asked earlier.

"So you'd like to know if Tuscans drink wine at every meal? Well, let's see how Chou, here," he says pointing across the table at me, "would answer the question since she's also a *straniera,* foreigner."

Because he is surrounded by such a rapt audience, this generosity with the floor is a surprising gesture from the duke and I'm pleased to take it. "I'd say it's difficult to talk about how a Tuscan drinks without talking about how he eats."

The Hollanders like the opening, another excuse for a cheer and the clanging of glasses. I continue. "A day's and an evening's eating and drinking usually goes like this. Upon rising, a man takes a *caffè ristretto corretto con grappa,* which is to say he holds the bottle of spirits over the small cup with the left hand where not more than two tablespoons of thick, almost syrupy espresso wait, while he makes the sign of the cross with the right hand. The perfect dose of grappa splashes into the coffee with only that gesture, which also performs as morning prayers. Hot milk and bread or marmalade-filled coronets complete the breaking of the fast. Then, at about nine, after three hours of work in the fields, a glass of red wine lifts the spirits and makes good company for a round, crisp roll stuffed with mortadella. Then, another espresso. Nothing much until noon, when one wants a light *aperitivo*—Campari soda, Aperol with a spritz of white wine, or even a quick *prosecco*. At the stroke of one, seated at table, a liter of local red is placed close to his drinking arm. The main meal of the day is long, rich in variety, but not weighted down in quantity. A plate of crostini or one of *salame* or a heft of cooled melon or a basket of figs, tastes of braised fennel or onions or eggplant. Then a thick soup or a plate of sage-scented beans, sometimes both of them, before a stew of rabbit with olives or veal with artichokes, maybe *porchetta* if it's Thursday. Roasted potatoes and spinach or beet greens sauteed with garlic and chiles are always there. Then, *una grappina*—literally, a tiny shot of grappa, but since Tuscans are not literal about such piddly things, they pour the stuff out into a water glass, filling it to the rim—is taken for digestive purposes before *il sacro pisolino,* the sacred nap.

"At three-thirty or four, an espresso and back to the fields or into the barn for mending and building projects until seven. A quick face wash, *un colpo di pettine,* a stroke of the comb, into the truck and back up to the bar for a glass or two of simple white, a saucer of fine, fleshy olives, focaccia, crunchy with crystals of sea salt and set down with a pitcher of oil for drizzling. A nice prelude to supper. But once back at table, out comes the red again, less of it, though, because supper is thin compared to the harvest table at lunch. Now there wait only a few hand-carved slices of prosciutto from the mandolin-shaped leg dangling conveniently overhead in the pantry. Maybe a mingy ten centimeters worth of dried sausage. Bread is near. Then a soup of *farro* or lentils or *ceci* with fat, roughly cut strips of pasta called *maltagliati*. *Leggera,* they call such a soup, light. Then *una bistecca* sizzling on a grate in the fireplace across the room or a breast of chicken braising away in the kitchen with red and yellow peppers and a handful of sage leaves. A few stalks of wild salad. The tiniest wedge of pecorino. A pear, skin stripped, its juicy transparent flesh carved into wedges, each of which is brought to the mouth on the point of his knife. A hard, sweet biscuit or two with a thimbleful of *vin santo*. A short bracer poured out from the grappa bottle to sip with the day's last espresso. All in all, a moderate feast."

I've barely, if at all, larded the truth in my telling of the story and am rewarded with polite applause and many repetitions of *incredible* in Dutch. I think the duke enjoyed hearing me recount impressions in Italian to Hollanders who speak the language in what he calls the *sopravvivenza,* survival style, when I could have spoken more easily in English, which they all understand and speak quite well. Of couse he takes this as a show of deference to him rather than considering that I might prefer speaking in Italian. Lulled, now, and deep into their cups, the Hollanders talk quietly among themselves, comparing their gastronomic culture to this Tuscan one. Pupa comes out of the kitchen wiping her hands on her apron, makes room for herself between two of them, asks Giangiacomo to open more wine. She points to the bottles in scandalous formation at the end of the table and laughs. She says she loves the plump sound a cork makes as it's urged, guided toward freedom. Her mother once told her that opening wine is like birthing babies. Everyone likes the metaphor, save one magnificently pregnant woman, her head wound in thick blond braids. She absorbs her wince inside a smile.

Fernando nods Barlozzo and me up onto our feet and, our good-nights said, steers us out to the truck. Pewter gauze drapes the moon. Dogs bark and frilled, parched leaves whir about this night of November. And as though he's finishing a sentence he'd begun a minute ago, the duke says, "What you should be doing is what you're already doing. You should be cooking for people. Just like Pupa does. Much better than traipsing all over the earth with strangers in tow, telling them things they won't remember and taking them places that are bound to come up short after that cruise to Cozumel or some whirl through Disneyland. Anyone with a whole soul and even the dimmest passion for adventure will find his own way through Tuscany. Write. Cook. That's what you love to do."

"We talk about having a little place of our own. We talk about it all the time," says Fernando.

"I can help you negotiate with the Luccis about restructuring one of the outbuildings, about putting in a kitchen and making space for a few tables. And the permits would be no trouble, since your house is already licensed as an *agriturismo*. It would take very little to set up."

"How is it that our house is officially an *agritursimo?*" Fernando wants to know.

"Another politesse passed to the nobility by the local authorities. Signora Lucci applied for funds to cover the costs of restructuring your house, signing papers that said the place would be used to attract tourism and to provide cultural activities. It's so that she could have a state loan with less payback. The system is called *i patti territoriali a fondo perduto,* terrirtorial incentive or loans that require only partial restitution. Haven't you ever wondered why she asks you to sign a different person's name each month in her rent register? She's covering herself should anyone come to check her records. By law, you're living in a country hotel. But running a hotel or setting up concerts in the garden would be too much trouble, so she just collects her rent from you—in cash and under the table—on an abandoned building for which the government paid part of the expenses to repair and put in order. Or almost in order. The whole scheme is fairly common in these regions."

I remember, now, the first day he visited us and what he said about Signora Lucci having done everything as cheaply as she could with the state's allotment.

"And you want a person like her to be our patron in a business as well as our landlady?" Fernando asks him.

"Her noble morals won't interfere with your less greedy ones. You can run your business as you see fit, as long as you pay her the way she wants to be paid each month. With a fat, sealed, unmarked envelope. I just want you to put your energies into something that will work, that will bring you satisfaction. Do something small, contained, and with the least possibility of failure. I want you to stay here, to prosper here. Isn't that what you want, too? You don't want to send me back to playing cards with that Brazilian. All I ask is that you just consider it." Caught by the wind, a brittle leaf raps fast against the window glass.

Consider it? I already know how it would look and feel and smell. A *taverna* it would be, a small room in a small town somewhere. The walls would be rough and washed in the color of ripe persimmons, the whole of it lit by a great black iron chandelier with forty candles and the flames of a fire. A single long table would be set before the hearth. Twelve chairs, maybe fifteen. That's all. I'd offer supper, one supper each evening built from whatever was fine and just harvested. Yes, supper made of soup and bread, some winey stew of game or lamb, pungent with wild herbs and my joy in fixing it. I'd set down a shepherd's cheese and then a nice slice of pie—one of berries, probably, or of opulent brown pears, their still-warm juices spilling over a yellow cornmeal crust and scribbling in the beaten cream beside it. Consider it? Yes, I promise I will. But now is the time for Fernando and me to invent something together. The *taverna* fantasy is mine. The project of the tours belongs to both of us.

We ask Barlozzo to leave us at the Centrale so we can walk up the hill. We kiss him good night, ask him to please stop fussing and ranting about what we should and shouldn't be doing, that we'll decide things in our own way, in our own time. Eyes full of woe, he waves, drives off. Fernando and I both feel the old duke's sadness, know that his discourse about our future, though sincere, was raised up tonight as smoke. Rooted deep as a weed in a wall is his anguish.

SINCE BARLOZZO CHOSE not to accompany us on the trial tour, we decide not to wait out the week. Next morning we're up at daybreak, packing sweaters and books and a few essentials, both of us excited about this journey. We close up the house and we're off to ride the most wondrous roads in all of Tuscany. Our first stop will be the thermal village of Bagno Vignoni, then on to Pienza and Montichiello, San Quirico d'Orcia, Montalcino, Montepulciano. Just outside of Pienza, we ride a zigzag road beveled into a rise and paraded on either side by a courteous rank of soldier trees, black and inevitable. The female cypress grows fuller with age, more round and lush about her middle, while the male stays thin and dry. Both stand watch. Made of savage land, tamed, is this Tuscany, instructed by a million hands into obedience. A dominion all of silk and velvet, the green and pink and tawny stuff of her bestrides the curve of the earth tight as new skin, rolling, riffling, then plunging deep into a blind, hiding from the sun, resting herself before a sudden surge onto a slope smothered in wild roses. High on a steep, sheep crop and chalky crags break the hills now and then, relieving the green that abides even in winter. The Tuscan light heaves glitter up at the olive leaves and they dance. In summer they dance as the poppies do and as the wheat does when it's ripe, all of them keeping time with the winds and the birds' wings beating. But today the branches are heavy with ready fruit, and so the leaves slow dance to a song of December. We wander in each of the villages, supping like warriors, drinking humble wines, astonishing wines. We sleep.

We telephone the bar each evening when it's nearing seven, knowing everyone will be gathered for *aperitivi*. As though we were calling from Patagonia rather than from fifty kilometers up the road, they line up to take a turn at shouting the day's news, which is mostly about what they're cooking or who's got the flu or how cold it was at dawn, always asking if there's anything worth eating so far away from home. Admonishing us to take care. And it's always Vera who reads our faxes to us. In a clear, official tone, she recites the English words as she perceives they should sound, pausing for punctuation and, at will, for gloss. I can hear how straight she keeps her shoulders, how high her chin. We understand nothing, yet we listen to her devotion. She will decode messages for two lambs in the wildeness, the wilderness which she is certain is everywhere away from her own doors.

One evening, it's the duke who answers, without a greeting and against a strangely silent backdrop, "*Torna subito. La raccolta è cominciata*. Come back quickly. The olive harvest has begun."

Castagnaccio

1 pound of chestnut flour (available in specialty stores and in every Italian grocery)
1 teaspoon fine sea salt
cold water
½ teaspoon sea salt
1 tablespoon extra virgin olive oil
½ cup pine nuts (optional)
2 teaspoons rosemary leaves, minced to a powder

Preheat the oven to 400°. Lightly oil a 10-inch cake tin. Pour the flour and sea salt into a large bowl and, in a thin stream, begin adding cold water, beating with a fork or a wooden spoon, until the batter takes on the consistency of heavy cream. Add the oil and beat for half a minute more. If using the optional pine nuts and rosemary, add them along with the oil. Pour the batter into the cake tin and bake for 30 minutes, or until it takes on the dark look of a crackled chocolate cake. Serve warm in wedges, as is or with a spoonful of lightly sweetened ricotta and a few roasted walnuts. A small glass of chilled *vin santo* goes well with it, however it's served.

Winter

10

Perhaps, as a Genus, Olives Know Too Much

So you really want to climb up into those trees when it's colder than hell, a basket strapped around your waist, and pick those olives, one at a time? Is that what you really want to do?" Barlozzo asked every time I reminded him to include us in the *raccolta*. And now, plumped three meters up into the saddle of a hundred-year-old tree, my bundled torso pitched about in the gasping breath of early December, my wish is granted. I'm harvesting olives.

Ears tingling under my old felt cloche, my fingertips are white with cold as they slide in and out of Barlozzo's gloves, which I've borrowed back from my husband. My nose runs. And all I do is send curses upon Athena. It was she who, posturing with Posiedon for dominion, sprung the first olive tree from the stones of the Acropolis, proclaiming it the fruit of civility. A fruit like no other. She said the flesh of an olive was bitter as hate and scant as true love, that it asked work to soften it, to squeeze the golden-green blood from it. The olive was like life and that the fight for it made its oil sacred, that it would soothe and feed a man from birth until death. And the goddess's oil became elixir. Soft, slow drops of it nourished ewe's milk cheese, a ladle of it strengthened wild onions stewed over a twig fire. Burned in a clay lamp, oil illuminated the night and warmed in the hands of a healer, it caressed the skin of a tired man and a birthing woman. Even now, when a baby is born in the Tuscan hills, he is washed in olive oil, modest doses burnished into every crease and crevice of him. On his deathbed, a man is anointed with the same oil, cleansing him in yet another way. And after he dies, a candle is lit and oil is warmed and kneaded over him, a farewell bath—the oil having accompanied him on all his journeys, just as Athena had promised.

BARLOZZO HAS DRIVEN Floriana to a doctor's appointment in Perugia, and Fernando is at home by the fire, aspiring to the grippe, so it's just me who's come to pick. I look about at my fellow harvesters. Primitive ornaments they seem, hitched up in the glittery ruckus of the leaves. Wrapped in kerchiefs and shawls, a layer of woolies, one of skirt, one of apron poufed out from under two of sweater, the women are a sturdy breed of sylph. The men, in the camouflage-green-and-orangeade regalia of the hunter, are less beautiful. All of them must be cold, bone cold, yet they banter and shout across winds, practicing a farmer's rite, perhaps the most ancient of all farmer's rites. They will have this year's green-gold sap as those have had it for eight thousand years before them. Still I'm thinking it must have been warmer during the harvest on the Acropolis.

Steeped in thin morning tea is the winter light, and the air smells of snow as we work in this small grove of some two hundred trees on the land of Barlozzo's younger cousins. Even in the teeth of the cold, I love my tinseled perch and the prospect over these lands. More even than vines and wheat, the olive is cherished here. From my high seat, I see far beyond the small estate where we work. I see the trees that plait the red earth of Tuscany, that climb her chalky flanks, flock fields and meadows, and roll over the hills of her. Loyal as the stars are olive trees. But even as they stand together, they are desolate, each one alone with some primeval keen. The old ones seem tortured, hulking grotesques. As though they've kept custody of too many stories, their chests are cleaved to bare their stalwart hearts. But even the young ones, new and slender and yet unwounded, are already marked with a tinkling wistfulness. Perhaps, as a genus, olives know too much.

A few kilos of each day's bounty are carried into a stone barn where a brunette donkey, harnessed to a rope, pulls seventeenth-century crushing stones round and round, her annual dalliance with show business. She whines and shrieks, flashing black velvet eyes on her adoring audience, which is made mostly of the very young and the very old. Round and round, she steps away the afternoon, turning the stones that press the porphyry fruit into a thick olive stew. The resulting mass is then spread between mats woven of hemp and crushed again, until the first reluctant drops begin to trickle into the old tub beneath them. This is a decidedly artisinal methodology practiced only as tribute to the past. Almost all of the olives are brought to the *frantoio comunale* in Piazze.

The olive mill is small, servicing only the local farmers or *padroni,* each of whom might have three or four hundred trees, less, perhaps, as Barlozzo's family does. The farmers often help each other to harvest, but there the sharing stops. Every farmer wants to be assured his olives—coddled and cared for better than anyone else's olives, harvested only at the moment of perfection—are pressed and returned to him as the jade fortune he deserves more than his neighbors do. And so he carts his own olives to the mill, sets them in *un posto tranquillo,* a quiet place, where he can guard them, protect them from ruffians while waiting his turn at the press. Finally, with a probing scrutiny he watches—as though he could recognize them—as every last one of his beloved purply fruits is heaved into the crusher to be pummeled and split between blocks of granite. He watches still, as the pulp is funneled into a vat to be agitated by steel paddles, to be warmed by friction so that the oil will drip less grudingly in the phase of *spremitura,* the pressing. Then the resulting paste must be forced through the mats, the debris left behind, so the oil can, at last, flow freely. Still he watches, until his blessed oil is funneled into bottles, which he will most often cork with his own hands, the very same hands that carved the corks, picked the olives, pruned the trees. The cargo is loaded into his *ape*—a three-wheeled motorized vehicle in which farmers are wont to terrorize back roads—or hauled up onto his tractor. Toward home now, he escorts his oil with the pomp of a crusading *cavaliere* returning with his spoils into a reddening sun. If I squint just so, the tractors fade, and I replace them with horses and wagons—a gentle tuning to turn things back half a thousand years or so.

During what can be hours and hours of waiting for his own moments at the crusher, *il frantolano,* the olive mill owner, ministers to his clients. The mill is built for business: cement clocks and corrugated roofing, a dirt floor in part, smooth white tiles paving the machinery areas. Yet, in the end farthest from the fray, there is a great fireplace. Flames leap in the hearth and under the raised and burning logs rests a contraption that catches the white-hot ash. Over the gentle heat of this ash is laid an old grill. On a nearby oilcloth-covered table there are several kilo-rounds of country bread, a great-bladed knife, a dish of coarse sea salt, whole cloves of peeled garlic speared onto several branches of rosemary. There is a demijohn of red wine cuddled up to a stone sink, on whose draining board wait thirty or so tumblers, turned upside down to drain from frequent rinsings under the tap. The farmers keep watch over their waiting olives, breaking the vigil with ritual refreshment. One whacks off a hunk of bread, roasts it on both sides over the embers, rubs it then with the garlic-rosemary branch, carries it, in his hand and with some ceremony, to the grunting press and holds it under the spigot for a few seconds to let drip a thick sort of cream composed of the crushed but not yet pressed fruit. One carries his treasure, with some ceremony, back to the fire, to the demijohn, filling his tumbler with the thick, chewy wine of the countryside. He quaffs with unhidden pleasure, eats with a burly hunger, returning to his surveillance, comforted. This solace might endure as long as a quarter of an hour before the next inclination for succor.

And so we sit together, the farmers and their families and I, as if in the waiting room of a wizard. And all we talk of is olive oil. At one point, looking to build a bridge between the old world and the new, I open discourse about America, saying that the medical community advises the consumption of extra virgin olive oil to help lower the evil side of blood cholesterol.

To a person, the circle looks at me with something near to mercy, and so I scurry on with news of the American posture that touts "the Mediterranean diet." "Constructed as it is of the freshest fruits and vegetables, complex carbohydrates, freshwater fish, sea fish, and a modicum of animal flesh—all of it laced with generous pourings of just-pressed olive oil and honest red wine—many American doctors call it the earth's healthiest eating plan."

Under darting gazes and fidgeting hands, I continue. "Of course everyone knows that eating this way discourages heart disease and obesity, chases free radicals, and promotes longevity," I say, but there is no one even pretending to hear me. My recital has fizzled as would a Tuscan's who, in the locker room of a Gold's Gym, tells his mates that lifting weights builds muscle.

The mill owner has wandered over to the fire and caught the last of my feeble delivery. "*Ah, signora. Magari se tutto il mondo era d'accordo con noi*. How I wish that all the world agreed with us. Here people die of heart attacks, but most often in their beds and long past their nintieth birthdays."

Chuckles bustle through the crowd.

"But you have some experience with olive oil. I can see it," he says.

In reflex, my hand reaches up to touch my face. Are there telltale marks of last evening's supper?

"*No, no, signora,*" says a man, perhaps the oldest one among the group. "There is no stain. He refers to your complexion. You have what we call here *pelle di luna,* skin like the moon. Your skin is illuminated. *È abbastanza comune qui,* it's fairly common here among the country women. It's the light that comes from eating olive oil all one's life. But is there olive oil in America?"

"Well, yes, there's olive oil in America, most all of it imported from Mediterranean countries, but I haven't really eaten olive oil all my life, unfortunately," I say. "But since I was a teenager, I've been washing my face with it."

This humble revelation of my toilette animates them. Six or seven stories are shouted out into the warm, winey, smoky precinct by the fire. One about a grandmother who died with skin sweeter than a baby's bottom is outdone by the telling of a great-grandmother who wore hats against the sun, cleaned her face with olive oil and rosewater, and died at 110 the day after someone mistook her at mass for her own granddaughter.

I'm on a roll here, feeling part of things, and so I venture further. "And I also make a pap with coarse cornmeal and olive oil and spread it on my face and décolleté, leave it to work like a mask, and then rub it off."

This inspires an even more vividly screeched series of stories. *Gesti di bellezza,* gestures of beauty, one of the women calls them. And almost to a person—the men included—each is willing to part with the most guarded, most effective, most ancient prescription for skin care that ever graced a countrywoman's face and body.

One cure asks that skins of just-crushed wine grapes be applied to the skin and left to repose for an hour or more, twelve days in a row. This makes sense to me, as I consider the current rage for alpha hydroxy acid, which is the chemical version of fruit acids, used to brighten and tense the skin by ridding it of dead cells. But there is another directive in this remedy, they say. One *eats* only wine grapes for the twelve days. One subsists on wine grapes, mineral water, and bed rest. The cure detoxifies, purges, purifies. And not only the skin, they say, shouting that fancy clinics up in the Alto Adige on the Austrian border offer the very same cure plus an hour's daily body massage and ask $10,000 a week. There's a great shaking of heads.

I listen intently to all the recipes for endless youth. I am entertained and informed by them, but one becomes my instant favorite. A gentleman who introduces himself to me as an "available widower" of eighty-eight years tells a story of his mother. "From a two-kilo round of bread held tight against her breasts, she'd cut thick slices, pulling the knife in a sawing motion, closer and closer in, putting my infant brother's nutritional future in great danger. She'd take the trenchers and soak them in fresh ass's milk. And, when they were wet with it, she'd take the mess to her bed on which she'd lie perfectly flat, make herself comfortable and then press the dripping bread to her face, over her eyes, finally covering the whole operating area with a small linen towel. She'd rest away the afternoon like that, quiet in her shuttered room, staying still as death, rising only when it was time to prepare supper. She performed this cure every time she had her monthlies, but of course I didn't understand that until much later, after she'd passed on the recipe to my wife. It didn't take much time before I began to make the associations between the ass's milk cure and my bride's weeklong cold shoulder."

"But did they both have beautiful skin?"

"The most beautiful of all, I'd say. Angels' faces, if not angels' dispositions."

Of both truths, there is a murmur of accord.

AFTER AN HOUR or so spent around the fire in the mill, I catch a lift home from someone who is heading into town and return to Fernando by about five. Gloating in insolence, he is where I left him, holding court before his hearth. And with not even a suspicion of flu about him. His cough is his habitual cigarette hack, dramatized now by melancholy. A Venetian prince protesting the winter, he sits primped on the sofa, his neck swathed in a fine, fringed woolen scarf, his body in a red silk quilt. How he hates the cold. And this is only the beginning of the dark, at least four months of it still ahead. But I know all will be well. Didn't Florì tell me it would? "*Tutto an-*

drà bene, Chou Chou, tutto andrà molto bene. Vedrai. All will go well. All will go very well. You'll see."

She's not been here for the past six or seven weeks, not since there's been some trouble in the family for whom she works. She stays all the week now in Città della Pieve, coming home only once a week for a few hours to take care of things here. But I haven't caught a single sight of her. Barlozzo says she just whisks in and out, that she's distracted and disturbed by the events in this family. I take to leaving her notes in her mailbox, which are always gone a day or so later but which she never answers. I miss her.

We pick the grove clean in three days, most of us working only one- or two-hour shifts, since there seems to always be a small army buzzing about, climbing up to retrieve full baskets from the pickers, spilling out the fruit into great plastic transporting tubs, and pulling out errant twigs and leaves. Even when my turn in the trees is finished, I stay in the grove, fetching and running with the others, then riding in the tractor to the *frantoio* at about three when the day's work is done. Barlozzo manages to stop by at one or two junctures, though not to pick or even to help much. He shakes hands, hugs people, asks after their families, rubs an olive or two between his thumb and forefinger, bites into them, rolls the flesh about in his mouth, chews it, shakes his head affirmatively, his tightly closed mouth turned down into an upside-down U, the almost universal Italian expression of appreciation. I watch his duke's prowess, how his presence enlivens these people. Still I can sense a skittishness about him. Someone asks after Florì. "Is she doing better?" the woman wants to know.

It must be some other Floriana, because Barlozzo, not having liked the question, rebuffs her. If it's *our* Floriana, why doesn't he just say the truth, that she's helping the family for whom she works to pass through a difficult period, just as he told us. But he doesn't say a word. I watch as he continues to look for half a moment at the woman. And then I watch as he walks away. Surely, it's *another* Floriana who has written this despair on the duke's face. Of course it's another one, I say over and over. But when he gets round to me, pretending to kiss him, I roar an icy whisper in his ear, "Tell me right now about Floriana. *Ti prego.* I beg you."

"*Ne parliamo più tardi.* We'll speak later," is all he says. Innocent words made of horror and tasting of metal. I run them about in my mind. I understand that he will say nothing more at this moment and I walk away from him.

As I'd done yesterday and the day before, I catch a lift home and go in to fuss over the melancholy prince. I go upstairs, then, to run a bath and sit in the heat until I'm weak and red and weeping. As it does always for me, this sadness comes not from a single hurt but from their gathering together, all of them come to crouch about me now like a congress of harpies. I miss my children. And something is very wrong around my friend with the topaz eyes. Something, and maybe the same thing, is very wrong around the duke. Now I know it was his grieving for Floriana about which he couldn't speak. And then there's whatever lurks about Fernando. But the cherry on the cake arrived today in the form of a note from our friend Misha, who lives in Los Angeles. A man made mostly of Russian gloom is Misha. The note says that he wants to visit in February. Only Misha would choose to visit Tuscany in February. And, though I care for him so deeply, I'm ready at this moment for neither his scrutiny nor his questions—which always come ready-packaged with answers—nor his punctilious surveillance. I can hear him now. "Ah, Pollyanna with the black-sugar eyes, what have you done with your life?"

Having nearly always disapproved of me, Misha has been asking that question for years. He's loved me, been my Greatheart, and yet he's been forever exasperated by what he scabrously refers to as my "spiritedness." How many conversations has he opened with, "If you would only listen to me?" I can't wait for Misha and Barlozzo to meet. Such a fine pair of sacerdotal cholerics they'll make. Now that I think of it, with the two of them plus the melancholy prince, I'll be cooking and baking for a weltschmerz congress. And beyond them, maybe this time some of the harpies's mewling is about me. About the haughty me. About the me who at this moment is faltering, stunned by the extravagant folly of my believing that I could make a life simply from the stark, unmixed desire for it.

When I take a bath alone, Fernando knows it's not the bath I want but the hiding. He waits a long time before he comes upstairs with two flutes of *prosecco* on a tiny tray. I continue the soaking and weeping. We sip the cold wine and then he rubs the vanilla water from me with a linen towel the color of parched summer wheat. I say all I want to say with no words. And he, knowing my silence has not been caused by a tough day in the olive trees, chooses silence, too. How I love that he doesn't ask what's troubling me, that he trusts it's a thing better kept to myself for the moment.

As I'm pulling his robe around me, I ask, "Are you hungry?"

"No, I'm not angry at all. But are you?"

"A little."

"Why? What about? Will you tell me what's happened?"

"I don't know what's happened. Nothing's happened. Everything's happened. It's eight o'clock and I'm hungry."

"What does the time have to do with your being angry?"

"Because it's about this time each day that my body is used to nourishment. Why all these questions? I feel hunger. A natural stimulus. It's very simple. I'm just hungry."

"I don't believe anger *è un stimolo naturale*. To be angry is to have an emotion. It's an emotional response to something or to someone, so tell me, *why* are you angry?"

"I'm just hungry. At least I *was* just hungry. Why must you examine such a simple statement, looking for some deeper meaning?"

"I'm not looking for deeper meaning, I just don't understand why you're angry. I just don't understand it at all. By the way, are you *angry?* Maybe it's just that you need to eat something."

When I go back downstairs to the fire, I find it stoked and roaring, the tea table set for a small supper in front of it. Every candle in the room is lit and Fernando is in the kitchen, foraging, fixing. A small sizzle of onion and butter wafts.

"Fernando, what are you cooking? It smells so wonderful."

"I'm cooking an onion."

"An onion?"

"It's just for perfume. I know how much you like the scent of onions cooking. *Onions frying in butter smell like home*. Isn't that what you always say? I couldn't find anything else to cook with it, and so we'll just have the onion. OK?"

"It's absolutely OK. I can't wait."

He's sliced a dried boar sausage and put it on a plate with a wedge of Taleggio and a few crumbles of Parmigiano, set out bread and a dish of the pear marmalade we'd made last October and one of crystallized ginger. And with a flourish, he brings out the onion. The *prosecco* leans in an ice bucket and we into each other, easy together. We laugh quietly about our continuing inability to understand the other's language.

"Do you know a couple who loves each other the way we do?" He's pouring out the last of the wine. "I wish I'd been around people who loved each other when I was growing up. Even if they didn't love me, it would have been comforting to know that there really was love."

"Actually, I did once know a couple who might well have been like us. I haven't thought about them in a long time, but when I was very young, they seemed like storybook people to me. And I wanted to be just like them."

"Who were they?"

"They were servants—the caretakers or perhaps the housekeeper and the goundskeeper—at a place in southern France, in the Languedoc not so far from Montpellier.

"I was twelve and a chum from school invited me to spend that August with her and her parents on what she'd called 'The Farm.' It was just outside the little town of Roquefort-sur-Soulzon. It turned out to be a rather glorious house, a turreted château, really, with hectares of gardens, not at all the sort of place I'd imagined. But there were a few sheep and a small vineyard. And there was this couple—Mathilde and Gerard—who watched over my friend and me when her parents went off on jaunts or to their offices a few days each week. I think Isolde and I must have been very young twelve-year-olds and not at all like girls of that age today. We played theater in her mother's long, swishy dresses and read *Fanny and Caesar* to each other while lying on our backs in the sun, each of us with a branch of lilac resting on our reluctant breasts—all the better to gulp the scent and sigh and scissor-kick our legs, then crumple into a swoon for the passion it raised up in us.

"I remember that Isolde asked me if I thought kissing a boy would feel as good as breathing lilacs, and I told her that I already knew it didn't: I told her that Tommy Schmidt had kissed me long and hard and more than once and that it didn't feel even half as good as breathing lilacs. With Mathilde, we baked endless peach tarts and broke them, still warm, placing the jagged chunks in deep, white café au lait bowls, pouring over thick cream from demiliter bottles and crushing it into the crust with the backs of our big soup spoons, then eating the sugary, buttery mess until we were breathless and fat and sleepy from the goodness of it. Nearly every day we'd follow Gerard into the dim, damp of the limestone caves that rimmed the far edges of the property where he went to inspect and turn the wheels of ewe's milk cheese he'd set to age. Sometimes we'd go into the caves alone and talk about menstruation or how much we hated Sister Mary Margaret, who looked like a reptile with a very black mustache, and how we just couldn't believe that Jesus would take her as his bride. But the most beautiful memory I have of that August is the one evening I spent alone with Mathilde and Gerard. I don't remember how it happened, something about Isolde having to accompany her parents into Montpellier, while I asked if I might stay behind.

"Mathilde and Gerard made their home in an apartment on the third floor of the château. I saw it once when Isolde and I were invited to tea. It was quite lovely, all painted in a pale, icy green with flowers and plants everywhere. But they had another space, one which they used as their summer house, and that was where we three had supper that evening. They'd fixed up the inside of one of the caves as a hideaway, and when Mathilde pulled back the heavy canvas curtain, I felt like I was stepping inside a doll's house. The color of the stone was light, as though it had been washed in something the color of roses. And it smelled like roses, too, and it was cool. Almost shivery cool. There was a dining table and two chairs, a small stone sink, and a day bed covered in purple chintz with brown satin flowers all over it. Bowls and baskets of melons and potatoes and onions and pots of mint sat on stones and on the earth floor itself, so there was almost no room to walk. The only light was from candles, crooked and flickering in a silver candleabra that seemed much too big for the table, though I thought it was perfect.

There was a stove outside the cave—some strange-looking thing Gerard had built and of which he was very proud. It contained a spit on which a scrawny chicken turned, its juices dripping into a pan set beneath it. On its single burner rice simmered.

"I watched while Mathilde readied herself for supper. Having peeled off her cardigan and hung it on a peg, she appraised herself in the mirror propped up against the stone sink. She washed her face and neck and décolleté, lathering with a thin wafer of soap sliced from a loaf of it she kept on a shelf, just like bread. She shook drops from several little vials into her palm, rubbing the potion with the fingers of the other hand, warming it, then patting it onto her just-scrubbed skin. Oils of roses and violets and orange blossoms, she'd said. Pulling out her small, golden hoop earrings, she threaded in little beaded ones that looked like tiny blue glass chandeliers and which moved every way she did. Undoing her hair, combing it, rebraiding it, twisting the long, thin plaits into coils and fixing them with tortoiseshell pins, she smoothed the sweet oil remaining on her hands along the part. She might have been ready for a waltz with a king. Or for supper, which I think would have been the same thing to her.

"Gerard performed his own abultions outdoors by his stove, using the water they kept in what looked like a holy water font or a bird bath, cracked and crumbling and wonderful. When he came inside, they greeted each other as though they'd been separated for weeks. They couldn't have been doing all that for show. They did it for themselves, for each other. They did it because that's what they always did. It was lovely for me that they stayed absorbed in their intimacy even in my presence, that they let me *see* them.

"Save a bit of the chicken and some rice, a few wrinkly, hard olives, and what must have been sardines, although I wasn't familiar with them at the time, I don't remember all that we ate, but I do remember the ceremony of the meal—the sharing of each thing, the changing of plates, the wine, the endless bringing forth of tiny morsels and tastes. She brought small clusters of grapes and a bowl of water to the table, dipping the clusters one by one and offering them to us. Then there were a few nuts warm and salty from her frying pan, cookies from a tin and sugared, dried figs cut from the string of them that hung near the canvas curtain. We talked and laughed. And they told me stories. I told them stories, too, the few I'd had to tell. Or dared to tell. But I liked the silences with Mathilde and Gerard, which sounded like smiles to me. I liked them most of all. In the candlelight of that snuggery, I believe it was the second time in my young life that I ever thought about how I wanted to be when I grew up. That evening I knew I wanted to be like them. And this evening I know I want to be like us. Which is to say, I did what I set out to do, they and us being of the same tribe, I think. I guess it doesn't matter that it wanted half my life before I did."

"You were way ahead of me," Fernando says. "I never knew anyone I wanted to be like before there was us. Anyway I think it actually works like this. You can't *become* like someone you admire. But if what you admire about them is already lurking about in yourself, they can stimulate it, inspire it, coax it out of you like the words to a song. Don't you think that's what we did for each other?"

"Yes. Surely that's what we did for each other."

"But when you were a little girl didn't you ever want to be a rock star or a ballerina or at least Catherine of Siena? Didn't you ever want to be rich?"

"I always thought I *was* rich. And when I was older, I knew it was true. But most of all, I wanted to matter. You know, really *matter* to someone. Once. Just once. But still I feel sad that most of us will never, not even for one of the suppers of our lives, dine as Mathilde and Gerard did, feel the nourishment of their food and their wine and their love as they did."

"Do you know why that's true, why most people will never have that?"

"Probably because simplicity is the last thing a person considers as he's madly searching for the secret to life. Mathilde and Gerard had so much because they had so little."

• • •

It's past eleven and I know by now it's not this evening Barlozzo meant when he'd said we talk later. We go upstairs, toting the priest with us. A rustic master stroke, a priest is a sort of metal lantern into which white-hot ashes are shoveled. The lantern is hung from a small metal arc and attached to a wooden base. Once assembled, the whole thing is placed between the sheets, creating a great bump in the territory of the bed and, in twenty minutes or so, warming it to welcome a shivering Venetian prince and his consort.

I place the priest on the floor and crawl up into the readied bed beside Fernando, who pulls me close, chortling with glee for the comfort of it and of me, he says. "But I warn you, this night you must not discover me. I don't like it at all when you discover me, pull the quilt away from me." In Fernandese, *discover* means *uncover.* Actually, I think I prefer "discover" in this context. Across the cultures, the discovering is never finished.

Between the tucks and folds of linen, how many battles and dreams have we played out upon the field of this bed, I wonder. How many crumbs have we shed from little feasts nibbled under the quilt? The scent of some spilled drops of good red wine, the scents of us. The parts of life left unsaid in other places we confide in bed. I hold the prince and the prince holds me. He unfastens the cord that keeps back the curtains, which hang from the four-poster frame, and the heavy red stuff falls about us. Clasped now in a candlelit tent, we lie on the inside of a cloud, flitting across the moon. He unties the ribbons on my nightdress, props himself on his elbow, and looks at me, running his fingers over me.

I ask him later, my voice small, whispering up from the darkness after the candle's long, slow sputtering, "Remind me to ask around where I can get fresh ass's milk once a month, will you?"

"Jesù."

11

December Has Come to Live in the Stable

The surgery was nearly two weeks ago, and soon she'll be beginning postoperative therapies both at the hospital in Perugia and in a clinic in Florence. Her doctors say it was contained, that there is every reason to expect a full recovery. Meanwhile her friends in Città della Pieve insist she remain with them so they might look after her, take her for treatments, follow her progress with the doctors. These people are family to her. And they understand her desire for seclusion. She's Tuscan. And one of the essences of that birth is the right to confront one's own life and one's own death in private."

It's the next morning and Barlozzo's face is broken granite, the pieces of it like shards put back together badly. He sits at the table and speaks of Floriana. He states facts, proffers all technical information, leaving nothing for me to ask save the questions I know he won't answer. I stay quiet and let him read me.

"It was her choice to shelter you. And not only both of you, but everyone else in town. But, of course, someone from the hospital talked to someone who talked to someone else and so in very little time the news arrived here. And besides, you and Floriana have known each other for only a short while. What is it, seven or eight months?" He looks at Fernando for confirmation. "She didn't want to worry you. But, more, I think she just can't imagine burdening you." Now it's just me on whom he flashes his gaze. "You know, you're not the only one among us who has a hard time believing anyone really truly loves you. When she's ready, she'll let you know how she's doing. Meanwhile, love her the way *she* needs to be loved, which may not be at all the same way *you* need to love *her*."

The duke has said everything, knotted up the argument all alone. Fernando asks some standard questions, which Barlozzo answers in two- and three-word sentences, as though we were suddenly in overtime. It's clear that anything more than he's already said is pure concession.

You know, you're not the only one among us who has a hard time believing anyone really, truly loves you. My mind repeats his words. And those words attach themselves to other, older ones. *I can make you feel loved but you can't make me feel loved. No one can. And if you try too hard, I'll bolt. I'm a runaway, after all.* Before knowing Fernando, this was my sutra, one of the self-observations I kept in a stash of secret aches. Maybe I'm Tuscan, too. And maybe it takes one to know one, and that's why Barlozzo knows me as much as I'm beginning to know him.

"Is that what you do?" I ask the duke. "Do you love her the way she needs to be loved, or do you love her in *your* way?" Silver swims in his eyes like minnows in black water, and he knows I'm not finished yet. "Why didn't you ever marry her?"

Wanting deliverance from me, he looks at Fernando, who comes to sit at the table now. "Why don't we talk about his some other time?" my husband suggests.

"I would like to talk about this. I would like to talk about it just as soon as I can." The duke tries a smile, opens the door to leave.

Frowning, stoking the fire, I see that Fernando is unhappy with my questioning of Barlozzo. But, for right now, I just don't have the will to defend my behavior or myself. I'm thinking that if I can't see Florì or talk to her, I'll write to her. I tear the first few pages from a small, leather-spined book in which I'd begun to keep notes for my next book. I'd bought it in Arezzo, taken by the rough feel of the handmade Florentine paper in which its cover is bound and by the pale reds and greens and golds of the Piero della Francesca madonna that adorns it. Now this will be Florì's book. And in it I can tell her what I'm feeling about her or thinking about her, or about anything at all I think she'd like to know. I may never give it to her; in fact, I doubt I ever would, but her reading it is not what matters about Florì's book.

December comes to live in the walls of the stable. The chill and the cold and the damp entwine and all of them prosper deep in the souls of the old stones. It's colder by more then ten degrees inside the house than it is outdoors, and the crusade we fight with fires and socks and warmed wine soothes us, but not always, and never for very long. Each morning we wake to vesperal light and a chill that compels us, like mountaineers, to move or perish. Up and out of our naked bundling into the breath of Siberia, where the floors are corrupted in the sheerest gray rime. Even the church bells sound cold, their ring funereal, as if veiled reapers had taken over the tower. Costumed against the freeze, we begin our day. Fernando sets the fire while I make the bread dough and race back up the stairs to place the bowl between the sheets and the quilt, packing our pillows around it in the bed so the stuff will have some hope of rising. I'm sure that our just-vacated bed is the warmest place in the house. The oven is a whimsy that takes an hour to heat but refuses to hold temperature for more than a few minutes unless something is set to bake in it. Otherwise it pouts and stutters, spends itself. Meanwhile the fire thaws the downstairs space enough so that we can pat the barely bed-risen dough into fat round loaves and set them near the hearth for a second rise. We perform the winter version of our toilettes, which means we brush our teeth and splash our faces and leave the rest of us to go French. We calculate thirty minutes of freedom to race up the hill to the bar for breakfast before the fire goes out, the bread rises, and the oven gets hot. I admit there is a certain awkwardness about our winter life here. Still, crack as firemen, we pull on boots and jackets and run to find our *cappuccini*.

Nothing much ever changes at the Centrale, the good forces of its gods being ever present and never minding the weather or what the calendar and the clock have to say. Some form of sympathy and of courage seems to offer itself in just doses, and so we sip or gulp from them according to need.

Back down the hill to stoke the fire, bake the bread, and turn on the computer. Cold or no cold, there's work to be done these days—a deadline for the book's edit; other, yet tighter, cutoffs for the bits and pieces of consulting work that trickle in and for commissioned travel articles and rewrites. I wear Barlozzo's gloves, leg warmers, the prince's fringed scarf, and I'm fine seated there before the fire in the waft of the bread's perfume and with a belly full of warm milk and coffee. Barlozzo gave us a space heater, a great hulk of a thing that sends up a hot, dry, choking breath for a few minutes before its greediness for electric juice kills off the computer and the lights and the oven and causes its own blustery death. Since the woodpile is diminishing at an alarming rate and—at least the way Fernando has calculated it—wood costs more than electricity, the heater is voted in. I must find a way to use it. Through trial and error I learn that if the oven is off, I can keep both the computer and the space heater. But so miserly tuned is this electrical system that I can't have lights. Who needs lights, anyway? Again, this is just a simple awkwardness, and I refuse to let it take on the air of an agony. Surely there are moments when I'd like a wolfskin cape, but things are OK just as they are. I think of my long-ago New York self fettered to a gray plastic desk in the poisonous stifle of a steam-heated cell as I sat spinning out clever text about Adolf's Meat Tenderizer and Welch's Grape Juice. I much prefer this workplace.

We discuss the wisdom of renting an office, but it's a consideration short-lived since we've portioned ourselves a hundred and fifty thousand lire—about $75—weekly for food and gasoline and wood. There is no money for any purchase or service beyond this unless we begin to pilfer the remains of our savings. I could set up at Barlozzo's place or even at the bar, but with the warmth I'd gain, it's privacy I'd lose. Besides, spring is three months away. And so, a willing, part-time anchoress on a cold hill in Tuscany, I warm my fingertips between my thighs. Now it's Low Renaissance architecture and pagan festivals, wild boar hunts and the one true formula for saltless Tuscan bread, the lords of Ferrara, the wines of Verona, and the alabaster mines of Volterra about which I write, pacified by the whoosh of the brutish heater, by Paganini and Astor Piazzolla, by firelight and candlelight and the shy winter sun that leaks between the yellow curtains.

SINCE THERE IS no market that sets up in San Casciano, on Friday mornings we head for the bawdy, spirited fair in Acquapendente over the regional border in Lazio and, on Saturday, to the picturesque market in Spoleto. Both are fine enough small-town markets, each of them boasting tables and stalls lorded over by the farm families, plying just-dug or harvested goods from their rich, fat earth. Surely we go to buy our daily food, but sometimes I think I haunt markets less for goods than for a few moments' fraternity with the farmers themselves, a daily indulgence of my Venetian life that stays pungent against time:

I hear it, feel it, the shivery pull of the Casbah, another call of the wild. I walk faster, faster yet, tilting left past a cheese shop and the pasta lady, finally braking in front of a table so sumptuously laid as to be awaiting Caravaggio. The farmers are sublime hucksters, rude, sweet, mocking. They are all of a seductive society, collaborators in a crack theater troupe. One holds out a single, silky pea pod or a fat purple fig with honeyed juices trickling out from its heat-broken skin, another whacks open a small, round watermelon called anguria *and offers a sliver of its ice, red flesh from the point of a knife. To upstage the watermelon man, another cuts through the pale green skin of a cantaloupe, holding out a salmon-pink wedge of it cradled on a brown paper sack. And yet another one shouts, "The pulp of this peach is white as your skin."*

When I lived in Venice, it was mostly about everyday life, about language and local culture and history, that I learned from my friends in the market and in the nearby *bacari,* wine bars. But in Tuscany, the lessons are all about food. As Barlozzo promised from that first day, for a rural folk, food is the fundamental theme of their lives.

It's different from that of the American who gets excited about the restaurant of the week or a holiday feast or a dinner party at which someone auditions a recipe from a just-acquired cookbook. Lunch and supper here compose a twice-daily-said mass. After all, here in the countryside, some people still grow it, gather, forage, and hunt for it. Often, they've transformed it from innocence into its supreme form, as is the case with the courtyard pig. They birthed him, fed him, raised him up into a fine, snorting creature, butchered him, salted his legs and washed them in wine, strung them up high from the eaves of their barns to swing in the Tuscan winds. Even now that most neither desire nor have need to follow each step of this getting-the-pig-to-table, they use this history, this sort of ancestral energy in other ways, as in the angst over the acquisition of the daily *etto di prosciutto.*

"From what position on the leg are you slicing? And will you slice it by hand or in the machine? Is that sweet or salty? Was it cured nearby? How near? If it's that too-sweet stuff from the Friuli, I'll take *nostrano,* our own. How long did it age? Is the flesh moist? Or is it dry? Is the grain of the meat smooth? Let me taste it. Let me taste the other one."

Munching dolefully, shaking his head in pig-inspired grief, he says, "*Che ne so, io? Dammi un etto abbondante di quello lì.* What do I know? Give me a hefty hundred grams of that one."

And these exchanges represent just one part of the *antipasto,* the "before the meal" dainties. Still there are the cheeses to ponder, the vegetables and herbs to rifle, the fruit to smell and press and pinch. And there's the bread.

"*Mi serve una pagnotta carina, non troppo cotta.* I need a pretty loaf, not too well cooked. No, no that one has no shape. And that one is worse. Crack the crust on that one over there and let me listen to it. *Eh, lo sapevo io, troppo croccante*. Ah, just as I thought, much too crispy. I'll have to content myself with that one."

"Which one?"

"That one, that poor thing there in the bottom of the basket."

All this huzza for a single meal. The dance and dialogue of it to be repeated next morning, if not again, in some diminished form, later that afternoon. And often there is a feigned hauteur between customer and provider, an authoritarian two-step complete with chest puffing, brassy voices, and hand jive. The great villagers' burlesque. Once I saw a butcher holding high a tangle of *pagliata*—suckling lamb intestines, their milk and pale blood still dripping—who said, "*Guarda che bello.* See how beautiful these are."

The potential buyer volleys, "If those are the most beautiful ones you have today, I suppose, ugly as they are, I'll just have to take them." It's the butcher's turn.

"How can you dare to call these ugly? I think it's you who are ugly," the butcher says, slapping the *pagliata* back into a ceramic bowl. "It's amazing how you managed to get so old and learn not a thing about quality."

"I'll show you what I know about quality, I'll take that second-rate *pagliata* and sautee it with garlic and parsley, I'll add a half-liter of my own white wine, just a spoonful of thick tomato puree, and let it all cook *pian piano* for three hours until all the people in my palazzo gather at my door to whiff and moan for the goodness of it. *Sarebbe splendido.* It'll be splendid. I'll bring a bowlful to you at 7:30, so wait for me."

The butcher barely smiles, not wanting to betray his glee at getting exactly what he wanted from his client.

One day, there is a four-year-old boy whimpering in his stroller as his grandmother pushes him about the marketplace. He begs her for another piece of the focaccia from the brown paper package in the stroller's basket.

"*Ma hai già finito quello con il Gorgonzola?* Have you already finished the piece with the Gorgonzola?"

"*Si, ma ero troppo piccolo. Adesso ne voglio uno con le cippole. Dai, nonna.* Yes, but it was too small. Now I'd like one with onions. Come on, Grandma."

She reaches inside the package and pulls out a ten-inch square of the flat, crunchy bread and says, "*Mangia, amore mio.* Eat, my love." I laugh to imagine the scene if *la nonna* tried to soothe his husky Latin hunger with a graham cracker or a plastic sack of Cheerios. Now, stopping the stroller in front of a pyramid of small violet artichokes, a half-foot of their curving and slender stems still attached, grandma rifles the heap.

The boy, focaccia in one hand, the other one free to flail at her, says, "*Ma ti dico subito, sono stufo di quei carciofi fatti in padella. Ogni giorno, carciofi in padella. Per carità, nonna, facciamoli fritti oggi.* But I'll tell you immediately, I'm so tired of those braised artichokes. Every day, braised artichokes. For pity's sake, grandma, let's fry them today."

Surely there is the impulse for change, but, where the table is concerned, rituals die hard, die slowly or, one hopes, not at all. And when I witness them, participate in them, sometimes I'm reminded of California. Beginning in the mid-eighties, I spent nearly eight years there, a journalist writing about food and wine during the glory epoch, the debut of the "new" California cuisine. Which wasn't really new, of course, as much as it was a deft repackaging of history, since cooking with the seasons was neither sprung up nor invented on the West Coast of America. I spent much time then with and among young chefs, fresh from culinary academies or an apprentice stage in starred kitchens, many of whom were bright and feverishly smitten with their work.

Certainly there were a few who searched their own mythic grandeur more than the satisfaction of perpetuating the mostly noble legacy attached to their titles. They thought to exalt themselves by riding Harleys, wearing alligator boots, and carrying Louis Vuitton briefcases. And it was they who believed their own press releases and perpetrated the fable that "fresh, seasonal cuisine" was a new idea, dreamed up mostly by themselves. But these were relatively few, and the rest of these young people, with a truly absorbing love of food, were exuberant, aroused by a fistful of herbs, lost in a quest for flavor. But the competition was horrific back then, as it is still, and the laws of winning and losing dictated, in error, I always believed, that the only way one good chef could distinguish himself from another good chef was to present dishes always more exotic, more shocking, more improbable, which might amuse jaded guests and keep them from a table next door. Where was the cachet in pristine, slender green beans, poached to a crunch, barely shined with sweet butter, and sparkled with a few crystals of sea salt when one could just as readily purée the beans with apples, mix the pap with minced oysters, bake it inside the belly of an artichoke, and present it with a basil and sweet-corn coulis?

More than once I have been seated before a primped and painterly plate, its elements so overworked and disguised that, try as I might, I could identify none of them. It might have been prop food for all its aroma. Enticed neither by swirls of kiwi purée forced from a plastic bottle nor by teetering constructions built from a puff of pastry upon which rested a grilled lamb chop upon which was piled a roasted pear, the pillar secured by spears of asparagus, which leaned fetchingly against it, a few hard-cooked lentils strewn casually about with the petals of a zinnia, I've always wanted food that sent a current straight to my loins. I'd find it exhausting, having to break down a still life before getting to my supper. There'd always be a suspicious moment or two, knife and fork arrested, some inquiry. Is the pool of "red stuff" made from suffered beets, or is it cherries? Maybe it's cherries *and* beets, an amalgam it once turned out to be, the duet swirled with a splash of fish fumet. And so it was that as chefs began to decompose the very molecular structure of food, recasting it into ever more bizarre forms and substances, it became harder and harder to stay excited about my job.

Why didn't more chefs and cooks and bakers walk in Alice Waters's footsteps, or, further north up the coast, in Larry Forgione's? And now I'm wishing I could scoop up all those men and women who began their chef lives as purists and bring them here to wander these markets, to stand in front of the burners with some of *these* chefs who change their menus every night so as to reflect that morning's market, and who are not quietly amazed by this fact as a proof of their own genius. They see themselves as torchbearers, passing down their gastronomic patrimony, getting beautiful food to the table and letting that beautiful food look and taste like itself, following the ancient, normal, natural, sensical rhythms of the good cooking that survive and flourish in even the humblest countryside *osteria* or trattoria kitchen in every region of Italy. And not one of them has ever puréed a beet and a cherry with the broth of a fish. Save those who've trounced their heritage and fashioned themselves after some of the Californians.

But in all the years I traveled on my stomach, almost wherever I landed it was the same lesson I learned. Foodstuffs the world over are as connected as the humans who survive by them. There's grain with which some form of bread is fashioned—flatbreads cooked fast over wood or coal or peat for the hungry and the fleeing, steamed breads, fried breads, baked breads. There are spontaneous grasses and herbs that shoot up through drought and blood almost as faithfully as they do in temperate fields. What a culture farms depends on its soil and rock and water. Upon the hands of its people. Upon its past. Every culture ferments and distills some fruit or vegetable or herb into spirits. And in all the places—however remote they might be from one another—where there are a pig and a cow, there will be some local, lush savory made from the flesh of the former and the juice of the latter. In Alsace it's *flammkuche,* in Umbria, it's a traditional bread that's fat with these two components, shaped like snails and hence called *lumachelle.* And how would America eat without ham and cheese? Ravioli are nothing more or less than kreplach or spring rolls, which are all kith to *canederli,* the dumpling of the Alto Adige, the Italian region that borders Austria. And when it wasn't gnawing the flesh of a beast, our race kept itself on cereal. Mush—a grain, any grain, softened in water. The Romans called it *puls,* which, even when the word slid to become *polenta* or *pulses* or *pablum* or *pap,* was still the same nourishing mush. One can see and taste the lineage of food as, for instance, in a menu offering "roasted polenta with arugula pesto," another reading of "grits and greens." The world's food is a story of mirrors and reprises, just as music is a story of what virtuosity, great or humble, can caress or liberate from those same eighty-eight keys.

And the selfsame normal, natural, sensical rhythms practiced in the restaurants here are practiced in the family kitchen. No one ever has to think too awfully hard about what to fix for supper. The day dictates. More specifically than the season, the determining factor of what makes it to the table is the weather within that season. Has there been rain, has the sun been hot enough to ripen the red peppers yet, or is there another day left for yellow beans and tiny new potatoes?

Here poor people eat far more magnificently than the rich in America. And so I ask myself—as I strain the cooking water from boiled potatoes into my bowl to enrich a bread, or let the juices of a once-a-week roast, as it turns on a spit, drip over and flavor a pan of potatoes, or stew hard bread with wild herbs and oil to make a soup—what does it mean to be poor? I think I'm learning how to live gracefully in need as well as in abundance. Essentially the approach is the same. But the trick is to define *abbondanza,* abundance. For us abundance has become a *giara* of just-pressed oil, far fewer *things,* a little more time. I remember Barlozzo telling us about the old days when accumulation signified three sacks of chestnuts rather than two. Different from the sort of accumulation some of my California acquaintances could carry off—1,000-square-foot travertine kitchens with three ovens, two dishwashers, and two refrigerators, fireplace, bar, and the cook's bath and changing room. There is clarity in this Tuscan life.

BESIDES, HOW COULD a person who has a wood oven in her garden ever feel poor? Even during these frigid months, we won't surrender our outdoor cooking, and yet we know some greater efficiency must be practiced to conserve the woodpile. We'll light it once a week and cook as much as we can in that single session—breads, *focaccie,* a braise or a roast, a stew of root vegetables. And in the last of the heat, we'll roast pears and apples hoarded in the barn or plump dried figs and prunes with a handful of cracked cinnamon bark and a good splash of *vin santo*. And each day and evening, we'll just take portions of what we'd like and gently reheat them in the kitchen oven. A perfect plan, until we consider storage for this wood-smoked bounteousness. Our refrigerator is barely grander than a good hotel room's minibar. But I've solved this problem before.

When the children and I lived in Cold Spring–on-Hudson, it was in a stone cottage, the gardener's house at the edge of an estate's park. The house was wonderful, but it was small, and everything in it was sized to a proportionately diminutive scale, including our refrigerator. In the winter, we'd cook and bake away all of our Sunday afternoons and then we'd store the lot in the trunk of the old Pinto. Pots of beef stew and chicken and dumplings, red peppers stuffed with sausage and bread, meat loaves wrapped in bacon, a corn pudding, a casserole of potatoes and Emmenthaler, or maybe one of spinach and cream—all of it packed like a puzzle, taut and safe, in my mobile fridge, the security of our suppers keeping me company as I drove to and from work each day, praying there'd be no thaw.

I tell Fernando this story and ask, "Why can't we just store the cooked food in the barn?"

"Because the local nocturnal animals would feast on it."

"Not if we build up a shelter. Bricks, logs, stones, we've got all we need to construct some simple food safe."

I prepare myself for a skirmish, but he's saying, "*Va bene*. OK. Barlozzo and I will put something together later this afternon. He'll love this idea. Also, he told me last night he wants to talk with us about Christmas."

I'm not so sure I want to talk about Christmas. Prescribed holidays can seem a sham to me. I'd rather have a dose of celebrating in each day, some small recognition of the miracles contained in it. The grand spectacles put me off. They end. And when they do, one often feels whittled down rather than refreshed by them. I like my daily life enough so that I'd rather live it even on Christmas. I want to light the fire, bake my bread, run up to the Centrale for breakfast, cook a beautiful lunch and dine with Fernando and Barlozzo, read and sleep by the fire, stomp through the woods and into the tangled, frozen fields until I'm breathless and aching with the cold and with the wonder of a black, starry night. Then I'd like to wrap my hands about a cup of hot, spiced wine and sip it together with our friends and neighbors who'll surely gather, at some point in the evening, up at the bar. As both the children are Christmasing with the families of their partners, perhaps a piece of this resolve is bravado, the result of my learning about and understanding that holidays must be shared when one's children are adults with complicated lives of their own. I know they'll be here with us for two months this summer, and that helps, if not so much. And I want to see Floriana. I sent a note to her through Barlozzo, asking if we might stop by. She has not replied.

It's the second weekend of December and every little village and *borgo* is celebrating their own newly pressed oil. Bonfires in village squares, great wood-fired grills set up on which to roast bread and sausages, whole pigs gilding on spits, makeshift burners to heat red wine, accordion players, mandolin duets, *mangiafuochi,* fire-eaters, *giocolieri,* jesters in medieval dress, tarot readers in satin skirts come to say the future and bishops in silk robes come to bless the oil and the souls it will nourish. Pagan rites, sacred rites embraced together in the warmth of the long, licking flames of a fire. Country festivals are cures. Sweet revels come to interrupt the constancy that life asks of a farmer. We will go to the *sagra dell'olio nuovo* in Piazze along with almost everyone else in San Casciano. Twill jodhpurs, riding boots, a white lace shirt, its collar tight and high as my chin, a soft leather jacket the color of sweet wine, my hair pushed up inside a brown beret. The night is black and scented in wood smoke and new snow as we jump down from the duke's truck on this Tuscan Saturday-night-at-the-world. In a wave of what seems like five hundred strong in a village where perhaps seventy-five people live, we walk in the dark toward the municipal parking lot, the scene of the *sagra*. We come upon the light. The first thing I see is the *paiuolo,* a cauldron rigged up over a fire that leaps from a pyramid of logs, waiting for a witch. There are beans cooking in it, red *borlotti* beans and the scored skins of a pig, branches of sage and rosemary, whole heads of bruised garlic, all of it bubbling in a broth of tomatoes and red wine. There are two narrow grills set up, each perhaps twelve feet long and glowing with the red and white ash of olive wood and vine cuttings. The crowd is thickest around them, waiting for the grilling of the bread, which would soon become bruschette. A man steps forward with a great basket of bread sliced into one-inch trenchers. With deft and flying fingers, he lays the bread along the lengths of first one and then the other grill, tilting around them to place a layer on the far side. The hot ash grazes the bread in less than a minute, and thus the man must race back to his first slice and turn it with the tongs just slapped into his hands as would be an instrument to a surgeon. In fact, he has two sets of tongs and uses them one after the other, never missing a beat. He is playing the marimba, turn, turn, dancing down one side of the grills and up the other in a thrillingly smooth glissade. When both sides of the bread are gently toasted, he lays the pieces onto restaurant-size sheet pans. Another dancer enters and drizzles gorgeous, thick green oil onto the hot bread from a two-liter bottle with a spigot, which he holds up a meter above the bread. The third dancer is behind him pinching sea salt over the oil, the pearly crumbles of it melting like ice on a griddle over the very hot bread. As quickly as he finishes one tray, someone passes it to the crowd, and then another one passes the next, until all the bread has been distributed and the marimba master is beginning his dance all over again.

There is a proscenium of sorts built up on cinder blocks. A tasting panel composed of four gentlemen who sit in front of a white-clothed table set with six clear glass bottles, each filled with the oil of a different consortium and labeled with a number. A line of glass tumblers is arranged before each man and, with the pomp of a Burgundian auction, the tasting begins. The judges are retired farmers, and since farmers hardly ever retire in these parts, I guess their average age to be near ninety. All wear hats against the cold, most of them the typical *colbacco,* a rabbit-lined wool cap with earflaps. One braves the night in a fedora. The first oil is poured into their glasses and the four dip their wizened, rough old beaks in to whiff the oil's perfume. They look at it in the dim light of the parking lot lamps and write impressions on yellow pads. They taste it, drink it in some cases. They write more impressions. They taste it on a piece of grilled bread and write again. There is no wine allowed on the dais, and I know this fact will cause a speedy finish to the event. Sure enough, the six oils are dispatched, smelled, tasted, drunk, and judged in as many minutes. The winner is announced and there is great cheering, whistling from the foot-stomping crowd. The oil from Piazze's consortium is the unanimous winner. Barlozzo says that's because it was the only one entered, that all the bottles held the same oil and that those ancients wouldn't know the difference between two oils if one of them was from Puglia. Or Greece, for that matter. Still he goes up to congratulate the judges and the mill owner. His fondness for his neighbors is as clear as is the false sarcasm he uses to hide it.

Attention is turned back to the dais as the mayor is announcing the winners of the evening's raffle, the proceeds of which are destined to cover the costs of whitewashing the interior of the chapel of Sant'Agata. The premiums are ported up onto the dais on the beefy shoulders of eight men, and the sight of the four whole *mortadelle*—each of them weighing in at twenty kilos—tantalize the screaming crowd into frenzy. First prize is two whole *mortadelle,* second prize, one whole mortadella, third prize, half a mortadella, fourth prize, the other half of the third prize.

A mandolin accompanies a whiskey voice torching out the evils of false love, and we wander toward the wine, served almost boiling from ceramic pitchers into styrofoam cups. Holding the hot things with two hands, sipping gingerly, we are warmed. We find seats at the communal tables, each of us in a different place. On one side, I'm snuggled close to the butcher who is wearing neither his cleaver nor his modish belt this evening; on the other side is a Roman who says he comes each year for this *sagra* on a bus with thirty-five other Romans. People at the table chide him for remaining a city slicker when life is so much more wonderful in Piazze. There is no trope, no satire but only a sincere desire to convince the Roman of what they believe.

More *bruschette* and jugs of wine drawn from barrels are passed about the tables, and now the beans are ladled out into white plastic bowls, the good spicy scent whipping our hungers. "*Evviva, i fagioli,*" shout the men as if they'd struck gold. "Eureka, the beans." Stewed and plumped to silk in the old cauldron, their flavor explodes in the mouth, then comforts, nearly like an unexpected kiss does from lips placed hard on the nape of the neck. A piece of bread, another spoonful of beans, now some wine, each food exalting the other. Beans and bread and oil and wine. So what does it mean to be poor? I ask myself once again.

BARLOZZO TOOTS HIS horn at 3:00 a.m. on Christmas Eve, ready to drive us to Norcia to hunt for black diamonds. Truffles. There in the southeastern part of Umbria close to the region of Abruzzo, the mystical tubers grow not so deep beneath the roots of oak, hazelnut, and birch trees. A local zealot called Virgilio—the duke's old chum—will lead us up into the hills. We meet him at the appointed hour and place. Wrapped in the traditional black wool cape of the *trifolau,* truffle hunter, a short-brimmed leather hat perched at an almost foppish slant, he and the camouflage-jacketed duke are an unlikely couple. We leave Barlozzo's truck in a field and climb into the back of Virgilio's pickup to sit among coils of rope and empty wine demijohns while he and the duke pass a grappa bottle back and forth up in the cab. As we begin our hike, Virgilio tells us he's been digging truffles for sixty years, that by now he can *sense* them even when it's this cold, as long as the ground isn't frozen. He says that his dog, Mariarosa, is nearly superfluous. "I've outlived generations of fine truffle-hunting bastards and I paid attention to every one of them, learned from them. The last one before Mariarosa was eighteen years old when she died. And as her senses dimmed, mine seemed to grow keener, as though she'd signed hers over to me. And so when she passed on, I just thought I'd carry on alone. That is until Mariarosa began following me one day. A small, bright bastard, just as any good truffle dog must be, she's more faithful than a wife," says Virgilio, who now seems tired from such a long soliliquy.

Barlozzo takes on the character of Virgilio, grunting answers to our questions, sometimes looking off into the distance when we speak, not hearing us at all. Or is it that I can better recognize Barlozzo's manner as it resonates in Virgilio? It hardly matters at this moment, in the powdered blue dawning of a Christmas. We tramp the mystical hills where once lived saints and serpents, and only our boots and our breathing and the cawing of some bird interrupt the whisperings of the snow. Mariarosa stops short by the roots of an oak, sniffs them. She barks then howls, prancing in ecstatic leaps, ears folded back in the wind, nose in the air. Mariarosa has found a truffle. Virgilio quiets her to a panting whine, kneels beneath the tree, gently scrapes away, with a trowel of sorts, at a point under some of the smaller roots. He uses the instrument as a shovel then, but takes only tablespoons of earth at a time, touching the place with long, searching, ungloved fingers and pulls up the truffle, shaking just some of the black, thick dirt from it, placing it carefully inside the canvas sack he wears across his chest. He feels about the spot once again, then covers it up, pats it as though in thanks, and walks on. He brings Mariarosa's snout down to scent the place where the truffle was found, pulls her close into his arms for an embrace, takes a biscuit from his pocket. Her prize. With only slight variations, Mariarosa and Virgilio repeat this magical performance four, five, six times before he announces it's time for his breakfast, that we're welcome to join him. He hands Barlozzo the sack to inhale and inspect and we huddle about him, yelping and groaning for the joy of such bounty, naming the dishes they'll grace over the next few weeks.

"*Calmatevi,*" says the duke, "calm yourselves. We'll see how many of them go home with us after they're weighed and priced."

We settle ourselves around a table in a small *osteria.* It's the last table, in fact, as the place is all abuzz with hunters, most of them stripped down to their woolen undershirts, at home in the smoky, steam-heated quarters, resting from their battles, quaffing liters of red, sitting in front of beefsteaks or bowls of thick soup and plates heaped with pasta. It's just after eight in the morning. But we, too, have been on the road since 3:00 a.m., just as they were in the woods or on the hills by then, and so this sort of early feasting seems just.

We begin with *frittata di tartufi*—a flat, thin, paper thin omelette, nearly orange in color from rich yolks given up by corn-fed hens—with fat black disks of musky truffle showing themselves all over it. In fact, it seems the eggs are merely transportation, a buttery, golden medium to get the truffles to the table. I reach for a first sip of wine but the duke stops me, says to wait. Cutting the great circle into four wedges, serving Virgilio and then us, delivering the last to his own plate with skill and pomp, he says, "Eat this immediately and with your eyes closed."

I slide down a bit in my chair, ravished and nearly disbelieving the sensations caused by an egg, a wild tuber, and a knob of sweet butter. Fernando sits dutifully with eyes still closed until the duke breaks the spell and says with glass raised, "*Buon Natale, ragazzi.* Merry Christmas, kids."

Even Virgilio seems pleased with our response to the first course of the breakfast, and he tells us, "This is the one truly perfect way to eat a truffle. The eggs are cooked over a low flame only to softness in good, white butter. And just at the moment they're about to set, one slices the truffle over all, as much of it as one can buy or steal. Cover the pan for a few seconds to warm the truffle, to release its power. Bring the pan to the table. But that's not the whole recipe. Everything else has to be just right, as well. No wine, empty stomach, ferocious hunger, fine company or no company at all. It's like making love, one thing out of place and it's all mechanical, no more exciting than potatoes and eggs."

Perhaps it's not so much that Virgilio is prone to silence as he is to saving his breath for plucking straight into the pith of things.

IT'S NEARLY DARK when we pull into the drive at Palazzo Barlozzo. The village is twilit, asleep beneath the fogs. I stand at the edge of the garden to look at her, watching as the windows, one by one, turn golden. Fernando and Barlozzo are making some sort of plans for later but I'm not listening. I throw a kiss to the duke and walk up the stairs, aching for a warm bath.

There's a tree in the tub. There are six-foot evergreens in jute sacks leaning in the bedroom, in the front entryway, on the landing, there are five of them in the stable and the whole place smells, feels like a forest, and I love it. Fernando is laughing and grinning close behind me as I discover his gifts.

"I told the *vivaio* to deliver them this morning. I left the key for him and a bottle of wine. Aren't they wonderful? After Epiphany, we'll plant them all along the farthest boundary of the garden and they'll be beautiful. It was the best present I could think of for us. *Un gesto simbolico,* a symbolic gesture, I guess. We'll transplant them like we did ourselves," he tells me.

I kiss him hard and long and then kiss him again. We take our bath, rest a bit, then dress and go downstairs to open some wine, but the duke is already there with a fire lit and the horrid, carbonated wine he calls *vino da festa,* festival wine, sitting in a bucket. A tall, fat silver fir, its tip bent by the too-low rafters, sits in a black metal stand in front of the kitchen door.

"I didn't know where to put it, so I just stood it there in the meantime. I know you're going to scream at me for killing a tree, but this is the first Christmas when I've *felt* like it was Christmas in a very long time and I really cut it down for myself and only brought it here because your place is bigger than mine," he says, grinning.

I tell him it's glorious and all of a sudden I feel like it's Christmas, too, and Fernando must as well because he's racing out the door to the barn to look for our decorations box from Venice. The search is futile and we think it must have stayed on the Albanians' truck, but it hardly matters, because the tree, the trees themselves, are perfect.

We sit there in our own private woods, we three alone in custody of the sour wine and the great dark fir tree and its kin, all of them ornamented only by the fire, their scent intoxicating our little parish, intoxicating us. We sit like this, staring and fascinated, not saying very much at all. I'm thinking that not a single sweetmeat did I bake, no gingercakes, no sugarplums, no pie, no roast, no wassail bowl. Save the trees and the truffles, no presents. Neither has there been agony nor temper nor fatigue nor a thin graciousness sipped with the eggnog. This is a good Christmas.

I struggle to get behind the big tree, trying to enter the kitchen to search some small tidbit to put before the men, but Barlozzo is saying, "Since we're due at Pupa's by eight and it's already seven, hadn't we better head up to the bar? Oh, and by the way, Floriana sends her good wishes, says she's doing just fine.

"Merry Christmas," he says in his proud English with the bedouin accent.

I think I'm beginning to like that he tells me only half his sentiments, while another part of them he simply lets me know.

The One and Only True Bruschetta: (brew-sket'-ah)
What It Is and How to Pronounce It

The almost universal mistaken pronunciation of *bruschette* by foreign visitors to Italy sometimes causes chagrin, but most often just quiet laughter from waiters and Italians who are dining close by. But whatever name one gives it, honest country bread, sliced not too thickly and roasted lightly over the ash of a wood fire, drizzled with extra virgin olive oil, and then sprinkled with fine sea salt, is a primordial gastronomic pleasure that is Tuscan to its core. The addition of chopped, fresh tomato is wonderful, especially in high summer, as is the perfume of a fat clove of garlic rubbed into the hot bread. But Tuscan purists will tell you that bread and oil and salt compose the best *bruschette* of all.

To make *bruschette* at home, find (or make) a dense, crusty loaf, slice it no more than half an inch in thickness, set it under a hot broiler or over a charcoal or wood fire, and toast it lightly on each side. Drizzle the hot bread with oil, sprinkle on sea salt, and serve immediately as part of an antipasto or, better, all by itself with a glass of red wine.

12

Supper Made from Almost Nothing

January arrives brooding. But we've settled nicely into winter, our tricks against the cold performed with ease so there is the illusion, at least, of warmth about the house. Fernando continues to read and work toward the planning of the "journeys project," as he's taken to calling it, while I write and edit and write some more. The village is quiet as a vapor. Even the bar seems in slumber, things barely stirring there except for an hour or so in the early mornings and for as long again at *aperitivo* time. Everyone is in recovery from the intemperance that began in September with the *vendemmia,* swelled into October with the chestnut and wild mushroom festivals, mounted, then, in November and early December with the olive harvest, all of it clinched in the keeping of the sweet, quiet rituals of a rural Christmas. Now, a long, delicious rest.

Fewer people come to Friday nights, muzzled up with their fires and televisions against the crisp ten-meter walk to the Centrale, but we persist in the ritual until the evening when we find absolutely no one in the bar except Tonino, deep in lesson planning for his Saturday class at the high school. Determined to dine out this evening, we just cart our basket back to the car, drive up to the overlook on the Celle road, indulge in the extravagance of leaving the heater on, open one window a crack, and set up for supper. The old BMW becomes an instant dining room. Always ready in the boot is a basket fitted with wine glasses, two of our most beautiful ones, plus two tiny Bohemian cut-crystal glasses, napkins made from the unstained parts of a favorite tablecloth, a box full of odd silver, a wine screw, a good bottle of red wine—always replaced immediately after consumption—a flask of grappa, a Spanish bone-handled folding knife, a pouch of sea salt, a small blue-and-white ceramic pepper grinder, plates of varying size, a tiny plastic bottle of dishwashing liquid, two linen kitchen towels and paper towels. Warm enough now, we turn off the heater, close the window and open the wine. Snow falls and swirls thick about the windows like curtains. Lifting the lid from the pot of sausages braised with white beans and sage and tomatoes, we decide to use it as a communal dish. We eat hungrily, digging for the pieces of sausage, feeding them to each other. There's half a sponge cake, split and filled with apricot jam and spread with hazelnut cream. We cut it with the Spanish knife, evening it out, then evening it out a little more, until only a strangely shaped wedge of it remains.

Too ugly to keep, we say, and we eat that, too. A sip of grappa in the Bohemian glasses.

ONE EVENING, WE convince Pupa to close her doors and come to supper with Barlozzo at our house and, over a soup of *ceci* and *farro,* the duke begins to talk about *la veglia*. Once *la veglia* was a way for farmers and their families to gather of an evening in the pitch of winter. Often one farmhouse was separated from the next by kilometers and, in winter, the only time neighbors saw each other was by plan. Apart from its promise of a supper of relative plenty, *la veglia* was hungrily anticipated to indulge social appetite. "And so folks would trudge through the snow with whatever they could spare from their pantries," he says. "Someone brought the end piece of a prosciutto, another a wild hare trapped in the gloaming of that morning, someone else lamb, another some part of whatever beast he'd been able to hunt, each one placing his offering into a cauldron set over a blazing fire. Cabbages, potatoes, herbs, heels of wine, and drops of oil flavored the great stew, which they called *scottiglia*. And while it all braised in symphony, people warmed themselves by the hearth, passed around a bulbous-bottomed wine flask in which white beans had been braised in the ash of yesterday's fire with herbs and oil and wine. Each one poured out a few beans onto his thick slice of bread, quaffed his wine, took a turn reciting Dante or telling ghost stories while they waited for supper. It was here that the old passed down stories to the young, saving history the way their elders had saved it for them. And when the last smudge of *la scottiglia* was finished, the wine jugs hollow as drums, the host, if he had them to spare, would pull blistering potatoes out from the cinders, giving one to each child for his coat pocket, a hand warmer for the long walk home over the frozen hills. It was understood that the potato was to be saved and, mashed with hot water or a little milk, eaten for breakfast.

"I always ate my potato when I got into bed, peeling back its skin and eating it like an apple. I loved potatoes so much I just couldn't wait until morning, even though I knew it meant my mother would serve me angry looks with my milk and coffee for breakfast."

"You must have been fairly well off as things went in those days," says Pupa. "We hardly had any meat at all. Where I lived, *la veglia* took on another form. Everyone would collect about the fire, all of them direct from their ablutions, hairdos in place, fresh shirts and smocks. Risen bread dough sat in the *madia,* the bread-rising cupboard, and the kettle hung in the hearth, ready to boil. The lady of the house fetched the dough from the *madia* drawer, placed it in the biggest bowl in the house, and set it on a table in front of the fire. Each person broke off a bit of dough and began rolling it between his palms into a short, slender rope, fashioning a rough sort of pasta.

Each piece of pasta was gently dragged through a dish of hard wheat flour and then placed on a tray. The process continued until all the dough was shaped into pasta. The trays full of pasta were then heaved into the boiling water, and as the pieces rose to the top of the pot, they were retrieved with a skimmer and placed back into the same bowl, warmed now and in which a small amount of good oil and a few generous handfuls of grated *pecorino* waited. A cupful of the cooking liquors, more cheese, a few more drops of oil, more cooking liquors, and pepper, freshly cracked with an exuberant hand, the whole was tossed about and served with a small wooden shovel. We called the confection *pizzicotti,* pinches. Supper made from almost nothing."

"Was it like that during the wars?" I want to know.

"Was what like during the wars?" the duke asks.

"I mean, eating boiled pinches and saving a scrap of meat to add to the neighbors' scraps of meat to make a supper."

"No. That wasn't wartime, it was life. Even when times were good they weren't so good," says Barlozzo. "The truth is that much of the time we were OK, but in great part it was because of our cunning as much as our fortunes. When the ground wasn't cold and hard, we had whatever we could forage—grasses, herbs, wild onions, chestnuts, figs, mushrooms, berries. We always kept some of everything apart, drying or preserving the bounty against winter.

And in the orchards when fallen fruit didn't suffice, we robbed the trees by moonlight. And so we had pears and apples, cherries, peaches, plums, and sometimes quince and persimmons and pomegranates. Again, we feasted on the glorious stuff, guzzling its ripeness, sucking in the sweet juices of plenty. But we saved some. We saved some for the other, less balmy time that always followed. Same with the things we grew. We had vines and my father and my uncles vintnered the gaunt, snarling red wine without which life was *impensabile,* unthinkable. It was food to us like bread, like the coffee, which most times we brewed from weeds and roots. We dried tomatoes and white beans and corn to grind into yellow flour. Not one of us having anything of money to buy what we needed or desired, it was by mutuality that we lived, everyone trading everyone else for what they didn't have, shuffling back and forth whatever they could grow up or gather or shoot or steal. But nothing was casual about the trading.

"There were regulations, firm and constant, honored by everyone. We bartered a two-liter jug of wine for a two-kilo round of new cheese from the shepherd. When we could, we'd bring him supper in the sheepfolds and he'd come by the next morning to return my mother's pot, filled then with soft, creamy dollops of the ricotta he'd just made by cooking part of the evening's milking over his wood fire, then adding some of the morning's milk and cooking it again until it curdled. It was the greatest of entertainments for me when the shepherd came carrying that pot full of cheese. And the canning jars and the canning kettles were like family jewels.

"My father would say that the canning jars were better dressed than I ever was, all washed and wrapped in clean rags and stored away against the wolf. But still, sometimes we were empty. The stores were finished before we could begin planting and harvesting a new season's food. We were hungry. Really hungry sometimes. Hungry enough so that the suffering was the only thing we felt. My mother would slice the bread, holding the great, round, now dwindling bulk of it on the shelf of her breast. She'd slice with her left hand, longwise across the loaf from right to left. I would sit there looking up at her. One night, I was feeling sick, and I told her so. As I remember, it wasn't only the hunger but the fear of this insufficiency that left me weak. I wasn't old enough to understand the rhythm of that life of ours. I didn't remember that it wouldn't always be this way. My mother came into where I was resting, the room dark and quiet and cold. She carried in something wrapped in a cloth, bearing it like a sacrament. *Tesoro, I have a surprise for you. Now, sit up and take this, open it up. Go on,* she'd said, as though it was true. I could feel it was only bread waiting under the cloth. Sullen, I stayed. *No, no, it's not just bread. It's bread and cheese. Look.* She opened the cloth. *See, here is the bread. And here is the cheese. Now close your eyes and taste how good they are together. It's a special supper only for you. Take a bite. See. It's a thick, soft slice of* marzolino. *Just like butter. Just the way you like it.* I closed my eyes, held her uplifted hands and bit into the bread she raised to my mouth. There was no cheese, of course, but only two slices of bread, stacked one on the other. But somehow her charm worked. I could taste cheese. I could really taste it. I ate slowly at first, then faster and faster until I'd finished it, keeping my eyes closed all the time. When I opened them, I saw that she'd been crying, smiling, sobbing. I think it must be the hardest thing for a mother, having both a hungry child and empty pockets."

THE DUKE SHOULD never have begun all this talk about a *veglia,* because now I ask him about it each day. "Who has a house large enough to hold a *veglia?*" I want to know.

"What sort of *veglia* are we talking about? If it's just twenty or thirty people, we can use Pupa's place, but if you want to invite the whole village, we'll have to hold it in the piazza, build a bonfire, and use the bar as an emergency room against the cold," he says as though we could truly execute such a party.

Knowing the very idea would be thrilling to me, he begins laughing out loud even before I say, "That's it. That's how to do it. We'll post a notice in the bar and—"

"And just say it's in honor of Florì's homecoming," he interrupts.

"What? When? Why didn't you tell me?"

"I'm telling you thirty minutes after she told me. She says she's feeling up to it, that she misses her little place. And most of us, I think, although she'd never say that. I'm going to pick her up on Wednesday morning. Let's let her just be quiet for a few days and set Sunday evening for the *veglia*."

I look for a long time at the duke and it's easy to see he's having a homecoming of his own, that he's consented to reinhabit his peace, to wash off the bad weather he's been wearing, in greater or lesser degrees, all these past weeks. We sit there grinning at each other, each of us sending out rounded daggers at the other, each of us trying not to be the first one to cry.

LETTERS AND NOTES are affixed to every centimeter of the small, sturdy mahogany door with the lion's-head knocker that is Floriana's. The three high cement steps that comprise her stoop are beset with flowers, mostly small nosegays of wild ones, the short stems of them twisted in aluminum foil or a dampened handkerchief. One of the village women has organized a troupe of cooks, each of whom will carry in Floriana's lunch or supper on a certain day of the week. I've been asked by the strategist to bring a sweet or some bread up to her *ogni tanto,* every once in a while, she already knowing my propensity to overfeed. Housekeepers, chauffeurs, handymen, woodcutters, ladies' maids who would see to her toilette, all have been anticipated and delegated with great care and affection. And, of course, Florì, with an equal dose of care and affection, demurs, then objects more animatedly, assuring the village spokespeople that she'll be the first to ask for help. If she needs it.

Her cheeks are flaming roses on the parchment skin of her face. A scarf, eerily russet as was the color of her hair, wraps her head and is tied jauntily in a grand, drooping bow in the middle of her forehead. Though the day is bitter, she wears only a cardigan and a thick, brown shawl over her gray wool dress. She has new shoes, pumps in soft black kid with a pretty, delicate stub of a heel.

"I got them in a shop in Perugia," she says giggling, Perugia being about the same thing as Paris to her and the ladies who are ogling them.

She does not look so different, no less beautiful, certainly not so very much thinner and yet there is less of her, as though a dimension was missing, as though she were an apparition of herself. Barlozzo husbands her along the few steps from the piazza up to her door, nods and softly speaks requests and directions to one person and another. They both smile and wave and go inside and I'm thinking how much they look like a bride and groom trying to go off to the privacy of their honeymoon. The only thing missing is a handful of rice, but even that appears, cooked in a soup, still warm in a lovely blue-and-white tureen enfolded in a kitchen cloth and pressed upon them by Vera as they close the door.

FLORÌ WALKS IN the village each morning, does her shopping, chats as reticently as she always did, takes her *caffè macchiato* as she always did, smiles and laughs as easily as ever. Neither mysterious nor voluble about her illness, she says she will continue with her treatments, that she feels quite strong. She says she is healing. She always wears the new black shoes.

Barlozzo says little more than Floriana save his expressions of faith, and even those he mostly flashes from his eyes. He's decided not to tell her about Sunday's *veglia,* reasoning that she'll be embarrassed for all the fuss. He says we'll just invite her at the last minute and say it's something we'd planned long ago. But he knows just as well as I that what was born as a poetical rebellion against the mopes of January has taken on Saturnalian proportions to celebrate Florì. And surely she'll know it, too.

THREE IRON DRUMS full of wood are set afire at the bottom of the hill that leads up into town and torches are set all along the way to the piazza, where more flaming iron drums are collected along the overlook wall. Something heathen flits about the scene. There's been some cheating in that there's much more to eat than the traditional *scottiglia,* though that very concoction bubbles gently in two huge pots on the back burners of the bar's kitchen stove. But there's *cinghiale al buglione,* wild boar braised with tomatoes and garlic and red wine; *ribollita,* thick with *cavolo nero,* black cabbage; *cardi gratinati,* gratineed cardoons, the pale green stalks poached and baked with cream and cheese. There are trays and trays of crostini, bowls groaning with *pici,* and barrels spewing wine. And Floriana takes it all in stride, tasting and sipping and saying how hungry she'd been for these foods, that though her Umbrian friends in Città della Pieve—sixteen kilometers distant from San Casciano—were fine cooks, she'd missed the Tuscan hand.

What she doesn't say is that even the Tuscan hand changes from province to province and sometimes even from *comune* to *comune,* family to family. She doesn't say that gastronomic regionalism is an abiding fact of Italian life. Every once in a while she looks down at her shoes and does a sort of two step, admiring them, I think. At the moment in the festival when the recitations are to begin, one by one, the elocutionists beg off, saying they can't recall their lines or that they've had too much wine, both excuses being one in the same, I guess. There is a lull, an expectation, but the duke fills it. "My father used to say that hell is where nothing's cooking and no one's waiting."

The lull lengthens a few beats before the applause, the cheers of agreement. It is a strange moment. It passes, though, immediately dissolved in the comfort of a great farrago. Fernando and I give each other a sign from our different places in the piazza. We agree that it's time to go. We slip off, not really saying good night to anyone, always preferring to exit a party at its peak. Leaving early and unnoticed feels like escape, and so we walk fast. We run, then, all the way down the hill, then up to our place. Slowing down, catching a breath, we walk beyond our house, up the Celle road. Fernando turns back to look at the village, says the firelight becomes the ancient stones. He kisses me gently and holds me.

"She's dying, isn't she?"

I just look at him for a while before asking, "What makes you say that? Barlozzo would never be so jubilant if he thought that was true."

"That's the part that confounds me, too, but still, when I look at her she seems haunted in a way, as though she's already gone but has been allowed back on some reprieve, given a dispensation so she could say good-bye."

"I think it might be only that she's been so very far away. She's been in a place we can't begin to imagine, and so now it's as though she's arriving back in pieces, in stages. She's just not whole yet."

"It all makes me think about us and what we would do if one of us was Floriana."

"We're both Floriana. Dying is what we're all doing, each in our own way. Anyway, death is just moving house. And we're getting very deft at that," I tell him, longing to leave this discourse.

"Just moving house, is it? Just another journey? Is that how you see it? Well, I don't see it that way at all. Besides, I like it here. I want to stay as long as you do, but not any longer. I want to stay right here close to you. What you do, I want to do. Wherever you go, I want to be there. But how can you be so unmoved by all of this?"

"I am not at all unmoved. It's just that I'm moved for Floriana rather than for you or me. And besides, I'm freezing and I think it's this talk of dying as much as the cold that's causing it. Please, let's go home." I turn back and walk fast.

"The truth is you're very frightened about dying," he shouts. Overtaking me, catching me by the arms, he walks backward so he can face me, wanting company for his own fresh terrors.

"No, that's not the truth. I think I'd be very frightened if I were facing Florì's particular moment. And you know I'm desperately frightened for her. But this is *her* illness. And everything about it belongs to her. And because we're her friends, our emotions must be about her rather than about us. Why do you tangle up what's happening to Florì with what's not happening to you or me? If you get sick or I get sick, then it will be time to practice for dying."

Under a raw blue sky sugared in tiny stars we walk back home in single file along the icy road, Fernando leading. We build up the fire and we sit close to it, sipping tea. Fernando is right. All of us consider our own lives when someone close by is losing hers. Or seems to be. And maybe he's right, too, about my appearing to be unsentimental, *unmoved,* as he called it. But I honestly don't worry about my own death. At least not since those days when the children were little and I plotted with the gods, struck all those pacts beseeching them to keep me upright until the babies were. I'd sworn to never ask more for myself. Truly grateful about how that all turned out, I've stayed respectfully hushed on my own behalf, even if I do still bargain from time to time regarding the well-being of the long-since upright children and, more lately, of Fernando. But for all my embracing of how this living and dying seems to work, it's as though I haven't yet applied it to myself. Caused less by the Narcissus in me, I think it's more the imprint of Pollyanna on me that lets me live as though I'll never die. Or is it that it's just fine if I do, since I've lived so long and well already? Surely I'd like to stay longer, though. When my own dying does pass through my thoughts, I think mostly about not wanting to miss out on life with Fernando and the children and my friends. I think about them saying their good-byes to me, then going off to supper. Without me. I'd be flailing my arms from wherever I'd landed, urging them not to go to one place but to another one, suggesting certain dishes and wines, trying to take care of them, even though the truth is they'd always taken care of me.

I try to tell Fernando what I'm thinking and he says he understands.

"I'm not so worried about my dying as I am yours."

"I think I'm safe for tonight," I say. "And if we work things right, we can turn the next few hours into a lifetime." Just as he seems soothed, I begin to cry. He thinks the tears are for Floriana and they are but, damn it, they're also for him. And for me.

13

Fasting Was How We Were Living Anyway

Carne vale, literally, "meat is valid." The eating of meat has long been consented by the Church during the festivals that herald forty days of purification via the tight and sober way of *quaresima,* Lent. *Carnevale* became the sweeping name for all such presacrifical events, including those other fleshly ones that took place beyond—and perhaps on and under—the table, the perspired cavortings of bodies, licensed by a mask. Once *carnevale* in Venice was celebrated for half the year and more—and a long and brazen mazurka it was, the canonical festal foods' only sauce glutted between the partaking of other plums. But here in the hills of southern Tuscany, *carnevale* has borrowed from Venice only the single, fried, and sugary pecadillo of *le frittelle,* fritters.

Little doughnutlike confections, they are piled up into fetching pyramids in every *pasticciera* window and sit, beckoning, on every bar. Filled with ricotta or marmalade or a satiny rummed cream, or empty except for sighs, dragged through warm honey or sugar or wet with the pink jolt of *alchermes*—an ancient herbal concoction used to flavor and color—one, maybe two bites and the wisps dissolve into memories only the thighs seem to recall. They begin appearing sometime in late January or early February, depending upon the date of Easter in a given year. And on *martedì grasso,* Fat Tuesday, *le frittelle* are presented for the last time, never again to be dispensed until next *carnevale*. I think it's their short, mandated season, like the one for local strawberries or asparagus, that adds to their lusciousness. Amnesty for a forbidden food.

And more than we ever did in Venice, we eat *frittelle.* We engage in "tastings" by bringing home four of each variety from the *pasticceria* in the village, thoughtfully rating them for crispness, delicacy, flavor. That sampling too small for serious research, we enlarge the field, braking for every hand-lettered sign announcing *oggi frittelle,* today, fritters, at bars and pastry shops from Chiusi, Cetona, Città della Pieve, Ficulle, Sarteano, Chianciano Terme. Sometimes we carry a few home for four o'clocks with Barlozzo or to bring to Floriana, both of them usually shaking their heads over the little morsels, bemoaning what passes for *frittelle* in this day and age. The two of them must have schemed on the subject because one day they *both* arrive at four, Floriana's market sack full and hanging from Barlozzo's arm.

"Ciao, belli," says Floriana, *"cosa pensate se facciamo una piccola dose di frittelle, al modo mio?* Hi, beauties, what do you think about our making a tiny batch of fritters, according to my method?"

Fernando is hugging her and I'm trying to peel off her coat from behind and the duke is already messing with the fire, saying, "I'll heat the wine if you've got any decent cinnamon."

We have to mix the fritters on the dining room table because Floriana and I can't both fit in the kitchen. We are constantly foiled by Barlozzo, who interrupts each phase of the operation, assuring us that his mother always did it differently. Fernando quiets the crowd by reminding them that he's the only Venetian on the premises and that *le frittelle* belong to his own culinary culture. He proclaims that Venetians won't tolerate raisins in their fritters. Floriana tells him that she knows very well it's *he* who won't tolerate raisins in his fritters and that he can't denounce the poor little fruits for the whole of the water kingdom. "And besides," she says, "these are white raisins that have been soaking in dark rum for half a year, and once you taste them you'll be begging me for the whole jar."

There's flour and potato starch, eggs and sugar and butter, the juicy zests of oranges and lemons, vanilla beans, fat and soft, which Barlozzo slits and scrapes with the tiniest blade on his pocket knife. We beat and spoon and fry the ravishing things, tossing them, hot, in a bag of pastry sugar, piling them up on a footed dish just like they do in the shops. We eat them then, and drink the duke's warmed wine, and there is a party in the stable that afternoon, a homespun sort of *carnevale* all our own.

Barlozzo and Florì take turns telling us stories of the old lenten fasts that, apart from penitence of the faithful, served a real purpose for the body. "Those fasts cleansed the innards, especially the liver, prepared one for spring tonics and for the hard work that lay ahead. Eating is all about rhythm, just like everything else. A body can't thrive eating the same things day in, day out. Eat with the seasons, fast for one dark month each year, and always rest for at least an hour after lunch and supper. Some of us stayed the forty Lenten days without sugar, meat, wine, or bread. We ate beans and lentils, sometimes eggs and whatever vegetables there were. Of course, there were times when fasting was how we were living anyway, so Lent was just another name for it," sums up the duke.

None of us wants to hear about supper after the *frittelle,* so we just sit and talk and listen to each other until Floriana says she'd better go. She is halfway out the door, Barlozzo already out on the terrace, when she turns to me saying, "You know, Chou, I'm sorry about leaving you with all those plums last autumn. You can't imagine how many times I've wished we'd made that jam. But I was lazy then. I think that's all it was. But now, I don't feel lazy at all. *Buona notte, ragazzi.*"

It is Ash Wednesday, the first day of Lent, and I think how quaint it is that Misha is arriving just as we go, spiritually, into the dark. Fernando and I are on our way to Florence to fetch him and, though we are happy for his coming, so are we agitated for it. He represents some strange conjunction of pugnacious coach, loving Jewish uncle, and Jungian, the last of which he truly is, a psychiatrist by profession. He has been my friend for many years and, during his two visits to us in Venice, he and Fernando struck the sparks of sympathy, though each with a hand on his dagger.

We tuck Misha into the backseat, his small black leather traveling bag next to him, exactly where he wants it to be. I breathe deeply and the scent of him comforts me. Always the same boarding-house perfume, it's made of old sweat trapped inside damp tweeds, the Cavendish shag of his pipe, and a single note of cabbage, stayed too long in a pot. As a young doctor, just out of school in Russia, he emigrated to Italy, living for many years in Rome before finding his way to Los Angeles, and it was in these Tuscan hills where he came often to walk and write and think. He is at ease throughout the ride home, saying, in his perfect Italian, how much he misses Italy, which is almost as much as he misses Russia. He neither asks trick questions nor ones to which he already knows the answers. I know that he's saving those, that he will spew them forth fast and sharp as a quiet serpent will his tongue. But I'll be ready for him.

He tours the house with Fernando, settles himself in a guest room while I'm in the kitchen, and when we sit down at table, I see he's pomaded his hair to a plumbago sheen and tied a handsome paisley cravat at his neck—battle dress, I think. I can't help myself from holding down one leg of the table, girded for the first blow. It comes in the form of "The house is charming and could be quite more so with a few changes. It's a shame it's not yours."

Fernando jumps in. "We've begun to look about for a house to buy but, actually, we feel no urgency about it. We don't feel the need to decide about that. Or about much of anything else right now. Besides, we're becoming quite affectionate about this place, and it hardly seems to matter whether it belongs to us."

"Living life on the social margins doesn't disturb you, then?" His glance is a sword, which I thrust back at him.

"I think 'social margins' is a subjective state, and if that's how our life seems to you, so be it," I tell him, getting up to pour more wine for him.

"You define 'social margins,' then," he says, not resting half a beat before he defines them for himself. "You don't have jobs and you don't have investments. You seem to have dissolved your professional histories and set up here among the olives, assuming a stance in the whirring diorama of village life. You are behaving irresponsibly at a time in your lives when such can be very dangerous."

"We don't have children to raise. We don't have debts. And it's living here and doing what we're doing that feels good right now," I tell him.

Fernando has taken on the crack rhythms necessary to converse with Misha, and he steps on my last word. "How many of your patients tell you they want to change things in their lives? How many of them keep those dreams locked in a box, only taking them out for a weekly airing when they come to talk to you? I honestly think I'm stronger for having 'dissolved my professional history,' as you say. I still have some paralyzing moments, times when I want things to be easier or clearer, but I had worse terrors sitting, day after day, in that office in the bank."

"But at least you had security then. Now, you have nothing. Prudent people *build* security rather than rip it apart just when they might need it most." There is an almost withering unction dripping from his eyes now. He places both hands on the table, palms down, long white fingers splayed.

"Do you really still believe in security? It's a myth, Misha. And I'm surprised you haven't understood that. It's a treacherous delusion. Do any of us need yet more proof that security can neither be bought nor built nor gained by deeds, good or evil?" I ask him, placing my hands on the table, miming his. "Shrink the complexities. Divine, distill, Misha. Cook the juices down to a syrup. It's sensations rather than things I'm after. Only the mysterious is eternal. I prefer to *feel* this life rather than to grow foolish enough to believe I own it. The only way to be safe is to understand that there is no safety."

Misha stays silent. Very quietly, then, I remind him: *"But to the other realm, alas, what can be taken? Not the power of seeing, learned here so slowly, and nothing that's happened here. Nothing."*

"Ah, now you quote Rilke."

"No, I'm quoting *you* quoting Rilke, the way you used to twenty years ago when I first knew you."

"But you quote us out of context. You rest your head in the brumes, Chou. You always have. And it seems Fernando has taken to the same airy comforts," he says quietly. "To the romantic, all things are romantic. To romantic people, only the romantic can happen. I think you must have been some species of an innocent abroad since your beginnings. I think you were born in a time very much out of harmony with your nature. But instead of that being a problem, you've just marched or danced or wandered through the eighteenth century. Or perhaps it's the nineteenth by now?"

"And now who are *you* quoting?" I ask.

"I can't remember, but it might be myself," he says. "But what I'm hoping is that you don't lean too much on this coupling with Fernando. I hope you understand that we're all, each one of us, alone." He says this looking poker-straight into my husband's eyes.

"I'm not alone now, Misha, and I think most people who are alone are so by choice as much as they are by fortune and destiny. There's a great humility about love. Before a person can surrender his aloneness, he has to care for someone more than he cares for himself." I get up to take away the untouched plates of soup, but first I hold Misha's face in my hands. "Please don't worry so much. I'm doing well. We're doing well. You know better than anyone that most of us are moved by the same desires and fears. It's the timing and the proportions these take on that separate us. Right now we're, emotionally, a little distant from you."

Misha looks at us, one and then the other. Still sitting, he takes both my hands and kisses them, gets up from his chair then and solemnly kisses Fernando on the shoulder, Russian style.

"Shall I fry the cutlets, or are your appetites confined to blood and wine this evening?" I ask. They say they're starving now that we've got past the welcome speeches. I melt sweet butter over a slow flame, add a drop of oil so the butter won't burn when I raise the heat. I slip in the pork, pounded thin and pressed all over with shreds of dried orange zest, fennel seed, and the crushed crumbs of cornmeal bread. I crust them quickly, one side, other side, turn them onto a warm plate while I build a sauce. Fernando and Misha have gone out on the terrace for a smoke, to make their own peace, and I'm thinking that perhaps I've been too hard on my old friend. For Misha, to torment is to love.

But he knows me so well, knows I've always tripped on ladders, corporate or otherwise. Never having quite seen the point in climbing north all the time, I rather liked moving through life in arabesques—a little turnoff here, another one there. Dallying it might have seemed sometimes, though it wasn't. I always finished things, rounded them out smooth as I could. I didn't rush, but I didn't sleep either. Besides, I never would dress for success. And I understand that Misha is not charmed by witnessing happiness. His pain is old, much older than he is, so that even the hypothesis of happiness seems vulgar to him. *Happiness is for stones,* he always says. And so for him, it's better to pass the time with a malcontent, a cynic. Someone loathe to lay down his burdens. Or at least someone who is still waiting for his happiness. Some people are afraid of joy. Terrified that they don't deserve it or that they won't be able to feel it, should it ever come to visit. Mostly I think people are terrified that joy won't stay, won't last. Another reading of Barlozzo's warning that says *Don't trust the peace.*

I notice that Fernando and Misha are no longer on the terrace. Since I don't see them in the garden, I think they must have taken a walk up into town. I slow the supper proceedings, pour a glass of wine, and sit by the fire, but as soon as I do, they appear, arms full of wood, cheeks reddened in winter.

"We've been in the barn, solving things," says Fernando.

"Your husband here is actually quite Machiavellian, Chou. I may have found my match in him. He can quote more passages from *The Prince* than I can. And we both agree that the only real bandits in life are those who believe themselves immaculate, without stain. Perfect people make us feel bad, isolated, punished. We agree on that, as well."

All this accord built in half an hour makes me smile. I go back to my sauce, but they follow me and we're so tight in the kitchen-that-was-a-manger that all we can do is laugh and say how good it is to be together. We decide to eat on our laps by the fire. I push them away to set things up while I heat the buttery juices from the cutlets, add a long splash of *fino,* two drops of red vinegar. When the mass begins to bubble I squeeze the juices from a beautiful blood orange directly into the pan. A grinding of pepper, a knob of butter for shine, and we're ready. I make pools of the sauce on the plates, lay the barely reheated cutlets over it. Misha carries out the dishes, sets them on the shelf of the hearth, Fernando brings the small bowl of celery root and mascarpone purée. And we dine.

The Machiavelli festival proceeds with the consideration of the merits of good and evil. I half-listen, since I've heard Misha's interpretations many times before. "All of us must be aware of our own capacity for evil. Evil is a skill, a defense, an art, a sport. One simply learns it, as one learns to shoot or to ride. Then one tucks away the skill, applying it as needed."

"But what does one do for practice? I mean, how does one keep the skill sharpened?" Fernando asks, but, like the duke, Misha answers only the questions that suit him.

"One who wants to be always good is inevitably ruined by those who are not good. I think that was your case, wasn't it, Fernando? There were those who abused your *goodness,* mistook it for frailty, yes? You may be the least frail man I've ever known."

"*Io lo prendo come un complimento.* I take that as a compliment," says Fernando. "But I think it's too late for me to learn evil. I'm having enough difficulty with English."

I kiss them, leave them to their cups, and take the priest up to bed.

"It has been an evening of unexpected beauty, Chou," Misha says as I'm climbing the stairs. Actually, it was, I think, as I tuck the priest under the sheets.

In half a day he's become the town *divo.* The San Cascienesi are all in a twitter over Misha, charmed by his truculence, marveled by his command of their language. *Un straniero,* a stranger who drinks and smokes and plays cards, who tells jokes in dialect and who is, most stupendous of all, *uno psichiatra Californiana.* Misha cuts *una gran' bella figura*. Did I notice more than one widow sliding off her kerchief and fluffing up her hair? I chide him on the way home, ask him if he wouldn't like to come and "live among the olives" with us, but he just tilts his head, not quite allowing himself a grin.

The five days he'd planned to stay with us spill over into eight or nine and I think Misha rather enjoys the celebrity bestowed upon him by the town as much as he does our cosseting of him. He keeps his dour face through it all, though, save when he can cajole Fernando into another Machievellian tussle.

Early on Misha and Barlozzo seemed to find sympathy in each other over their sunset grappa up at the bar or sitting by our fire, but the two wear neither long nor well together, Misha saying Barlozzo is a Spartan, too repressed in his general discourse. Barlozzo lets his feelings be known by simply interrupting his visits to us and taking polite leave from the bar as soon as we enter with Misha in tow. Fernando says they are like two bull moose, staking out territory. He says they are jealous of each other. Perhaps he's right. But even so, when Misha is ready to leave, all packed up in the Renault he'd rented in Chiusi so he can travel about a bit before heading to Rome and his return flight, I think I can read some joy in his old face. It's not so with the duke.

I don't know whether it's the aftermath of the horn-locking with Misha or unexpired emotion over Floriana's plight or some other calamity, real or perceived, that causes the shades to cross his face again. But there they are, gnawing into the hollows about the duke's eyes as we sit, on the same afternoon of Misha's departure, in the plush blue of a sofa in Florì's little parlor. We're waiting to take her shopping in Città della Pieve.

"There's a place I'd like to show you," he says.

"What sort of place?"

"Just a place. A house. Or what's left of what was once *una casa colonica,* a country house," he says.

"Is it nearby?"

"It's not too far away. Do you remember that bend in the Tiber just a few kilometers before the turnoff up to Todi, where we collected the stones for the fire ring? It's near there, on the other side of the road, about five hundred meters into the woods," he says.

"And you want us to see it? I mean, are we going to visit someone?"

"No, we're not going to visit anyone. No questions, please. I just want Floriana and you and Fernando to come with me tomorrow. See if you can't arrange things with her," he says, nodding toward the next room, where Floriana is muttering about the whereabouts of a glove. "Set it for either tomorrow or Saturday. We can lunch at Luciano's and then stop to see this place for a few minutes. I know I'm being mysterious, but it's just that I want to talk to all of you about something and I can't do that until I show you this house. Will you just do this for me?"

"Of course I will. Or I'll try," I tell him.

But Florì wants no part of this *gitarella,* little journey, saying she loathes that road as much for how it winds and twists as for the memories of riding it to the hospital in Perugia every week for the past four months. Now that those horrors are past, she says she doesn't care if she ever sees that road again. She'll stay at home and cook a little supper for us, have things ready for when we return. "Tomorrow will be a perfect day to stew a hen," she announces as she marches downstairs, on her way to the butcher.

Barlozzo is gracious about Florì's refusal, saying it's probably better if we three go alone anyway, calling us the "front guard" and almost relishing the perplexity he's causing.

It's just after four as we climb down from the truck into a bluish light. Following the duke up a dirt path trampled in goat and sheep hooves, February's wind is a banshee's wail, the howling up of a thousand wolves broken by the brio of a lone bird squalling. The path is hardly steep, but still I'm breathless from going against the wind as Barlozzo stops in sight of a ruin. Tall and narrow as a tower, it is made all of chimneys, the caps of which rise above the flat roof and form a crenellation. Grasses grow high up and into its long paneless windows, the past sucked tight into the stones. We walk closer, wander inside and about it, up the stairs, down a different flight of stairs. It's a big place and I count seven fireplaces, maybe ten rooms. There are two small barns and a winemaking shed, complete with a rotted press and a row of dark, green demijohns dressed in straw jackets.

"There's not much land, except the few hectares of dormant vines up the hill, but there's more than enough for a vegetable garden and a good patch for flowers and herbs," Barlozzo says, as though he's trying to sell it to us. "In that barn over there," he says pointing to the farther one, "there's a summer kitchen with a wood stove, which I could re-vent and convert into an oven. I've studied it carefully." Now I'm certain he wants *us* to buy the place. "But whose house is this?" Fernando asks him.

"This hasn't been anyone's house since after the last war. There's a chance it might be mine. And Florì's, if she wants. And for you two, if you're willing. The chance of my buying it at this point is still small, but I'm in discussion with the owner, a Roman who's never even been up here to look at the place since some uncle or great uncle left it to him last year. His relatives keep dying and he keeps inheriting their properties and this is one of the few he seems willing to surrender from his growing realm," he says.

"Why would you want to be so far from San Casciano?" I ask him.

"It's not that I want to be so far from there as much as I think I'd like to be here. At least some of the time. I'm barely free of the preliminary stages in what might be years of negotiating," he says.

"Years?" Fernando and I ask together.

"What's this? You doubt my immortality? I say let's take it while we can, and when we're gone, the almighty sheep can have it. I don't mean it to be anyone's 'principal dwelling,' as the lawyers say. This could be a place where one of us or all of us comes to be alone or to be together. Even when we're all here at the same time, there would be no dearth of privacy. Like Fernando's trees, the house is a symbol. Whatever else happens, it will be here," he says lighting two cigarettes at once and passing one of them to Fernando.

"But why would you want to take on such a project?" I ask.

"That's a strange question coming from you. Besides, I'm not thinking of it as a *project*. I'd tile the roof, fix the floors, rework the plumbing. I wouldn't even think of a heating system, what with all these fireplaces. I've been meaning to find something like this since my father died, and that was more than forty years ago. He left me a humble stake, which I've yet to touch. I think it's time I did. *Parva domus magna pax*—in a poor house there is great peace. And Jesus knows this is a poor enough house," he says, just standing there smoking, waiting for us to say something. We're both too stunned for much more than awkward laughs and professions of disbelief.

"You just have to promise me one thing, Chou. We'll have to ration your fabric and I must ask you to respect the limits set by the rest of us. I won't have this place looking like some baroque drawing room. No tassels, no fringes, *neanche un putto,* not even a single angel."

We're still not saying much. He talks some more.

"What I'm wanting to do here is to make a home, a second home, if you will, an alternative home, if you must, where all of us can spend some time together. As much or as little as we might desire. My motives are purely selfish. My place in San Casciano is more a den than a house, and that's all it will ever be. Floriana's apartment is wonderful, but it sits right in the middle of the village and, especially since she's been sick, I think she often feels too much on view, like she can't take a walk without collecting an entourage of well-meaning invaders. And, last of all, I don't like it much that the only place you call home belongs to the Luccis. That's a feeling born of very old rancor, which nothing and no one can soften. I know full well that you're in your vagabond phase and that by this time next year you might be living on Elba or Sicily or somewhere in the south of France. But wherever you are, Floriana and I and this place can still be here waiting for you. Now, there's nothing you have to agree to except, when the time comes, to take a set of keys and make yourself at home. I would not be opposed to your helping me with the work, but all the expenses involved, as well as what it will cost to maintain the place, belong to me," he says.

He's picking up twigs now and making a pile of them. "Let's try out the little fireplace. It's too cold to stay out here any longer. I've got some logs in the truck and a pair of bottles." He and Fernando go to fetch the wood and the wine and I roam the house. When they return, Fernando begins to set the fire and the duke opens the wine, pours it out into paper cups, passing one to each of us. He and I sit on a couch covered in a blanket, which I gingerly pat into some order, not lifting it for fear of seeing what might be living beneath it.

"Why did you let someone else marry Floriana?" I ask him without picking up my head from the blanket fixing. Fernando turns toward me from his bending over the fire and bores into my eyes with his blueberry ones. But I keep going. "Once upon a time, you and Floriana were in love, weren't you? And you are still. What happened to you? Why didn't you marry her?"

"I've already told you that the answer is very long," he says. "It's a story that began years before Floriana's and mine began. And it's a story that nearly everyone in town knows except you two, even if no one knows it from my telling of it. But I want to tell it to you. I've wanted to tell it to you since long before you began asking me to tell it. And now I will."

The flames leap and lick at the old, blackened hearth walls, yellowing the light around us. The duke rises from the couch, gives his place to Fernando. He goes to sit on a pile of rags, which once were pillows and, slouching in the spectral dark of the fire, he begins to talk.

"You already know a great deal about my mother, but I don't remember if I've told you her name. Her name was Nina. And my father was called Patsi. Patrizio. Since I have no experience in recounting these particular events out loud, I'm not certain where to begin, but I think this part of the story began when Nina told Patsi about the soldier. Yes, surely it began when she told him about the soldier. She just couldn't *not* tell him any longer. And as though there was nothing else to do for it, Patsi shot her. He shot her while she slept. He dug a grave a few meters from the house, the house where you live now, and he buried her, artfully covering up his deeds. It was early spring and he'd sent me to my great uncle's for a day and a night on the pretense of my helping him to put in tomatoes and peppers and beans. And when I came home, he told me Nina had gone away, that she'd packed some of her things and taken the train to Rome to look for work. He said we'd hear from her when she'd had time to reflect. But, of course, we never did. I was sixteen at the time. It was three years later, when he was dying, that he told me the truth.

"He said, *You know, son, a person can die of shame and she'd been dying of it, in one form or another, for all the time I knew her. She was my brother's* fidanzata, *his girlfriend. He loved her, or at least he did for a while, until he met another girl he thought he loved more. But he wasn’t quite ready to let go of Nina. My brother finally decided which one of them he wanted when Nina told him she was pregnant. Nina lost. I’d been watching all this, almost predicting it, a* cavaliere *at the ready. I’d loved her since she was ten, since I first saw her sitting in church. I remember she was wearing a white beret. It was pulled way down over her forehead so all I could see were those eyes. Those endless black eyes. Just like yours. But I was a big guy of fourteen, much too old to be thinking about babies like her. As we all grew up a little, she and my brother fell in love and well, now you can put the pieces together for yourself. Do you understand that her troubles began long before she took this man, this Tedesco, into her bed? When she couldn’t have my brother, she took me.* Secondo scelta, *second choice, I was, and there were very few days when I didn’t sharply feel that fact. She was a good wife, dutiful, correct, often even sweet, but her broken heart kept spilling out old dreams and she was mostly busy picking up the pieces, endlessly sorting them out into different configurations, never knowing quite what to do with them. So when she told me what happened while I was away, it wasn’t the shock a man might feel if he and his wife had been mad for each other or even reasonably content with each other. She’d been betraying me always. Is emotional betrayal any less real than the carnal sort? And so for me, this other betrayal was not altogether unexpected. But it was more than I could contain. I was weary of forgiving her for not loving me. Weary of loving her with every breath and surviving on only her merciful kindnesses. Not even you were mine. Even you were someone else’s. I’d agreed to take over where my brother left off, but that pact did not include my suffering yet another man.*"

Barlozzo has been saying all this in a voice different from his own. An older, more feeble voice, and perhaps in the way his father might have spoken it for himself. Now his own voice returns. "What Patsi committed was known, in those times, as *un delitto d'onore,* a crime of honor. When a man was wronged, cuckolded, it was socially and morally acceptable for him to defend himself. An outgrowth of dueling, I think. The state silently condoned those acts, while Mother Church shook her head and turned away. Until the fifties, that's how it was all over Italy, and until much later in parts of the south where the code of silence still prevails. Surely the village knew of the events; they knew what Nina did and they knew what Patsi did. Of course, no one has ever trespassed upon the subject with me. No one ever will. It's just something that happened. A fact of local history.

"Do you remember what I said at the *veglia? My father always said hell is where nothing's cooking and no one's waiting*. That was the first time I've ever mentioned my father to anyone since the day he died. And certainly I chose a rather strange quote of his to pass on. But it just sort of slipped out, uncensored. That was the reason for the silence up there that night. All this is why, or at least most of the reason why, I've stayed alone. You see, I was afraid of loving a woman as completely as Patsi loved my mother, but I was more afraid of loving someone less than that. Both doors opened onto the lion's den. You might say that I refused Florì way back then. I believed those feelings I'd had for her were passing ones, like some small bewitching from which I'd soon awaken. I never called it love. But instead of the feelings passing, only time did. So much time, and all the while I was perpetuating the legacy. Or at least helping it along.

"Floriana spent twenty years with her *seconda scelta*. And I've spent my much of my life in a great, long de profundis. What I've done, mostly, is to surrender my own turn at having a life. I let Nina's and Patsi's lives wash over into mine, transfusing it with their pain. And as though it were my salvation rather than my ruin, I've been holding on to that pain like a trust, holding it so tight to my chest there was no room to hold anything or anyone else. Under the weight of lesser or greater fortunes, I think what happens to a great many of us is that we really don't know what we want or with whom we'd like to have it. Nothing seems real until it's already gone. Until it's sealed up tight, out of reach. Until it's dead. Be it a person or a dream. And then the light comes, and so we mourn.

"Floriana is all the women I've ever loved or wanted to love, meant to love if I'd only known how, or would have loved if I could only have managed to find them. And when I thought she might be dying, I felt as though I wouldn't be losing just her but everyone. Floriana is everyone. Though we'd never been together for anything more than the most public of occasions before she became ill, she was always near. We've lived two hundred meters apart for most of our lives. And I'd convinced myself to settle for that proximity, to mistake it for some form of intimacy. I told myself over and over again that the nearness of her was enough. But when she came back home from Città della Pieve, all I wanted to do was to begin *living* this love for her. At last I would submit to it, devote myself to it, trust it and her and myself with my whole heart. It seemed natural and right that I should be the one to care for her. It must have seemed natural to her as well, though we never discussed it. Never *decided* about it. I don't even know if she'll let me stay close to her after she's regained her strength. But I think this house might help us. I would go mad, now, trying to live without this connection to her. Haven't I told you that all my motives are selfish?"

As he's wont to do, the duke is moving too fast for me. I need to understand more than I do. I ask, "Why didn't you ever tell your father about the soldier?"

"I was eleven years old when all that happened, Chou. And my mother treated his presence in our home and in our lives so undramatically that I did, too. She never told me to keep anything secret from my father, but somehow she must have known I'd never say a word, she being certain that I knew it would hurt him and hurt her.

She knew I would protect her and protect my father without asking me to. I just followed her lead for those few weeks that he was with us. I accepted him, enjoyed him. I heard my mother laugh and I liked that. She seemed like a girl, and that made me think I could stop trying to be a man. His name was Peter.

"As much as I can piece it all together now, he must have been a deserter from the troops stationed at La Foce, the Origo estates that sit between Pienza and Chianciano. I think he just walked away one day and came down through the woods, over the mountain roads. He must have simply showed up at the door one day. Situated as we were outside the town, our house—your house—would have seemed a relatively safe one in which to ask for water or a place to sleep. Perhaps she was out in the garden hanging the wash and he caught sight of her. She was beautiful. All that dark hair piled up on top of her head, eyes like a doe. He would have found her irresistible. That part of the story is hardly rare.

"And maybe the rest of the story, albeit in less treacherous forms, is also not so rare. Casualties of war. Nina was twenty-eight, and I think Peter must have been younger, perhaps not more than twenty. And so all three of us were children, really. Frightened, hungry, not knowing what was next and when that might be."

"Did you hate your father?" Fernando asks him.

"No. It's a horrifying thought, but each of us is responsible for our own judgment. No one else knows what we know about ourselves. Even when the state takes over, it still remains a private thing in the end. Besides, I think my mother lived her whole life in those thirty-three years. Sometimes I think she'd lived all of it by the time my father had returned from the war, that those intervening years must have truly been a death for her. And so I closed my father's eyes, lit a candle, washed him in oil, wished him peace. I arranged to have Nina buried properly, but not in the same place where I buried my father. I just couldn't do that to either one of them."

We are silent now, staying so until the fire burns to ash. The dark is thick and cold as we find our way out into the night, starless and waiting for the moon. Back in the village when we leave him, the duke asks, "Don't you think it's strange that, of all the farmhouses in Tuscany, you two chose to come and live in the one where I'd lived? I mean, I understand that my having lived there was unknown to you, just as I was unknown to you. But if you look carefully you'll see there are the pale tracings of a circle about us. Nothing much at all is accidental in a life."

Spring

14

Virtuous Drenches

Bursting in upon the pitiless winter, the torrid breath of Africa rises up to warm the afternoons. Each day's good news of Florì the duke carries to us like flowers, settling himself near our fire after he's said good night to her. He continues negotiations to gain the pile of stones with the seven fireplaces and the sleeping vines. *L'eremo,* the hermitage, he's taken to calling it. The Vulcan seems sluiced out of him. Surely the crust and the grit remain, but the ghost is gone. And in its place there has sprung up an old, gangly chap who sticks close to us as a night-spooked child.

He rings the buzzer early one morning while we still sleep. And when we don't answer swiftly enough, he pounds urgently at our door. Something is very wrong. I turn myself face down into the hollow where Fernando had lain, my heart thudding loud as Barlozzo's fist.

"*Le erbe sono cresciute.* The weeds are up," I hear him yell as though the British were coming. It's only grass he wants to talk about.

Minutes later we are trudging behind Barlozzo over the back meadows and into the new light. A cloth sack over his shoulder, trowel and knife handles protruding from his jacket pockets, he folds himself neatly in two over every bright patch of hours-old green, loosening, digging, pulling some of it up with its roots, cutting others at the quick, bundling like kinds with lengths of kitchen string and flinging the muddy faggots into his sack. He hands us tools, but I'm all thumbs when I dig, my movements neither sure nor quick enough to sustain Barlozzo's patience. "You hinder me more than you further me," he says.

And so he and Fernando go on ahead. I take my time, separate leaves I can recognize such as wild arugula and dandelion from those I only think might be worthy of a salad or a session in the saute pan with wild garlic and oil and at least one fat red chile. The sun is awake now and so am I, grateful for Barlozzo's invitation to this dawn sortie. I'm walking along feeling the softening earth under my boots, composing menus, feeling gallant about my new life as a forager, singing a little. And I'm laughing, too, at a long-ago remembrance of the frantic Saturday lawnmowing scenes in my surburban Saratoga County neighborhood. The sinister whacking of the electric weed eater, the great toxic puffs of spray choking children and choking dandelions, the same race of dandelions that, today, will compose my lunch.

I'm having a lovely time when I'm interrupted by the sound of whopping and shouting. I think they must have excavated a lode of Etruscan jewels, but when I finally get to them, they're busy tying together bunches of scrawny brown stalks that look like perverted asparagus. They are *brusandoli,* wild hops, a whole patch of them. Barlozzo is already touting how he'll cook them for our supper. "First we'll have a salad of dandelions and other field grasses with a good spoonful of ricotta mixed with salt anchovies on top. Then we'll eat the hops, barely poached, drained while they're still a little crunchy, tossed with the thinnest shreds of sharp spring onion, dressed with only the squeezing of a lemon. Then we'll fry some in the best oil, add some white butter, beat this morning's eggs and pour them in only when the butter begins to talk. A little sea salt. And when the underside is deep brown, I'll toss the frittata in the air, catch it on its other side, and just when the vapors of it begin to make you crazy, I'll set it on the table and we'll eat it straight out of the pan. Very cold white wine is permitted, but no bread. Nothing else. Florì will want to stir them into rice or some other insipid pap, but just ignore her."

"And since when did you begin reciting preludes to supper?" I ask him.

"*Va bene,* OK, take credit for my poetry, but I do find that saying my plans out loud does stimulate the appetite more than just thinking them."

On another morning when March feels warm as June, Fernando is under orders from the duke to head down near the thermal springs to find wild garlic and herbs for the brewing of tonics. I stay behind for the bread vigil, and when it's done I slip a jacket over my night dress and pull on my boots, take a basket and scissors for flowers, and walk down to meet him. It's a rare morning during these days when Barlozzo is not present looking for cheer or balm in ever-increasing doses. I'm feeling blissfully free of him for a few hours, like a beleaguered mom when the Irish au pair takes over. Looking around me, I'm thinking there is nothing at all here that bespeaks an era, sets a date on this morning. It could be fifty years ago, two hundred years ago, many more ago. Just earth and sky and wild roses budded, sheep grazing.

It's so warm I take off my jacket, leave it on a rock for later. I think I see Fernando not too far ahead and, in my gauzy white dress, I am Diana invoking the chase, flailing arms, calling to him. Nothing. It's too warm to walk farther so I'll lie here in the spicy grass and wait for him. Now I hear him coming closer, singing "Tea for Three," as usual. I'm still and quiet, sinuously arranged in pastoral goddess pose, ready to devastate him with my supine self. He'll fall to his knees and cover me with kisses. My heart beats like a child's when she's playing hide and seek, but all my husband says is, "*Ma cosa fai qui? Alzati, ti prego. Sei quasi nuda e completamente pazza.* But what are you doing here? Get up, I beg you. You're almost nude and completely crazy."

"I'm just feeling playful, that's all. You were without the duke for once, and I thought I'd surprise you. Just you."

"But you'll get sick lying on the damp ground," he says bending down to hug me. "And you know as well as I do that our rascal child is stalking the meadows somewhere near. I don't want him or anyone else to see you wandering about in your night dress."

I try to rise elegantly but I step on and finally trip over the Diana dress, falling, catching the heel of my boot in the hem of it, ripping the thing, trying again to get up, falling again. Some pastoral goddess, I tell myself, clumping back up the hill, up into the garden, up the stairs, damning my even fleeting faculty for self-deception. As I'm fastening my skirt, I can hear the duke shouting to Fernando from the back meadow: "Sorry I'm so late."

THE CHEESEMAKING SEASON is underway, with the ewes feasting on the same newly sprouted grasses as we do. And though it's late this year, the first cheese of the season is called *marzolino,* little March, a *pecorino* eaten white and sweet and fresh, after only a few weeks of aging. Partnered with a heap of fava beans still in their pods, the cheese is dressed with oil and grindings of pepper.

We slip the favas from their pods, ignore the still-soft inner skins, and eat them, on a hillside, with the *marzolino* and half a loaf of good bread. Perhaps an even better accompaniment to a fine *marzolino* is honey. Long before beekeeping became an art, bees still made honey and shepherds risked wrack and ruin by plunging an arm into a hive for a piece of comb, breaking it, scraping it, and eating it with their fresh sour cheese. An early *dolce-salata* dish. It was the shepherds who knew most about life. Shepherds who were born, lived, and as often died under the stars. They followed the pastoral ritual of the *transumanza*—the shepherd's crossing with his flocks from summer mountain pastures to winter lowlands and back again, journeys of three hundred kilometers or more. As solitary as was his life, a shepherd was a bon vivant of sorts, a nomadic storyteller who carried news and folklore into the even greater isolation of the villages he passed, remote hamlets from which people never ventured from one mountaintop to the next. Welcomed as an entertainer, invited to sit around the fires of the farmers and the woodsmen, he traded tales for bread and wine and oil. An ancient supper from the days of the *transumaza* is one that a shepherd made with his own ricotta. He mixed the ricotta with a stolen egg or two, formed dumplings from the mash, dropped them into a kettle of water boiled over his fire, drained them, and finally dressed them with a piece of hard bread rubbed between his palms and, if he was lucky, a few drops of bartered oil. As I imagine this, I wish it were possible to trade one comfort for another as the shepherds did, as Barlozzo's mother used to trade a pot of soup for one of ricotta. I would trade bread for secrets.

BARLOZZO HAS FORMULAS for tonics and all sorts of virtuous drenches he mixes and ferments in a hideous vat. A wet and rusted tub on wheels, he parks it in our barn and heaves what look and smell like lawn trimmings into it, pounding at them with one of his hand-hewn tools. With the garden hose, he douses the mash, lets loose the vat's metal cover, and says,

"We'll need to let it sit for a week or so."

I'm untrusting of the murky potion afloat with slime and foam until I taste the clean, sharp freshness of it. He empties the vat from its spigot into a pail and begins the process all over again with a different composition of materials. As each batch is brewed we filter the stuff through cheesecloth, pour it into scrubbed and sterilized wine bottles. Each one corked and labeled according to its particular benefit, we lay down some of the bottles on the bottom shelf of the refrigerator; the remainder we store in the armoire. Wild chicory for internal cleansing; wild fennel and dandelion, a general panacea; *rucola* and wild onion to cleanse the blood; passion flower, valerian root, and wild garlic to lower blood pressure; wild borage for the skin.

"These don't age like wine, you know. Drink them all before the heat comes—a glassful, cold and neat, three times a day." I fear for my bowels, having felt the ravages wreaked by quick sips, yet I promise to take the full cure.

One Saturday at the market in Cetona I'm in a rapture over a wooden box of lettuces, little ruffled nosegays of them. Leaves like satin cream or yellow speckled in winey red, some of them green as limes, frilled in pink. I want to just look at them, I want to draw them. Most of all I want to feel them in my hands, taste them. Maybe it's true that life is a search for beauty, for the harmony that comes from the mingling of things. Maybe life is a search for flavor. Not the flavor of just a food but of a moment, or a color, a voice—the flavor of what we can hear and see and touch. Certainly good cooking is about flavor. About the liberation of flavor, the suspension of it, and, finally, the release of it. One liberates the flavor of an herb by gently bruising it, thus freeing its natural oils and essences. Next, one suspends those oils and essences inside other components. For instance, to make a basil pesto, one pounds garlic and basil to release their oils and essences. Then one captures, holds those flavors by suspending them inside olive oil, forming an emulsion, a thick, smooth sauce. But this sauce has yet to rerelease all those flavors one worked to liberate and suspend. The sauce needs heat, contact with heat. First, taste the sauce cool, just as it is, from a spoon or your finger. Certainly it's wonderful. But then toss the pesto with just-cooked pasta or spread it on a roasted tomato, hot from the oven. The contact with heat intensifies the flavors of the sauce to their fullness. The business of cooking has much in common with the business of life.

A Tasting of Pecorino Cheeses with Chestnut Honey

Approximately 3 ounces of cheese per person

A basket of thinly sliced artisanal breads
Dark honey, preferably chestnut or buckwheat, lightly heated
A bottle of *vin santo,* chilled

In lieu of a sweet, this is wonderful thing to carry out at the end of a Tuscan supper. The only work it asks is the shopping or the bread baking, if you wish. Collect as many varieties of pecorino—ewe's milk cheese—as are to be found, trying to find both fresh, soft varieties as well as those drier, crumbly ones with a bit of age on them. Tuscan pecorinos are more readily available now in America than they were a few years ago when only the Roman, peppercorn-studded varieties, best used as grating cheeses, were to be had. Two soft varieties and two more aged ones compose an honorable field, yet serving one or two, especially paired with a pot of dark, rich chestnut honey, some dark, whole grain breads, and a bottle of chilled *vin santo,* will be quite enough to please.

15

Florì and I Are Shelling Peas

"You haven't said much about the house. I mean, do you like it, do you like the *idea* of it?" I ask her. Florì and I are shelling peas. Sitting on the terrace steps between the two pots of white hydrangea we've just planted, our frilly spring dresses ruched up on our thighs, the jellied peach light of five o'clock stroking our bare legs, bare feet.

"It's a fascinating old place and I think it could be beautiful. But I'm not excited about it in the way Barlozzo is excited. Of course, he'll see the process through and have it in the end. But, Chou, it's enough for me when the daylight comes."

Barlozzo's been up terrorizing the butcher into carving lamb ribs, which he'll grill out in the fire ring for our early supper. Toting his prize, he strides up from the drive and stops a little way from us. "*Poveri fiori,* poor flowers," he says, "having to sit so close to the two of you. They might as well be swamp grasses for all anyone could notice of them. *Belle donne, buona sera*. Beautiful women, good evening."

He and Fernando set about bathing the ribs in oil and white wine. Pulling stalks of it from his ever-present canvas shoulder bag, Barlozzo tears the leaves of *mentuccia,* wild mint, he'd gathered on the hillside, pressing them onto the scant flesh of the lamb. They stoke up the fire and Florì pours some white wine into a pot, setting it over the grate to boil. She poaches the peas in the wine, drains them—saving the cooking liquors—and smashes the peas to a paste.

Meanwhile, I'm sautéing onions in a soup kettle with olive oil, sprinkling on some cinnamon and a few grains of sugar, sea salt, and grindings of white pepper. It takes a long time to caramelize the onions, to cook them down to a jam. Leaving the stirring to the duke, Floriana and I set the table and open some wine. Earlier, she had climbed the hill with a dish of eggplant, tiny white ones she'd roasted whole until their flesh collapsed. When they were hot from the oven, she'd poured over a sauce of crushed new garlic and olive oil and marjoram picked from the windowsill pot in her kitchen, piercing the skins of the eggplants so they could drink in the savory juice. I keep eyeing the old iron dish of them sitting on the table. How gorgeous they look. A fat round of potato bread, crusty and brown, rests on an upturned basket over a branch of rosemary, the scent of which it will take in as it cools. A bowl of young lettuces waits to be dressed with the drippings the little ribs will surrender into a pan set below them as they grill. There's nothing to do but finish the soup. I ladle veal stock into the cooked onions, add the smashed peas, the reserved pot liquors and a bit more wine, stirring the mass to blend and heat it. Carrying the pot directly to the table, I add a handful of pecorino to the soup and then spoon it out into shallow bowls, threading each portion with oil. The *carabaccia,* as it's called, should be eaten tepid. And so we let it cool while we begin with the eggplant. Each of us tears away at the skin of one, spreading the perfumed cream on a piece of bread, eating it out of hand between sips of wine.

"I'll take another dose of nightshade, if you don't mind," I say, reaching for the eggplant. "*Melanzana,* a bastardization of *mela insana*. Literally, 'unhealthy apple.' That's what we're eating. A part of the nightshade family, as is belladonna." Eggplant was a centuries-old staple of Middle Eastern cuisine by the time it was introduced in Europe, but here it was shunned as food, revered as a table ornament. "I guess someone got hungry enough to eat it one day and here we are."

"Belladonna," says the duke sotto voce. I'm sorry for the old chap who first called poison a beautiful woman."

Florì and the duke say good night before the sun sets. They walk down the drive, climb up into town and we watch them until they vanish among the new-leafed trees.

The next afternoon, Florì and I walk along the Celle road. I tell her that Barlozzo has told us about his mother, his father.

"I was certain, sooner or later, he'd tell you. He's never talked to me about it, you know," she says, stopping to look at me, facing the sun so her long skittish eyes are yellow as saffron.

"Maybe he never needed to talk with you," I say. "He trusted that you knew it all. And, too, he trusted that you understood it had always been the obstacle between you."

"I suppose that's true. And it's also true that, in the deepest part of me, I've always known that he wanted to love me. But maybe it was me, my inconsolable fear of what I knew must be his torment. I never felt wise enough to help him wash all that away so I could find his heart. So, you see, I was as much an obstacle as were Patsi and Nina. I never knew how to begin. I never knew what to say. Why can't we talk to each other, Chou?" She asks the question for all of us.

We've walked only half a kilometer or so when she laughs and says, "I'm tired. Spring fever. I think I'll just take to my bed for a few days, let everyone fuss over me. I can do that now that I know I'm well. Before, when I wasn't sure, the idea of everyone being around me seemed too scented in farewell. But now I think I'm ready for a week of women's care and company."

The word goes out, and next morning five of us are gathered in Florì's small apartment, each of us getting in the others' way, cleaning, cooking soup, keeping her company, painting her toenails, listening to her stories. She looks at me, tells me to come closer so she can ask me something important. She says she wants me to put makeup on her face. She wants mascara and a touch of powder, "*e un pò di ombretto, appena, appena,* just a very little bit of eye shadow." But what she really wants are red lips. As though they were a sin, she asks for them in a hoarse whisper, pointing to mine—colored, as they always are, red as an anemone—then pointing to her own. I run up the hill to get my kit. I smudge and draw and brush about her eyes and face, paint her mouth and, when I finish, I hold a mirror for her inspection. She is silent. She closes her eyes. I sit next to her on the bed, holding her hand. We stay that way for a long time. When we look at each other, I see her face is wet and warm, her powder streaked, her mascara slipping into black puddles in the deep half moons under her eyes. But her lips are perfect. I tell her that and she answers, "Yes. They are perfect."

I fix the damage before calling in the others to admire her. They shout and scream and say they all want red lips. One by one, I paint them until we're all sitting there around the bed and on the bed, giggling, passing the mirror, telling first-time stories about lipstick and secret love and high heels and wedding dresses. Somehow the telling of memories gives way to a round robin of sorts whereby each one shares *un detto,* a quote from scriptures or from literature. But here, more often the phrases are formed of succulent observation. Florì calls it saying truths.

"Tradition, whether the gastronomic kind or the lovemaking kind, is perpetuated by daily application."

"Beware of the tyranny of the giver. The giver has more cards than the getter. Or perceives it so. Yet how often is the giver giving to gain control, or at the least, the sanction to plunder the givee's life, how and when he may."

"When choosing a mate, be certain it's the one with whom you want to share your dying as much as your living."

"The greatest emptiness comes to us when what or whom we thought we understood cheats us by being something else, someone else."

"Sarcasm is a dagger honed from fear."

"When you get old enough, you discover your sons have become the husband you'd like to forget, while your daughters are eerily the same as the mother from whom you ran. Life is just a series of strange tricks."

"Don't be afraid of your children. If they're going to love you, they'll love you on their own, without your having to pander to them. If they're not going to love you, there's nothing to do about it."

"Most of us are rationed three silver bullets in a life. Each of them wants quiet deliberation before firing."

"Every once in a while some small vendetta can do your heart good."

"Why do we want them so much more than they want us?"

It's my turn. "Too much sweet is bound to finish in despair. Balance the sweet and the salty. I knew a French woman, a cook in a tiny place in the village of Poissy, who would rub a few grains of coarse salt over the tips of honeyed plums or figs just before she'd shove a great tart of them into the oven. *The salt exalts the sweet,* she'd say, licking her fingers like a cat."

After Florì takes a turn, there's nothing left to be said.

"Do you know it was hard, some days and some nights, just to get through the hours. I was always looking for things to do to fill the spaces before lunch or to keep myself still before dawn. Now, all I long for is time. So short and fast is this life. And it's not that I would have wished to slow it down as much as I would have wished to understand about the speed."

When she thinks we're ready for her, a woman called Tullia says, "What we should be doing is dancing, Florì. It's *la tarantella* we should be dancing to drive the demons mad, to remind them how much stronger we are than they."

A dance of rebellion against pain and death, a willful dance, arrogant, seductive, smashing bounds, tearing masks, shaking fists and shaking hips. It's a dance Greek and Bohemian, Arab and African. A gypsy's dance. Yet in this group of sober Tuscans, only she, born and bred in Salerno, only Tullia knows *la tarantella*. But like all southerners, first she wants to talk. She tells us that, after the war, when she was thirteen, there was no one left in the two-room apartment where she'd lived with her parents. No one save the uncle who'd come to take care of her when her mother died and her father didn't come home. But he had hands large and quick, she says, and she knew her fate if she stayed. So she stole from him before he could steal from her. She stole enough money to ride the train from Salerno to Florence, where she was sure to find work as a housemaid. Too, she stole half a loaf of bread and the three cuts of *salame* wrapped in brown paper he'd left in his pocket for his supper—he, as usual, not caring much what she ate for supper. Inside a tablecloth she'd tied these along with the red cotton skirt she'd outgrown but loved too much to leave behind, a nightgown she'd bleached white in the sun and patched with very small stitches, her mother's black silk dress with the shoulder pads, the crucifix from over her bed. And a tambourine. Having no shoes, she'd scrubbed her feet in vinegar, straightened her pinafore as best she could, placed the bundle on her head as though she was taking it to the public fountain and, instead, walked away to the station. Bread and courage and a tambourine. Seeds to grow a life.

Only Tullia knows *la tarantella*. "Show us," we ask her. "Show us how."

Nearing seventy now, perhaps more, she stands up to her full height, which might be approaching five feet. She removes her pink cardigan, baring a sleeveless woolen undershirt, edged in lace. And in her slippers and elastic stockings, her prim navy skirt pulled up above her knees, Tullia strikes a pose. She closes her eyes, staying still as stone, listening for the music, I think. Listening for her youth. When she's ready, she throws back her head, thrusts out her chin, raises her arms and begins a slow, deliberate series of turns and slides and more turns, accompanied by her own whispered hisses and long, gutteral groans. I want to see the scenes that must be passing behind her clenched eyes, hear the sounds. Plump and elfin, she is neither lithe nor clumsy. And surely she is beautiful.

"*Ma, ho bisogna del mio tamburello.* But I need my tambourine," she says breaking the spell, putting the sweater back on and wrapping herself in a shawl. "*Vengo subito*. I'll be right back."

Meanwhile some of us begin to try out the moves, but like all folkloric dances, this one must be danced from the inside. And so, before Florì's bed, three of us dance strange amalgams of jitterbug and cha-cha while, in my fashion, I tango, it being the only dance I ever wanted to know. When Tullia returns, she claps away our folly and begins, in earnest, to teach us. She tells us to think erotic thoughts, angry thoughts, vengeful ones, loving ones, sad ones. She tells us to mix them all up together like they are mixed together in life, and then, she says, we'll be ready to dance. There seems no hope for us as Tullia slaps her tambourine.

Someone says, "I don't think I've ever had an erotic thought, the nuns having slapped them out of me before they were even formed."

And now Florì, rooting hard, says, "Dance for me, if not for you."

"Oh, no. It doesn't work that way. Get up and dance for yourself," says Tullia.

Florì walks to the armoire in the corner, opens it, takes out her now not-so-new black pumps from Perugia. She sits down on the bed to slip them on. In her white flannel shift, the long, narrow lines of her body and her large, full breasts evident, she stands before us. And before her very own troupe of demons. Black shoes. Red lips. Now Florì dances. She'd been paying attention, because she's truly dancing, the staccato of her heels keeping time with the tambourine, the sounds surely waking the devil, then taunting him, just like Tullia said they would. And when she's pink and breathless and dripping with the sweat of triumph, she opens her eyes and weeps old tears. She asks for wine.

All our thirsts and hungers have been whipped by the talking and dancing and it's more than broth and white rice we crave. Some one begins to heave flour onto the kitchen table, building it up into a hill and urging a crater into its middle. Another one is ready with eggs and milk, butter, softened yeast. Four hands, mine and Tullia's, work at the mass, kneading and slapping it into pale satin. Covered in a white cloth, the dough rests. Someone else is already heating fat over a low flame, a liter and a half of sunflower oil in a heavy, shallow pan. I wash my hands and dry them on the apron Florì had tied around me and think that it's this, it's this *connection* that I need and desire most from this life. Humble as it is, this is my legacy. I'm a cook and a baker. Such an ancient metier is mine, descended from the loaf-givers, the keepers of the fire, the distributors of largesse. I'd always known I was playacting whenever I'd tried to learn more about business, to "ask for the order" or "go in for the close." I never fooled myself any more than I did other people. And so it's good to be home. This is what I've wanted to do and how I've wanted to be.

Flori's gone to fetch *la ciliegina,* dry white wine scented with cherry leaves. She'd brewed it a year ago, set it in a cupboard to age. This is the occasion of its debut.

"This is the first time in my life I've ever drunk wine when my husband was not present," someone says.

"Here's to the next time!" says another.

We take turns cooking the *cincialose,* tearing pieces of the dough, stretching them with our fingertips into uneven little cakes, slipping them, then, into the bubbling oil, watching them rise and blister and turn to gold. Each of us cooks six pieces, drains them, sprinkles them with salt or sugar, as requested, passes them out. The next one does the same and the next one, too, biting into the hot, crisp stuff between sips of the cool, sweet wine. Erotic memory for all of us.

16

The First of the Zucchini Blossoms Are Up

April had been feverish. The sirocco pumped wild and hot from the south and some days it brawled, head on, with the *tramontana,* the reckless northern wind not yet ready to rest. And so everything happened in April. Storms ripped, winds gasped. And in the lulls, the sun practiced for August. Now the cherries are ripe, the wild strawberries, too. Basil and borrage and small green-fleshed melons are in the markets, ripe wheat in the meadows. And on this first day of May we're half-heartedly packing to leave it all.

I don't want to go away right now any more than Fernando does. He's thinking we can wait until the autumn to begin the research I must do for the book on southern Italy. But I know I can't. I've drawn a work plan and it tells me, plain and simple, it's time to begin or be crushed at deadline. We'll be gone nearly two months, moving through Campania, Basilicata, Puglia, Calabria, and into Sicily, returning here just a few days before the children arrive for the summer. Routes are mapped and colleagues have prepared insider paths to cooks and bakers and winemakers. "It's time to go."

"Yes, yes, of course it is. It's just that it's so beautiful here."

"It's always beautiful here. The beauty will still be here when we come home," I tell him, trying to fit my ruffled lace skirt into the single suitcase we've alloted for me. It fights, though, with all the other skirts and jackets and shawls I'll probably never wear betwixt the goats and the oranges. Still, I like to be ready. Fernando's case is half empty. I fill it up with the apricot-colored lace and the sandals with the ties that wrap like ballet shoes. He always chooses the big red case for himself, knowing I'll run out of room, liking that I'll mix my things with his.

"I'm just happy you've stopped carrying around the ball gown," he says hugging me, smoothing my hair.

We've invited Barlozzo and Florì to lunch, so I get to work. There'll be *frittatine,* small omelettes stuffed with the tender, thin stems of new garlic sautéed with borrage flowers, and suckling lamb braised in butter and onions until the flesh nearly melts. A salad made only of basil leaves, whole and sweet, and wood strawberries. A drizzle of oil, a few drops of old balsalmic, some pepper. A decidedly un-duke-like menu. But Florì will love it.

It's the front door buzzer that breaks through my singing and Fernando runs up the stairs two at a time, knowing it's announcing some playful intrigue of Barlozzo's.

"It was early this morning as far as anyone knows. Barlozzo went to bring her the paper . . . the priest . . . a doctor . . . an ambulance."

Wiping my hands on my apron, I walk to the foot of the stairs. I don't recognize the voice of the visitor, and hearing but pieces of his words, I take in nothing but chill. There's noise, then, behind my eyes, like something made of steel and spinning hard, shutting out the light, and I know it's the truth that Florì is dead. Fernando's arms are around me, his hands pushing my head to his chest, covering me, rocking me.

The afternoon of the red lips and the cherry wine was nine days ago. Today she's dead. We run down the hill to the curve, up the steep into town, but it's just as true there. Florì is dead. When people say something, it's a broken phrase, a thought choked off somewhere in its middle. We drink the water Vera offers. Someone says there will be a procession from the church to the *campo santo* tomorrow at sunset. There will be a mass in the morning. No one speaks of what or how. In a starched white shirt and dark gray trousers, his freshly washed hair combed back straight from his broken brow, Barlozzo walks down into the piazza from the lane that winds up beyond it. From her house. He shakes hands and woodenly accepts hugs as he proceeds. As he approaches the entrance to the bar, Fernando walks out a few steps toward him and I walk behind Fernando. The two of them speak and I reach around my husband to take Barlozzo's hand, parched skin over long bones. He holds my curled hand tight in his curled hand as he continues to speak to Fernando. He and I don't look at each other. *"Ciao,"* he says. *"Ciao,"* he says again, gorging the word with all the other words he can't say.

When we're back at home, Fernando goes directly to the desk, begins to write notes to people who'll be expecting us at our first few stops, notes he says he'll fax from the bar later on. We won't go away. We open every door and window in the house, wanting the weather to take us over, to make the noise, to cover the noise. We take off our clothes and climb back into our unmade bed.

"SHE WAS GREEDY for death. A month ago, maybe less, when she'd gone for her scheduled check, the scans showed new masses. She was reaching for her purse, her sweater, as the doctor was explaining the next procedures. She thanked him. She smiled as though it had been such a lovely visit. And both he and I knew she'd already made up her mind to die."

It's just after dark now, and we sit on the terrace floor, Fernando and I with our backs to the stones of the stable, the duke facing us. "It wasn't long after that when she called all of you in to play house with her. I think she'd already begun to hear that tumult, that whirring that comes with dying. People know. She knew. But it wasn't until she saw those ghostly films hung up there in the white light that she began to *listen* to what she knew. I knew she believed that her long, slow dying was not the best way to love me and so I never begged her, not once. I never got angry with her, never asked her why. And fast as she could, she slipped away. No fear. No hope. An ancient way of facing life and facing death. But there was nothing of despair in these last days. I did my crying apart from her. And if Florì cried at all, she cried alone. She wanted to wash the walls, all the walls in her house, and so we did. She'd work on the bottom parts then stand back and look up at where I was scrubbing, tell me the spots I'd missed. It took all day, and when I asked her why she was so worried about having clean walls she said, 'Because it's something I can decide.' She said she didn't want stains on her walls any more than on the beauty of these past few months together. I think she was satisfied. She'd lived the life she'd longed for since she was a girl and it mattered less to her the length of that life than that it had finally become real. But I was sure we had time. I began thinking in terms of months, maybe a year. Sometimes I would dare to think about more. No matter when it came, I would never have been ready for this morning. And she knew that before I did. She kept telling me how much she loved me. She'd say it and say it again like she was trying out the words in all her voices, her girl's voice, her young woman's voice. Her voice before she got sick. I think the pain and the pleasure came out even for Florì. She left me a note." Taking a small envelope out from his white shirt pocket, the kind of envelope that comes with flowers, he removes the card. "She left me seven words," he says, *"I wanted death to find me dancing."*

THE SKY PROMISES stars, the first ones glinting even as a red sun still soaks the Tuscan hills. Each of us holds a candle. In his purple robes, the priest waits, the altar boys light the censer. When no one else can be seen coming in from the village, the litany is said. Frankincense mists tremble over the grave and flowers are dropped in, the first ones slap hard against the metal: the rest make a sound like *hush*.

BACK AT HOME we open some wine and talk a little. I tell Fernando that Barlozzo looked like a child to me this evening. "I wish I could have picked him up, folded all that length of him into my arms, told him that the pain would go away."

"He knows it won't. But at least it's *his* pain. Finally it's his and not his father's, his mother's. Just as the duke said it had for Florì, I think the pain and the pleasure will come out OK for him."

We sit there by our fire, telling each other it's the last one of the season. We say that every night when we don't set the fire outside in the ring, never wanting to relinquish the ritual of one fire or the other. "Are we waiting for the duke?" I ask.

"I think we are, even though we know he won't come."

We take our supper by the hearth, cover a bowl of soup with a plate and set it on the ledge. A snack for Santa Claus, I think. Fernando thinks it, too, and we laugh. It feels so good to laugh. Like a swallow of strong spirits makes room for more supper, laughing seems to make room for the rest of the tears. Fernando and I have another thought in common.

Sweaters tied round our shoulders, we don't have to wonder where to look for him. We walk to the *campo santo.* It's not hard to locate the grave, since it's the only one lit by a torch, a man digging in its light. "I thought she'd like to sleep with the pomegranates," he says, leaning on the shovel. The tree he is planting looks to be a meter or so high, but already its limbs are thick and twisted, the bark of its trunk black and rough. A tree to reckon with. Not at all surprised to see us, he continues to work, dumping earth from a plastic sack, patting it gently against the roots, filling the hole, patting the earth again and again. He has a demijohn of water in his wheelbarrow, and he bathes the tree, waits for the earth and roots to drink, pours on more. Two dwarf pomegranates are planted in terracotta urns and he moves them to flank the bigger tree. He's finished. At least for now, I think, wondering if he has plans for an olive tree, a grapevine or two. Surely there will be roses. He sits on the shorn grass, knees pulled up to his chin, lights two cigarettes, gives one to Fernando. "I'd like a cigarette this evening," I say, and he offers me one from his pack, no questions asked. My husband lights the cigarette from the ash of his, puts it between my lips. We all sit and smoke and no one cries until he's home.

NEXT MORNING ON our way up to the bar, we meet the duke coming the other way. His favorite blue plastic carrying case is under one arm and full of flowers. "The first of the squash blossoms are up, *ragazzi*. They're beautiful, all feminine."

"Does this mean I'm cooking lunch?" I ask him.

"Not for me. Not for a while. Maybe when you come back from the south."

This is his way of saying we should leave, not suspend our plans any longer.

"We'll be getting on the road soon enough," Fernando says, offering his friend the chance to change his mind.

"But these were to be my going-away gift," he says, placing the carrying case in Fernando's arms.

"OK, then. We'll come to find you early in July." He and Fernando have settled it.

I hand the keys to our house to the duke. To Palazzo Barlozzo. "Just in case you get to missing the velvet and the brocade," I say standing on tiptoe, pulling his face down to kiss. What I'm thinking is that he might like to sit in Florì's chair under the window in the upstairs hall some mornings, to read a little. Refusing to let the duke see his tears, Fernando walks straight ahead toward the house. I'm crying too hard now to care who sees me and so, wrapping my arms as far up onto his chest as I can reach, I hold the duke tight to me. I hold the duke tight for all I'm worth, and he lets me. I look at him. "*Ciao, bestione, ciao,* great beast. Remember how I love you."

"*Ciao, piccola, ciao,* little one." Lifting his face to the sun and away from mine, he stays that way until I reach the house and go inside.

WE'RE PACKING UP again, making the final check, carrying things out to the car. We'll leave at dawn. We've dined on the last bits and pieces left in the cupboards, a supper made of stones. A lone sausage, a sprouted potato, and three lamb chops we cooked over the fire outdoors. The car duly loaded, we go back to the garden with the last of our wine, not at all ready to go indoors. Fernando pulls me close to him so my back nestles into his chest, and we sit like this on the packed May earth. Twilight is a woman. And she's a long time in leaving. Like the train of a wedding dress, she drags pink clouds across the darkening, never minding the hard blue night at her heels. Rain falls like a blessing, the mizzling of it polite, not disturbing the fire at all. A new moon sickles, polishing the stars, and I sit holding my face up to the rain, to the light, letting a quiver of wind, like a faithless lover, kiss me on his way to someone else. *This is what I've wanted to do and how I've wanted to be.* There is nothing vainglorious in my thoughts. My small life would hardly stretch to fit the needs and desires of many others. Still, I want what I already have. But I know there's no holding seawater in your hands, no fixing the moon. All of life is nothing more and nothing less than a few short strolls around the park, a sashay or two around the fire.

"What are you thinking?" asks Fernando.

"That life is this marvelous and terrifying mystery."

"Don't you ever think about anything *big?*" He tightens his arms, kisses my hair.

I sit in the warmth of him, his heart beating through me and into mine. And I wonder why it is that, of all the thousands upon thousands of people who pass through one's life, most leave not a trace. Into abandon and oblivion they are consigned, as though they were never there. And more curious, why do those few, only those few, stay somewhere safe, dying, even, but never entirely so, engraving the heart, deep and smooth? The cut of the eyes, some voluptuous sting, one exquisite phrase, a voice like chocolate just before it melts, a laugh like thin silver spoons chinking across a marble floor.

The way the sea crashes into crisp champagne pools behind him as he kisses you. A hand resting on a hip. One mesmeric glance, brown or black, green, topaz. Blueberry.

Without warning the rain turns hard. We run to gather dishes and glasses and the spoils of supper. We make two trips each and slam the stable door against the thrashing water. The electricity has blown, but still we laugh as I light the candles in the wall sconces on either side of the mirror and Fernando lights the ones on the table.

"*Siamo salvi,* we're saved," he says, pouring brandy into a great crystal snifter, offering it to me with both hands. I sip and then he does, just as Aeolus screams, flings wide the stable door, crashing it against the wall, the blow crushing its hinges, the furious draught guttering the candles on the wall, cinnamon wax spilling from their wounds, the flames leaping like Cossacks, dancing. The door won't shut but partway. As we begin heaving furniture against it, the wind goes soft and the rain spends itself in a dwindling gasp. We say let's leave the door hanging as it will for a moment, let the strange evening come inside. We're pattering about the room and, with the tail of my eye, I catch us in the mirror.

Framed between the flames, peaceable now, we are a portrait. But those two, could they truly be us? The candles light up the raindrops that form crowns of tiny amber beads in our damp hair. Ripened, whole we are, and made of velvet, of vintage stuff—worn, still lustrous, faded like blowsy August roses gone to bronze. Fernando doesn't see the portrait and moves in and out of the picture. I stop him, pull him back a step, holding him around his waist so we can look together at us. "See? Stay still for a moment and look at us."

He gazes at us, looking hard and then quizzically as though he can't decide if we're a memory or a dream. He tells me this and I say I think we're both a memory and a dream. And that, as well, we're real. He looks for a long time. He blushes, as though the mirror was a camera. We look until the exhilaration, the flash is past, and we've both grown timid, somehow embarrassed. Or is it that we'd glimpsed our secret selves, the best of us distilled in a moment, a fugitive moment, a dissolving moment, seeping, spilling over into the next one, just as time has always moved, never waiting for us to catch up. Barlozzo said it. *Time is a blackguard, Chou.* And, of course, he's right. There goes time, running like hell, looking back at us, taunting, as we fumble, trying to save him in a jar. Trying to tuck him forever under the bed, fix him tight inside a red satin box. Trying to string him like pearls. Enough pearls to make a life.

Acknowledgments

Rosalie Siegel,
donna nobile

Sharona Guri from Tel-Aviv,
Isabella Cimicchi from Orvieto,
muses, both

Sandra and Stuart Roth,
beautiful hearts

Lisa and Erich,
cherished babies

Fernando Filiberto-Maria,
the all, the everything.
The everyone

A Thousand Days in Tuscany

Marlena de Blasi

A Reader's Guide

A Conversation with Marlena de Blasi

Jennifer Morgan Gray is a writer and editor in Washington, D.C.

Jennifer Morgan Gray: *A Thousand Days in Tuscany* is an autobiographical chronicle of your time in San Casciano dei Bagni. Did you keep a detailed journal during the time covered by the book? Was there one image or person in your life that compelled you to begin writing this memoir?

Marlena de Blasi: Friends keep giving me these lovely leather-bound journals, as though the empty books themselves would insure that I'd keep writing. I have quite a collection of blank ones and sometimes I recycle them, give them as gifts to others. But I did keep a journal of sorts during the San Casciano days, if not a particularly detailed one. I called it Florì's book. It was a way for me to tell her things even when we couldn't see each other or talk.

I suppose I was the one who compelled the memoir, if "compel" is indeed the right word. I just wanted to tell my stories.

JMG: Do you view this book as a companion piece to *A Thousand Days in Venice*? How did you seek to make it a stand-alone work? Were there other titles you considered for either book and then abandoned? What is the "bittersweet adventure" of the book's subtitle?

MdB: Surely it's a companion piece to the first book. It begins on the very day we left Venice. But one who reads *A Thousand Days in Tuscany* first will not be at a disadvantage. I didn't have to try to make it stand by itself. It's a different story, albeit with two of the same protagonists. It recounts a whole other part of my life.

A Thousand Days in Venice was my working title, my only title. The title I would never have considered changing. I was lucky that my publishers didn't ask me to. But *A Thousand Days in Tuscany* is a title of which I'm hardly very fond, but my publishers loved it. The title is not even true since the book covers only a single year. But I guess "*Three Hundred Sixty-five Days in Tuscany*" doesn't have the same ring. Apart from that little ruse, the book is not about Tuscany in the way that *A Thousand Days in Venice* is about Venice. The second book is more about people than it is about place. The original title was *Dolce e Salata*. Sweet and Salty. "That's how life tastes to me," I think I say at some point in the text. *A Thousand Days in Tuscany* is not another finding-the-villa-and-choosing-the-marble-for-the-staircase sort of story, or one about the darling peasants who come to clean the house and cook the suppers. The story is as much about pain as it is about beauty. All sugar or all salt—both end up as oppression. Even in Tuscany.

JMG: You discuss your husband, Fernando, and his "Quicksilver" nature at great length, beginning on page 93. What was the most difficult aspect of dealing with Fernando during those episodes? How did your relationship evolve during that time?

MdB: Once we'd been in Tuscany for a few months, Fernando began to blossom and the Quicksilver in him faded rather fast. The episodes I write about happened very early on in our Tuscan days. These were backlash events, the result of his unmanaged expectations more than anything else. He wanted his peace to arrive with our baggage. I think many people suffer delusion if they are convinced that serenity is geographical. The "If only I lived in Tuscany or Paris or Rio, then everything would be fine" song.

As for what I found difficult during those periods, I think they were actually much more instructive than they were difficult. I learned that it was wrong for me to expect Fernando to be anyone but himself. In addition to his character, his very culture played a part. It's simpler to quote the text.

These crises of his, which feel oddly like betrayals, cause desolation in me. And I have to push hard at that desolation so I can remind myself of how he is *made*. All this behavior is an expression of his character, inexorable as bones and blood. Besides that, Fernando is Italian, and he knows what I can't learn. He knows that life is an opera that must be shrieked and lamented and only once in a while laughed.

I must tell you that having lived for almost twelve years in Italy now, I've become a bit unused to all this therapists' lingo about "relationships" and such. Here there's much less of that. Here people deal more in emotions than in excavation. We leave the digging to the archeologists. What I will say is that love—the real kind that happens only when both people love each other more than each one loves himself—ALWAYS grows. ALWAYS gets stronger. Nothing and no one can do much damage. And of course the converse of that is also true—if it's not love, it can't become love, no matter who the therapist is.

JMG: Barlozzo takes you and Fernando under his wing from the beginning of your time in Tuscany. Why do you think he immediately did so?

MdB: I think that in the text I talk about how Florì viewed Barlozzo's attraction to us. She said that he liked us *a pelle,* from the skin. It was an instinct, much like falling in love is instinctual. Indeed, it was love that we all felt, and still feel, for one another. That's what Florì meant when she called us "complicit." Over the years, I've come to understand that—at first sight and more thereafter—I reminded Barlozzo of his mother, who died when she was not yet thirty. I think I talk in the text about his comparing me to his mother. Eyes, voice, mystery. He said we were very much alike.

JMG: What about Barlozzo was compelling to you from the outset? How do both of you "trust risk more than comfort"? How was Barlozzo's relationship with you different from the one he enjoyed with Fernando?

MdB: I say in the text that it was always "high noon" when Barlozzo arrived on any scene. I say that he looks a little like Gary Cooper. Now if you put both of those images together, perhaps you can understand why I found him mesmeric, gritty. I think that just as he was drawn to us instinctively, so were we drawn to him. A purely emotional response. Many readers want to know if I saw him as my father figure and I suppose I did, and do, but he's much more than that to me. I guess I'll save the rest of the answer for another book.

As for our mutual trusting of risk more than comfort—neither one of us believes in the myth of security. I think a person can chase safety—in a relationship, a job, a house, a bank account, any number of things—for all his life, as though safety were life's entire goal. As though there were some prize for arriving at the end of life with all that "safety" intact, even if one also arrived not having lived that life, never once having walked to the edge. In the book I'm writing now, there is a part where Fernando and I have just spent an evening with two very old sisters who live in one of the grandest *palazzi* in Orvieto, women who've played things close to the chest for eighty years, never risking so much as their children's wrath or a single strand of rubies, I tell Fernando, "Poor souls, they've had a safe life. Now they're old and sad, their mettle untried."

As for how Barlozzo's relationship was and is different with Fernando—well, the two of them are children together. They both immediately become about ten when they see each other. It's a gift each of them gives to the other. Now with me, Barlozzo gets to be old. Maybe even older than he really is. He gets to talk about dying and being fearful. He gets to talk about the past. And I get the same things from him.

JMG: On page 215, you write, "Mathilde and Gerard had so much because they had so little." Similarly, how did living in San Casciano give you perspective on what was truly important in life? What do you think is most alluring about the prospect of living "the simple life," and what are its challenges?

MdB: I honestly don't think that the people of the village gave us perspective. Remember that at least some significant percentage of them was trying to "escape" village life. Traditional life. They wanted to trade medieval life for "the pink and yellow cement palaces in the post-war part of the village." What some of them might have done for us was to present, close up, images of who we wanted and didn't want to be as we grew older. Everything is distilled in a hamlet of two hundred souls.

But I think there's evidence on almost every page of the book of our perspective on the simple life. We never really measured our choices in a clear-cut "allure versus challenge" sort of way. We never got out the yellow pad and drew two columns. I, more than Fernando at the beginning, was in thrall with the idea of weeding and scrubbing at life, of making it smaller, in a sense. Relieving it of things and thoughts and pursuits that didn't add to our peace, and even relieving it of a few people who we knew could only continue to be themselves. And the smaller we made our life—no job, no house, not much money—the larger it became in terms of appreciation. There is a sense of privilege rather than of deprivation which comes with simplicity. Bread and oil and wine are a feast. A length of silk is a treasure. A day, a whole string of days spent walking and thinking and lying down in a field or wading in a river—not knowing if it's the wind that makes you shiver or the revelation that this,

this is how you really want to live—these composed our perspective. None of this is to say that in dreams there are no responsibilities. All dreams, at least the ones you really want to come true, begin with work. And so one invents the next thing to do. And the next one after that. Simplicity is not for the faint-hearted. Nor for the feint-hearted either.

JMG: Were you surprised that you so easily fit into the rhythm of the town? Was there a particular point when you really felt as though you belonged?

MdB: No, I wasn't surprised. I would have been surprised not to have felt comfortable. I've traveled alone so much in my life, found myself in situations both awkward and marvelous, grim and enchanting in so many places in the world that, somewhere along the way, "fitting in" became natural. When strangers sense a person's interior comfort, they become much more at ease themselves and differences—even in language—diffuse. Besides, the truth is that we're all much more alike than we're not.

Another truth is that "belonging" is a rarity even among people who have been together forever—living, working, being neighbors. They are almost never a cohesive tribe, if you will. So the desire for a societal belonging has never been an issue for me. I know that I belong everywhere as much as I know that I don't belong anywhere.

JMG: As I was reading, I found myself wincing whenever Misha opened his mouth! And it seems as though others, like Barlozzo, did as well. How is such a contentious person such a source of comfort—and a great friend—to you? Has he been to see you since his inaugural visit?

MdB: As you might recall, Misha was a psychiatrist. Can you imagine being one of his patients? Barlozzo and Misha locked horns. In some ways they were just too much alike. About the same age, each one sprang from a very different culture and each one also lived through some stunningly difficult times. Years before, when I lived in California, Misha and I had become friends. In fact, at one point he believed he had fallen in love with me, though that idea passed quickly enough. But there always remained some wisp of jealousy from him where I was concerned. He showed it when he first met Fernando and, in a sense, when he met Barlozzo—though for an altogether different reason. He felt that Barlozzo had usurped his role as general sage and guiding spirit in our lives. Also, Misha knew when he came to visit us in San Casciano that he had only a few months left to live. He never told us this, not until he'd returned to

California. And so the intention of his visit had been to "knock some sense" into us while he still could. But his letter from California said, among many other things, that he'd gone away from us with great contentment. Strangely enough, Misha and Florì died within a few days of each other.

JMG: What do you think incited Barlozzo finally to tell you the story of his family? How did his past weigh him down? And what do you think finally prompted him to live beyond the secrets and demons of those who lived and died before him?

MdB: Going back to that sentiment of instinct about which we spoke earlier, I think it played its part at this point as well. He felt safe with us. He'd carried the demons about with him until he found a safe place to put them down. To close the door on them. In the book I'm working on now, there is a scene that might help to explain "how his past weighed him down." He tells me, "I wish I'd done what you did." He whispers this. "I wish I'd loved someone more than myself. Myself whom, over time, I couldn't distinguish from my sadness. As though I was made of sadness and there was nothing to do about it, and so I got used to it. Came to cherish it. Obedient as to a king, I followed where it led me. I thought it was me who was obliged to shelter the past. To keep it burning at all costs. A fire in the rain. Except for Florì, the sweet respite of her, my life has been made of other people's lives. I wish I'd done what you did and claimed one for myself."

JMG: Were you surprised when Barlozzo suggested he might buy a house for the four of you—him, Florìana, and you and Fernando—to spend time together? What about that gesture was characteristic and uncharacteristic of him? After Florìana's death, did he follow through on those plans?

MdB: Yes, Fernando and I were both stunned on the day when he first brought us to see his "ruin." What I think he was after was to make up for lost time. At that point, he and Florì had finally begun to live the love they'd had for each other for forty years. Rather than like a man beyond seventy, he was behaving like a young man in love, wanting to buy a house for his "bride," wanting to have "children," wanting to "settle down." He wanted all the things he'd never had or thought he could have. So, it was a magnificent gesture. Heartbreaking, really. He thought he would live with Florì, share the house, from time to time, with us. And this sweetness is both characteristic and uncharacteristic of him. Florì called him *buono come pane,* good as bread. And that's what he was and is. But he'd become very good at being rascally, too. At hiding his vulnerability behind the guise of a scoundrel.

As for whether he followed through on those plans—well, the dream died with Florì. But in the book I'm writing now, you'll see what happens with the "ruin."

JMG: Do you think you and the other women would have gathered around Florì's bedside had she not asked you to? How was it a cathartic experience for all of you? And how was it just a fun party that captured her spirit?

MdB: We were all happy when Florì said she wanted to be fussed over for a few days. We'd all been longing to take care of her from the first day she came home from the hospital. But she resisted us then, remained thoroughly self-sufficient. I believed her when she told me, "I can do that now that I know I'm well. Before, when I wasn't sure, the idea of everyone being around me seemed too scented in farewell." So, no, I don't think we all would have arrived at her bedside unbidden.

I don't think the event was cathartic as much as it was nourishing, enriching. No one left behind their delusions or their pain or their memories in Florì's bedroom that day. Rather, we came away with an exalted sense of our courage. We were all in the Red Tent together in tribal celebration of our childhood and our womanhood.

How was it just a fun party that captured her spirit, you ask? In no way was it that. No way at all.

JMG: How did you feel about leaving on a three-month trip to research a book in the wake of Florì's death? Do you think you would have done so without Barlozzo's approval (whether tacit or overt)?

MdB: When Florì was sick and I wanted to go to the hospital to be with her, Barlozzo admonished me to love her the way she wanted to be loved rather than in the way I wanted to love her. In other words, she needed to be alone, and so the best way to love her was to let her be. It was much the same after Florì died. All I wanted to do was to keep Barlozzo close to us. To grieve with him. But that's not what he needed from us. He needed to be alone. The best way to love him at that moment was to let him be. A loud resonance there.

Too often, when someone is ill, others relate that illness to themselves. Either thinking: "What if it happened to me?" or, perhaps worse, "How will their illness, dying, and death affect me?" Or, the absolute apex of egotism, "I can't take all this suffering." The person who is ill can't even be the protagonist in his own illness.

As it turned out, by asking us to let him be after Florì died, by his telling us that he would much rather be alone, what Barlozzo accomplished was to strengthen the intimacy among he and Fernando and I. More about that in the next book.

JMG: I've read that you and Fernando have launched the project of leading tours together. How do you enjoy working together as a team? What do you think the most important element of exploring a new place is—in other words, do you have a philosophy on how to best enjoy traveling?

MdB: Well, as far as our working together, that's the lovely part. I do the talking and the cooking and Fernando does the charming and the driving. Succinctly put. But the truth is, we don't have all that much time for that part of our lives at the moment. I'm always writing the "next book." At this point, we usually program no more than six to eight weeks a year for touring with our guests. With very few exceptions, this work has put us together with some of the most magnificent people we'd ever hoped to meet. In the book-in-progress, I do tell some of the stories surrounding these tours.

JMG: How was writing a memoir different from the food-based writing—including cookbooks and criticism—that you usually do? What were the challenges of the memoir? How did you find it a liberating project?

MdB: This is a great question because normally one would expect that the leap from food books to memoir would be a giant one. But in fact, when I was writing cookbooks, they weren't cookbooks at all but a collection of recipes with memories. Now that I'm writing in the memoir genre, I include recipes. In a sense, I've always done both. Even when I was a food critic for all those years, I always wrote about the history of a place or of the chef or of his grandmother. So my writing life has always been very much of a piece. Only the balances have shifted.

The challenges of a memoir? To tell other people's stories along with your own. More than your own. To develop all the players. To let yourself be seen in resonance, reflection rather than under hot, white light. Some writers are too busy with their own lives to be collecting impressions about others. When they set about to write their story, the result can be one long egoistic narrative. Not so many of us live such fascinating lives that the telling of them can stand alone.

Was it a liberating project? Well, everything one does passionately is liberating, isn't it? I love my life, I love to write. I love the hard parts about being a writer more than the easy parts, though. And there are lots of hard parts.

JMG: Do you have any special writing routines or methods that facilitate the process and stoke your creative juices? Do you cook a great deal while you are writing?

MdB: I cook a great deal when I'm writing and when I'm not. I cook and bake with great constancy, shall we say. Fernando rations my flour during writing periods so I get only a kilo a day. Two decent loaves. One for a neighbor, one for us. I rotate my bread route. I even bring bread to the baker, trade him for flour. But as for routines—no. I write mostly in the very early mornings (while waiting for the bread to rise; didn't I tell you that my life is all of a piece?) but sometimes I don't sit down to write until late afternoon. I would feel throttled by a routine of any kind.

As for stoking the creative juices—I have trouble the other way. I find inspiration in the smallest events and so my fingers are always trying to catch up with my racing mind. As for methods—Do you mean going to writers' conferences or joining writers' groups or taking classes and such? Well, I've never been to a writers' conference and I hope to continue to evade that experience. All those churning, churlish, starving people waving manuscripts at one another. And most writers' groups are not peopled by writers at all. As for creative writing classes, well you can't teach a body to write words any more than you can teach it to write music. You can teach a person to write poetry because poetry has more technical flesh on its bones. You can teach someone the rudiments of how to put color on a canvas (not teach them to paint, mind you) since there's technical skill wanted for that, too. Same thing goes for all the fine arts. But I've never known a writer who learned how to write. Though I have known a few who became decent plagiarists. If you're a writer, you write.

JMG: Do you try to sit down at your computer and write for a certain amount of time each day? For instance, are you predisposed to writing in the evening, the morning, or just whenever, as you say, your fingers are itching to catch up with your mind? Are there any writers you love to read when you're about to plunge into crafting your own words?

MdB: No, there's no preordained plan as to when or for how long I'll write. But since I'm not a sleeper and am awakened by the muses at no later than five each morning, I already know—before sunrise—if it's a long session I'll want that day, a shorter one, or just an hour or so to read what's already there. That daily-changing sense of things is what gives my writing life its shape. In the same way that I don't sleep much, I don't rush much either.

I read at least half the time in Italian. Mostly classics, once in a while a contemporary work. Rarely, though. Italian literature has been in a slump for years. Maybe centuries. I read happily in Italian, although I do so, in part, because I live in a place where books in English, at least good books in English, are hard to come by. My non-Italian reading is often dictated by the secondhand books my friends send to me or by the care packages posted by my British and Australian editors. From my own stacks, I read and reread the dead Europeans. And the Russians. All of them.

JMG: What can your readers expect from you next?

MdB: I'm working on a third memoir, the working title of which is: *In via del Duomo 34.* Our address here in Orvieto. It's a continuation of *Tuscany,* just as *Tuscany* is a continuation of *Venice,* but, too, it's a story unto itself.

Reading Group Questions and Topics for Discussion

1. This book is titled *A Thousand Days in Tuscany: A Bittersweet Adventure.* What do you consider to be the "bittersweet adventure" of the subtitle? What would you call a book that chronicled the past thousand days of *your* life?

2. San Casciano is itself a living, breathing character in the book. What is your most vivid impression of the town? How is it similar to, or different from, impressions you had about Tuscany prior to reading this book?

3. How do the author and her husband adjust to living in the rustic world of San Casciano? What does de Blasi see as the most rewarding and challenging aspects of this new life? In your view, what would be most appealing about living a similar existence in a simple, rural town? What would be the most frustrating?

4. How does de Blasi reconcile the tension that sometimes exists between "the simple life" and the march of progress, especially as she acclimates to her new environment? How do the villagers respond to this conflict—of "tradition versus the new"—in their own ways? Have you ever struggled with a similar tension in your life?

5. The author has said that this book is a companion piece to *A Thousand Days in Venice*. How does the book function as one standalone memoir, and how does it provide another piece in the puzzle of the author's life? Do you think all readers would benefit from reading these books in tandem? If you've read both books, does de Blasi's mindset change from one to the next, with her change in location?

6. *A Thousand Days in Tuscany* is separated into sections delineated by season. Discuss this organizational technique. How does the framework of the book mirror the way that rural Tuscan life unfolds? Could you imagine this book organized in any different way?

7. On page 99, de Blasi writes, "Right now all I know is that in love there must be some form of desperation and some form of joy." Do you agree or disagree with this idea? How is this statement exemplified by the relationships in the book, particularly the one that

de Blasi shares with her husband and the one between Barlozzo and Floriana?

8. De Blasi develops a passionate relationship with the land itself. Why does she so enjoy the grape and olive picking she becomes a part of during the course of the book? What connection does this give her to the earth? What activities do you enjoy that might impart that same sort of feeling?

9. "Both my clothes and I are survivors of some other time," says de Blasi on page 133. How do the clothes that the author chooses to wear evoke her personality and character? Why does she choose to wear one particular ensemble per season?

10. How does de Blasi's discussion of food throughout this memoir impact your understanding of her life? Do you plan to try any of the recipes that the book includes?

11. Why do de Blasi and Fernando nickname Barlozzo "the duke"? Why do you think Barlozzo immediately takes de Blasi under his wing? What characteristics do the two share? How does Barlozzo's counsel and involvement shape the life that de Blasi and Fernando construct in San Casciano?

12. How does Barlozzo's story about his past give clues about the formation of his adult personality? Ultimately, how is he constrained by the ghosts of his parents, and how is he able to triumph over them? Have you ever felt a similar struggle with the past?

13. What about Florìana was so compelling, and to the author and Barlozzo in particular? Why do you think she was so private about her illness? How did her fellow villagers respect her need for privacy and, ultimately, for companionship?

14. The note that Florì leaves for Barlozzo reads, "I wanted death to find me dancing." How does Florì's attitude about death mirror the one she holds about life? If you needed to leave someone a similar note at the end of your life, what would it say?

15. In which ways are de Blasi and Fernando a study in how "opposites attract"? How do their different personalities and cultures play a part in their relationship? How are the two similar, both in their approach to their relationship and to their new life in San Casciano? How does their relationship evolve during their time in Tuscany?

16. De Blasi tells Misha that security "is a myth." Do you agree with her statement? What prompts Misha's concern about his friends' safety and security? Do you think that Misha fears change? Why? Does de Blasi value "risk more than comfort," as Barlozzo contends? What is the largest risk you've taken in your life? How was it rewarding?

PHOTO: FERNANDO DE BLASI

MARLENA DE BLASI lives in Italy with her Venetian husband. She is the author of four memoirs—*That Summer in Sicily, A Thousand Days in Venice, A Thousand Days in Tuscany,* and *The Lady in the Palazzo*—as well as three books on the foods of Italy.

ABOUT THE TYPE

This book was set in Perpetua, a typeface designed by the English artist Eric Gill, and cut by the Monotype Corporation between 1928 and 1930. Perpetua is a contemporary face of original design, without any direct historical antecedents. The shapes of the roman letters are derived from the techniques of stonecutting. The larger display sizes are extremely elegant and form a most distinguished series of inscriptional letters.